THE
OUTSIDE
HANDYMAN

THE
OUTSIDE
HANDYMAN

A step-by-step guide to maintaining
and improving the outside of your house
and your garden

John McGowan and Roger DuBern

ARCO PUBLISHING, INC.
New York

Published by Arco Publishing, Inc.
215 Park Avenue South, New York, NY 10003

First published in Great Britain in 1984 by Windward
an imprint owned by WH Smith & Son Limited

© Swallow Publishing Limited 1984
Conceived and produced by
Swallow Publishing Limited
32 Hermes Street, London N1

Managing Editor
Sarah Snape
Editor
Richard Wiles
Art Director
David Young
Designer
Caroline Courtney
Design assistants
Laurence Grinter, Susan Brinkhurst
Picture research
Liz Eddison

Library of Congress Catalog Card Number:
84-6214

ISBN 0-668-06229-0

Typeset in Plantin by Dorchester Typesetting Group
Printed in Italy by S.A.G.D.O.S., Milan

Contents

Introduction

Nearly everyone has some experience of home maintenance inside the house – papering walls, painting doors and ceilings, rewashering a leaking tap and so on. Most of it is fairly straightforward, involving basic materials, equipment and skills, and most people cope to a greater or lesser extent.

But it is a different story outside. The list of jobs which anyone is likely to encounter can seem daunting, involving anything from replacing a chimney pot to clearing the drains. Outside maintenance requires the homeowner to be a 'Jack of all trades' – painter, plumber, roofer, bricklayer, carpenter, and a lot more besides. It is a tall order for anyone with little experience.

Any job can be done well if it is tackled with confidence. And true confidence stems from having the knowledge and skill to cope with the task in hand. That is where this book comes in. It has been especially planned, designed and written to give any householder the advice, guidance and knowledge needed to maintain the outside of the house to the highest possible standards. Armed with the information contained in its simple, no-nonsense approach to each job, the reader will be able to carry out the

work with complete confidence in the end result. Each job is described in easy-to-follow stages, with each instruction so clearly explained that there will be little room for doubt. Whether you want to know how to patch a leaking flat roof, lay foundations for a wall, or simply paint a window frame, you will find all the information you need here.

Of course, a house cannot be separated from its garden, and if you are taking the trouble to keep your house in tip-top condition then it makes sense to do likewise in the garden. That means building and caring for walls, patios, fences, greenhouses and so on. Again you will find all the information you need here, together with a host of useful tips and advice direct from the experts.

There is planning and practical advice too, for anyone intending to redesign either a small area or a whole garden. You can learn how to deal with a sloping garden, how to build steps, a fish pond, or simply a herb seat or sand pit for the children to enjoy.

In short, *The Outside Handyman* provides a wealth of information and advice that will prove invaluable in every home.

Conversion tables

LINEAR MEASUREMENT

1 inch	25.40 millimetres
1 inch	2.54 centimetres
1 foot	30.48 centimetres
1 foot	0.305 metres
1 yard	0.914 metres

AREA MEASUREMENT

1 sq millimetre	0.00155 sq inches
1 sq centimetre	0.155 sq inches
1 sq metre	1.196 sq yards
1 sq inch	645.2 sq millimetres
1 sq inch	6.452 sq centimetres
1 sq foot	0.093 sq metres
1 sq yard	0.836 sq metres

WEIGHT

1 gramme	0.0353 ounces (ozs)
1 kilogramme	35.27 ounces
1 kilogramme	2.205 pounds (lbs)
1 kilogramme	0.019 hundredweight (cwt)
1 kilogramme	0.00098 tons
1 tonne	1 ton
1 ounce	28.35 grammes
1 ounce	0.0283 kilogrammes
1 lb	0.454 kilogrammes
1 cwt	50.80 kilogrammes
1 ton	1,016 kilogrammes
1 ton	1 tonne

THICKNESS

Millimetres	Inches (Approx)
0.8	$1/32$
1.5	$1/16$
3.0	$1/8$
5.0	$3/16$
6.0	$1/4$
9.0	$3/8$
12.0	$1/2$
15.0	$5/8$
18.0	$3/4$
22.0	$7/8$
25.0	1 inch

CAPACITY

1 litre	1.76 pints
1 litre	0.22 gallons
1 pint	0.568 litres
1 gallon	4.546 litres

1. Maintaining your house and garden

A house has to be kept in good shape if it is to withstand the all-round barrage it receives from the elements. Rain, snow and wind batter the walls, windows and roof while, from below ground, moisture rises to complete the attack. In the garden, outbuildings, fences and walls take the full brunt of the weather and early deterioration is inevitable without protection.

Routine and regular maintenance is the simplest and most economical approach to house and garden maintenance. Preventing problems occurring and anticipating likely troubles takes up little time – just an hour here or a morning there. If you allow a minor defect to flourish, there may soon be a major problem to deal with.

Planning considerations
Organization of your maintenance workload is important. Assuming that there are no immediate problems requiring attention, you can split up the work into a convenient pattern to suit your own spare time. For example, set aside one summer for roof and chimney repairs, the next for general garden work, the next for painting and so on. Your timetable will depend on the condition of the house and garden, the improvements to be undertaken, your own working speed and, of course, the household budget.

Setting up a job, gathering the necessary tools and equipment or buying materials takes up a lot of time. If you have to do roofwork, for instance, you will need to erect the essential ladders or scaffolds and these may have to be hired or borrowed. It is a waste of valuable time and money to set up a scaffold and roof ladder in order to replace a chimney pot (see page 78), then to have to go through the whole routine a month later to replace some roofing (see page 66). It can be wasteful of materials, too – you could find yourself with a half-used bag of cement after repatching the flaunching of a chimney stack (see page 79) and find it has gone hard a couple of weeks later when you need some concrete to fix a new fence post (see page 116).

Relating jobs
Since so many of the same tools and materials are needed for various jobs around the house and garden, think in terms of relating jobs to save time and money in the long run. Take, for example, the house gutters (see page 82). These have to be cleaned out in the autumn to get rid of leaves and other debris, and any defects such as leaking joints or loose brackets put right. To carry out this work might mean assembling a whole list of items – such as screwdrivers, drill, mastic (caulking compound), hacksaw, screws and so on – and so this is a good opportunity to inspect the gutters on the garage, shed or greenhouse.

Another example is sand and cement mortar. This is mixed up, albeit in different proportions, for a number of jobs. So when you find that a patch of rendering (stucco) has to be replaced on a house wall, have a look for other defects such as crumbling brickwork pointing, a crack in a concrete path or a loose paving slab which can be repaired at the same time.

Link materials together, too. Metal items are found all round the house and garden – windows, gutters, downpipes, railings, gates and so on. Rust attacks iron and steel items, so these have to be checked regularly for signs of corrosion. The remedy is always similar; wire-brushing to remove the rust, followed by repairs to holes, and finally a coat of rust-inhibiting primer followed by paint. So again, tackle the whole lot together.

The normal winter protection for unpainted metal is oil or grease, so, if you are greasing some gate hinges, assemble any gardening equipment such as lawnmower, shears or fork and treat these too before storing them away for winter in the garden shed.

Wood has to be protected from decay by paint, varnish or preservative. So if a fence has to be treated with preservative, tackle the shed at the same time. Hardwood window and door frames are varnished, so it may be that there is an item of garden furniture that can be coated at the same time.

Buying materials
Materials are expensive nowadays, so do not waste anything. Think in terms of economy. Buying in bulk is always cheaper in the long run. Hardware such as screws and nails will last indefinitely, so too will building materials. Chemicals and liquids such as adhesives, varnish and paint have a long shelf life provided that they are stored properly. If you have to buy something that will not keep very long once opened you would be wise to think of doing at the same time all the jobs it might be needed for rather than having to throw some away.

On the following pages there are checklists of likely maintenance jobs to look out for in the house and garden. You would be wise to keep a small notebook as a reminder of outstanding repairs so that you will not overlook a related repair when the time comes.

Checking the defences

Often the best way to check a roof is from the inside on a rainy day. Look and listen for any drips and trace them back to the point of entry using a torch (flashlight).

Flat roofs are troublesome; if water does not drain away and lies in puddles it can eventually seep under the waterproof covering and travel some distance before it appears as a damp patch on the ceiling. Nevertheless, a flat roof on an extension is easier to inspect than a pitched roof: you can walk about on it safely and examine suspect areas at first hand.

Examine the chimney stack for loose or cracked pots. The sloping layer of cement mortar (flaunching) into which the pots are bedded can be similarly damaged. An ordinary brick stack, or one that has been rendered or pebbledashed (finished), can suffer the same defects as house walls – cracked and missing, or 'blown', patches. At the base of the stack, where it meets the roof, there is a lead or mortar strip, called the flashing, which seals the small gap. Check that it is sound.

The house walls may have no obvious signs of damage, but moss or mould growth indicates wetness, which could be caused by rainwater penetration or leaking gutters.

Inspect the house gutters at least annually for blockages. Any leaks or overflows are usually detectable on rainy days. These can be caused by decay in an old cast-iron system or faults such as loose gutter brackets, which causes sagging. The downpipes and drain gullies into which they lead must be kept clear so that water is able to flow quickly away.

Around the rest of the house wood and metal parts (door frames, windows and so on) have to be checked periodically for flaking paint, rotting wood or rust, as well as any cracks or unwanted gaps that could admit rain.

Whereas repairs are spasmodic, painting has to be tackled on a regular cycle – the number of years a sound coat of paint will last depends on how much the house, or just one elevation, is exposed to the elements. The part of the house which receives the sun most of the time or stands in the path of winter winds is not likely to last as long as a sheltered side.

Roof
Check for cracked, slipped or missing slates, tiles, or shingles

Downpipes
Ensure that the tops of the downpipes are not blocked by leaves, birds' nests or other debris

Doors
Rainwater blowing under the door indicates that you need a weatherbar (a strip of metal or plastic angled to repel rain). Check for gaps between the door frame and the walls

Drain gully
Keep these free from leaves and other rubbish, which could cause a blockage

Chimney
Look for cracked or loose pots. Check the flaunching (the sloping layer of cement mortar into which the pots are fixed) to make sure it is not cracked or loose. If the chimney stack is made of plain brickwork, check to see if the mortar joints between the bricks are solid. If the stack is covered with rendering or pebbledashing (stucco), look for cracks, bulges, or missing patches

Flashing
At the base of the chimney stack inspect the flashing (the material that stops rainwater running down between the stack and the roof). Check that there are no cracks in the flashing and that its top edge is anchored well into the stack

Gutters
Keep gutters free from blockages. Inspect metal gutters for rust damage and, on rainy days, check for leaks from the joints between sections of the gutter. Make sure that the brackets supporting the gutter are securely fixed and that the gutter slopes slightly towards the downpipe to enable rainwater to flow away smoothly

Walls
Look for loose, crumbly mortar pointing between the bricks, cracked bricks with flaking faces, or more extensive cracks in the wall which could indicate subsidence. If the walls are rendered or pebbledashed (stuccoed), check for cracks, bulges and loose or missing patches

Drives and Paths
Look for cracks, pot holes or broken sections, particularly at the edges. Loose paving slabs are a trip hazard and must be fixed immediately. Puddles forming after rainfall indicate hollows, which must be levelled out

Airbricks
Airbricks are usually seen on older houses with suspended timber ground floors. They must be kept free of obstruction (such as piled-up earth or garden debris) so that air flows below the floor to keep the timber dry

Damp-proof course
Make sure that there is a gap of at least two bricks depth between the damp-proof course (d.p.c.) and any path or patio abutting the house wall. Check too that the surface slopes away from the house to carry away rainwater. Never build rockeries or pile up earth against the wall

Windows
Faults to look for are cracked or broken glass and loose or missing putty. Gaps between the frame and the wall must also be sealed. Clear out the indentation (called the 'drip groove') on the underside of the sill. Inspect wooden-framed windows for rot; metal windows for rust

Looking after the house

Damp is the greatest enemy of a house. There are basically two types – penetrating damp and rising damp. Rain that enters through the walls, roof and windows is called penetrating damp. It is usually caused by leaking gutters, poor pointing between bricks or damaged roofing, and can be cured when these defects are corrected. Potentially far more serious, however, is rising damp, which works its way up from below ground. This can eventually cause dampness to take hold in the structural timbers of the house – typically the floor joists. When this happens and is allowed to go untreated, it is likely that wet or dry rot will follow.

Identifying rot
Wet rot is the lesser of these twin evils; it is likely to be contained in areas that are definitely wet, such as windowsills and door frames.

Dry rot is a major problem. It is so-called because it has the ability to spread itself from wet timber onto adjacent dry timber. It does this by growing thin strands, which are capable of transferring water from wet to dry timber. Since it can travel through walls, it can climb all around the house if left unchecked. Dry rot is often called the 'cellar fungus' – cellars are usually damp, unventilated places and these are the conditions in which dry rot thrives.

Damp in cavity walls
Modern houses are less likely to suffer from dampness. To start with they have cavity walls – the exterior wall is actually comprised of two walls with a 50 mm (2 in) gap between them. In theory, moisture which seeps through the outer wall will be unable to cross the gap and so reach the inner leaf, which forms the wall of the room.

Unfortunately, errors during construction can cause a breakdown in the structure's defence against moisture penetration. Mortar dropped into the cavity as the walls were being built is a chief cause of trouble; if it collects on one of the metal wall ties used to link the walls, or is allowed to pile up on the ground, moisture can use the mortar as a 'bridge' to cross the cavity and show itself on the inner leaf.

Damp in solid walls
With solid walls (these have no air gap), which are found in older houses, it is the density of the bricks which repels the damp. In wet weather the moisture *does* sink slowly inwards, but not too far; then along comes a spell of fine weather and the wall dries out. But if there are any cracked bricks, missing rendering (stucco) or crumbling mortar joints, the moisture can travel through quickly. Sometimes, though – especially if poor quality materials were used – the walls

simply prove to be too porous and even a well-maintained wall can be affected.

Protecting the floor
The floor of a house has in-built defences, too. In modern houses with solid concrete ground floors, there is a damp-proof membrane (vapor barrier) which, if properly installed, will prevent moisture from below ground rising any further. In many older houses there is no membrane (vapor barrier); the thickness of the floor slab and its density are relied on to keep out damp. As with walls, poor installation or lack of density can lead to a breakdown in the defences.

Timber floors will stay dry provided that they are ventilated through the air bricks in the house walls and rest on strips of bituminous felt (or slate in older houses) placed on top of the 'sleeper' walls, which support the joists.

Sealing points of entry
Doors and window frames are typical points of entry for moisture. Usually they are simply screwed to the perimeter of the hole cut in the wall and – even though some incorporate bituminous felt strips to keep out moisture – this is where the problem usually occurs. Windows in modern houses are usually sealed with a bead of flexible mastic (caulking compound), which forms a seal; older houses will benefit from this treatment also.

Seasonal Timetable – The outside of your house

SPRING
It is too early to start painting since the weather is likely to be unsettled and frosts can still occur, which will result in a poor finish. However, it is a good time to make repairs in preparation for redecoration – replace damaged roof tiles, repair defective gutters, renew broken glass or faulty glazing putty, fix window and door frames. While the weather is still cool, arduous jobs such as laying a concrete path or building a patio can also be tackled.

SUMMER
The painting season. Tackle walls first, and leave woodwork until later in the summer so that it will have had a chance to dry out completely. Avoid redecorating in full sun, however, as excessive heat can ruin a freshly painted finish.

AUTUMN
Tackle repairs to paths, drives, fences and gutters. Apply preservative to bare timber, and re-treat previously preserved wood. Check all metalwork for rusting. Check and repair sheds and greenhouses.

WINTER
The weather limits the amount of outside work possible. Prepare for the cold weather by checking the roof, walls, windows and doors for defects likely to admit moisture, and remedy such problems immediately. Clear gutters and drains of fallen leaves and other debris. Drain and/or insulate outside taps. Remove or prune trees where necessary. Certain jobs such as repairs to gates can be tackled, since these items can be taken off their hinges and brought under cover. Preparation work, such as digging and shaping the ground and laying hardcore for patios or paths to be laid the following spring, can also be undertaken.

Looking after the garden

As well as caring for the house it is important to make sure that the garden is up to scratch, so make a careful appraisal of the area to see just what has to be done in the way of maintenance, repairs and general improvements.

Maintaining fences
Outdoor woodwork is particularly susceptible to the effects of the weather. Examine boundary fences for signs of deterioration. If any posts can be rocked from side to side it is likely that the timber has rotted below ground level. It is important to repair a broken or rotten post immediately; if left, the rails and panels will eventually break and the entire fence may fall down in a high wind. There is no need to go to the trouble of replacing a single broken post unless the whole fence shows signs of failure. An effective and long-lasting repair can be made by cementing a concrete spur into the ground alongside the broken post, and bolting the two together.

Check the rails, feather-edge boards, and panels for damage. If any have worked loose, renail them before the wind breaks them away completely. The ends of rails or panels that have come loose can be refixed with galvanized steel repair brackets, which are screwed on as a brace for the loose joint.

Discoloration is a prelude to decay setting in. About every two years treat the fence with a good quality wood preservative – much more effective than creosote in preventing timber decay and prolonging the life of the fencing. Most preservatives are harmful to plant life so the best time to treat the fence is in the spring when the timber is dry and plants in the proximity of the fence will either be very small or can be cut back without being harmed. However, you must protect any plants and soil against the fence with polythene (polyethylene) sheets to prevent them being splashed.

Problems with outbuildings
Sheds and other timber garden buildings should also be treated with preservative and rotten sections replaced. Examine felt-covered roofs for tears that can admit rain and repair the damaged area with a patch. If the damage is widespread you may even have to renew the entire roof coverings.

Deteriorating surfaces
Paths and drives also need regular checks. Paving slabs can sink due to poor foundations or settlement of the ground; any unevenness can be dangerous, but the slabs themselves can also crack. Unless only one or two slabs are affected, there is nothing you can do except lift and re-lay the entire path on a firmer base. Watch out for crumbling edges to paths: they are a hazard which should be repaired immediately.

Dangerous steps
Steps that are in a bad state of repair are also lethal, so check them for loose or broken treads and repair them immediately. If the treads are slippery or uneven it is best to re-lay them with a textured, non-slip paving.

The rust menace
Wrought ironwork – railings, gates, etc. – is another area requiring regular attention. Rust spots should be brushed down with a wire brush and treated with a rust-inhibiting primer and two coats of paint as soon as they are spotted and before the corrosion takes hold thoroughly.

Efficient garden drainage
The success of your garden could depend on how well it stands up to the onslaught of the weather. Rain can be a particular problem: puddles that take a long time to dissipate could indicate a fundamental problem with the way your plot drains. If the problem is not a man-made one – a poorly laid patio with dips and hollows, for example – the solution lies with improving the land's natural water table. This could mean restyling the entire profile of the plot or installing land drains.

Seasonal timetable – Your garden

SPRING
Commence outdoor building work such as building walls, laying paths and drives, as soon as the danger of heavy frost has passed. Erect fences while plants are still dormant and not easily damaged. This is a good time to erect garden buildings, such as sheds, greenhouses and summerhouses. From late spring onwards it is safe to lay concrete and cement mortar without danger of cracking. Treat outdoor woodwork with wood preservative and repair any broken fence posts and rails. Examine garden furniture and repair any damage, or repaint as necessary.

SUMMER
Try to enjoy the fruits of your labour as much as possible; bring garden furniture out of store. Complete major garden improvements such as levelling ground and digging ponds before the soil dries out, making digging hard. Avoid laying concrete in high summer unless the area can be covered with polythene (polyethylene) to slow drying out. Carry out path, drive and step repairs. Repaint ornamental ironwork.

AUTUMN
Complete concreting and brickwork as soon as possible (be prepared to cover new work with cloths or straw if frost threatens). Heavy rain can also ruin outdoor concrete and cementwork. Isolate mains water to outside taps in case of freezing. Bring garden furniture under cover if possible, together with children's garden play apparatus. Repair any damage before storing items. Store away the garden pond pump, and float a ball or polystyrene block in the pond to absorb expansion of ice if the pond freezes.

WINTER
Prepare on paper a plan of garden improvements to be carried out in spring. Avoid concreting and bricklaying at this time. Tackle drainage problems, indicated by puddles and waterlogged soil remaining for long periods after rain has fallen. Prune and fell dangerous trees.

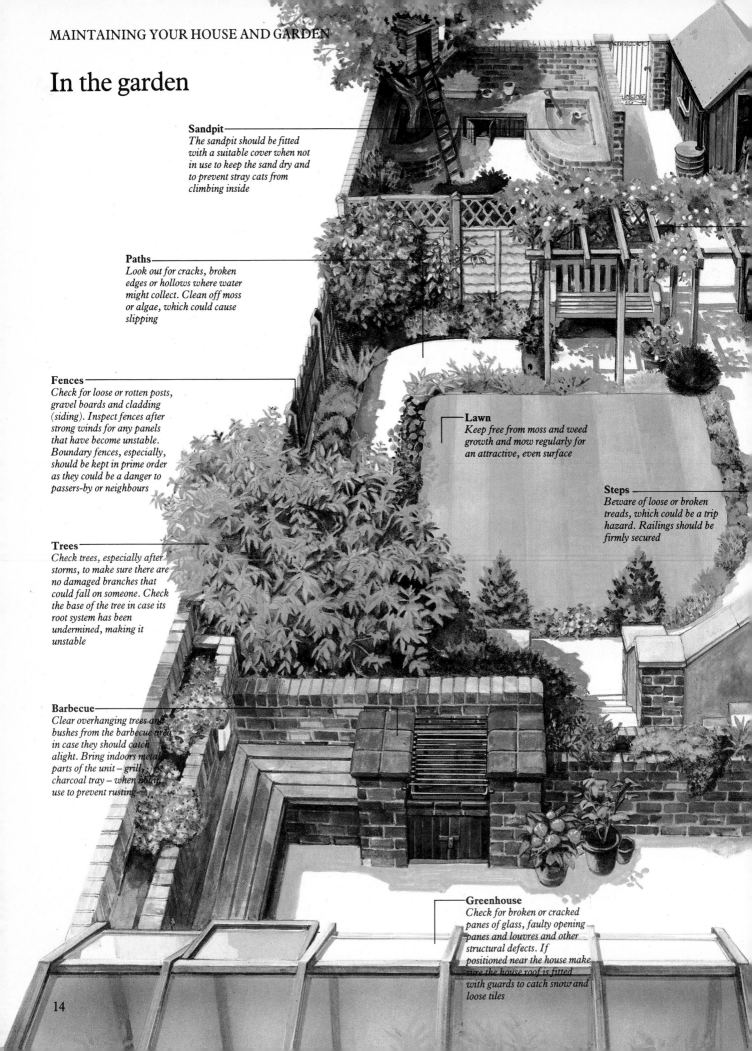

In the garden

Sandpit
The sandpit should be fitted with a suitable cover when not in use to keep the sand dry and to prevent stray cats from climbing inside

Paths
Look out for cracks, broken edges or hollows where water might collect. Clean off moss or algae, which could cause slipping

Fences
Check for loose or rotten posts, gravel boards and cladding (siding). Inspect fences after strong winds for any panels that have become unstable. Boundary fences, especially, should be kept in prime order as they could be a danger to passers-by or neighbours

Trees
Check trees, especially after storms, to make sure there are no damaged branches that could fall on someone. Check the base of the tree in case its root system has been undermined, making it unstable

Barbecue
Clear overhanging trees and bushes from the barbecue area in case they should catch alight. Bring indoors metal parts of the unit – grill charcoal tray – when not in use to prevent rusting

Lawn
Keep free from moss and weed growth and mow regularly for an attractive, even surface

Steps
Beware of loose or broken treads, which could be a trip hazard. Railings should be firmly secured

Greenhouse
Check for broken or cracked panes of glass, faulty opening panes and louvres and other structural defects. If positioned near the house make sure the house roof is fitted with guards to catch snow and loose tiles

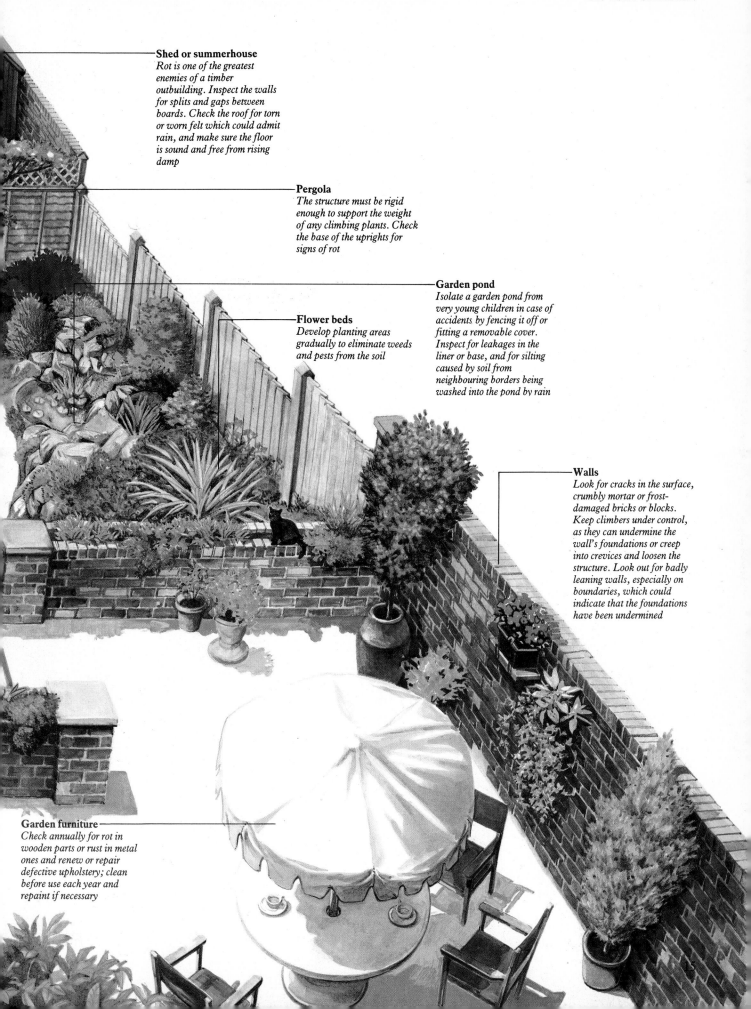

Shed or summerhouse
Rot is one of the greatest enemies of a timber outbuilding. Inspect the walls for splits and gaps between boards. Check the roof for torn or worn felt which could admit rain, and make sure the floor is sound and free from rising damp

Pergola
The structure must be rigid enough to support the weight of any climbing plants. Check the base of the uprights for signs of rot

Garden pond
Isolate a garden pond from very young children in case of accidents by fencing it off or fitting a removable cover. Inspect for leakages in the liner or base, and for silting caused by soil from neighbouring borders being washed into the pond by rain

Flower beds
Develop planting areas gradually to eliminate weeds and pests from the soil

Walls
Look for cracks in the surface, crumbly mortar or frost-damaged bricks or blocks. Keep climbers under control, as they can undermine the wall's foundations or creep into crevices and loosen the structure. Look out for badly leaning walls, especially on boundaries, which could indicate that the foundations have been undermined

Garden furniture
Check annually for rot in wooden parts or rust in metal ones and renew or repair defective upholstery; clean before use each year and repaint if necessary

2. House walls

Curing defective brickwork

The brick walls of your house are a vital barrier against the elements, so it is important that you examine their condition regularly. Old bricks are particularly prone to cracking, and may have lost their waterproof qualities through years of exposure to the weather.

Any bricks which have started to crumble or flake can be cut out and new ones inserted. Try to obtain old, matching bricks from a brick supplier or demolition site.

Slight decay – chips, cracks and flaking faces, for instance – can be repaired by hacking out the damage and filling with coloured mortar (coloured pigments for adding to mortar are sold both as liquids and powders).

The mortar between the bricks is another area where age and exposure to extremes of weather can have a detrimental effect. The mortar joints can be raked out, refilled with new mortar, then shaped to match the surrounding wall.

Replacing a brick

1. Cracked, flaking or badly damaged bricks should be removed and replaced with new, matching bricks. To remove a single damaged brick, drill through its face many times using a masonry bit in an electric drill, to weaken it further.

2. Chop into the brick using a cold chisel and club hammer and remove fragments as the brick crumbles. Hack off the old mortar joints around the brick, taking care not to damage adjacent bricks.

3. Clean up the hole then dampen the surface with water. Spread a layer of bricklaying mortar – use a ready-mixed type, available in small bags – in the bottom of the hole and 'butter' one end with mortar.

4. Take your replacement brick and spread a layer of mortar on top. Butter one end, by scraping the mix onto the brick from your trowel. Insert the brick in the hole, buttered end into the 'clean' end of the hole, mortared top to the top of the hole.

5. When the brick is fully inserted, scrape off any excess mortar that was squeezed out and tidy up the mortar joint around the brick.

Cracks *running through a brick wall, defective mortar pointing and cracked and crumbly bricks can spell danger in the form of damp penetration*

Repairing perished mortar

1. Chip away the old mortar using a slim cold chisel or special raking chisel and club hammer. Work carefully to avoid damaging the bricks. Cut back the mortar to about 12 mm (½ in).

2. Brush away all dust and loose material and dampen the joints with water to stop the dry surface sucking too much moisture from the filling mortar, which could cause it to crack or fall out of the joints.

3. For repointing, use a mortar mix of 1 part cement; 1 part lime; and 6 parts soft sand. This is not a strong mix intentionally, since the mortar has to be weaker than the brickwork. A stronger mix would cause excessive shrinkage and cracking later and would impede the drying out of rainwater soaking into the wall. Keep the mortar fairly dry. If it is too wet it will run down the wall and stain the bricks.

Apply mortar to the joints using a small pointing trowel. Load a sausage-shape of mortar onto the back of the trowel and press it into place

4. Load the mortar onto a hawk then cut off a sausage shape using a pointing trowel. Press this into the joint. Fill the vertical joints first (A), trimming off excess mortar as work proceeds, then complete the horizontal joints (B).

A

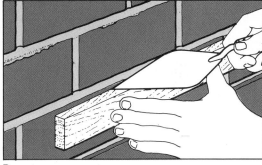

B

5. Shape the joints to match those on the surrounding wall. Flush pointing, formed by rubbing the joints with a thick rag or wad of sacking, is usually used only on garden walls. Weathered pointing leaves the mortar set at a backward angle to shed rainwater from the wall. A rounded profile is achieved by drawing a piece of 19 mm (⅜ in) diameter steel pipe, wood dowel or plastic hose along the joint.

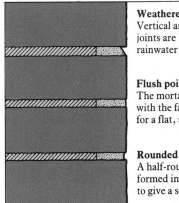

Weathered pointing
Vertical and horizontal joints are bevelled to shed rainwater from the wall

Flush pointing
The mortar joints are level with the face of the bricks for a flat, subtle effect

Rounded pointing
A half-round profile is formed in the mortar joints to give a soft, recessed look

6. If repointing is done in hot, dry weather, sprinkle water on to the joints for a few days afterwards to prevent moisture from the mortar being drawn into the bricks too quickly.

Repairs to rendering (stucco)

Rendering (stucco) can lose its grip on brick-work and may even fall away – sometimes in sizeable patches – due to dampness in the bricks or a fault in the render mix itself. Tap suspect areas with a light hammer: a hollow sound will reveal blown render.

Damaged areas should be cut back to leave a sound edge, using a bolster chisel and club hammer, then patched with new render.

Rendering should always be carried out in warm weather, but in an emergency where moisture is penetrating the walls during the winter, try to dry out the wall first. This can be done by applying heat from a blowtorch or hot-air gun. Alternatively, brush dry cement on the wall and leave it to soak up as much moisture as possible. Then brush off surplus powder before rendering the wall. If it is absolutely vital to work during frosty weather, you must include an anti-freeze additive in the render (stucco) mix. Do not, however, work in severe frosts.

Materials for rendering

The success of the finish depends on the suitability of the mix. The cement should be ordinary Portland cement. If it has to be stored for a few days before use make sure it is kept dry. Stack it off the ground and under cover. Sand must be clean plastering sand, not loamy building sand, which would cause the mix to shrink and crack on drying out.

You can add hydrated (powder) lime to the mix, to help to keep the material flexible and easier to use. The normal mix is 1 part cement; 1 part lime; and 6 parts sand. A coloured finish can be obtained by using an additive. Colours, however, are inclined to fade in time. Never mix large batches of mortar, even for a large amount of rendering damage. The mix will start to set in about 20 minutes, so it is better to make up smaller batches, which can be used up quickly. Do not be tempted to add more water to enliven a mix that has started to dry: you will only succeed in weakening it.

If the wall is to be left unpainted, the finishing coat of rendering must be a uniform colour. Sometimes, however much care you take in measuring out the ingredients correctly, colour differences can occur between small batches. So, if a large area is involved, make the whole lot at once but add a little more water to make it softer. This will delay the setting time and any slight weakness will be tolerated.

A steel float, *passed over the render when it is almost dry, will give a smooth, flat finish; lubricate the trowel by splashing on water*

Render is usually applied in three coats – a base coat, a 'floating' or levelling coat and a finishing coat. The first coat is about 6 mm (¼ in) thick and is applied as evenly as possible with a steel laying trowel. The surface is then scratched to make a key for the second coat and left to set for at least 24 hours.

The floating coat is applied and levelled to about 9 mm to 12 mm (⅜ in to ½ in) thick. It, too, is scratched and left to set. The finishing coat, which is about 6 mm (¼ in) thick, is applied last.

You can, however, apply only two coats for a successful finish: use a thicker first coat and a finishing coat about 6 mm (¼ in) thick.

Preparing the surface

Brush the wall with a stiff hard brush to remove loose material. Any holes in old brick or stone walls can be filled with a stiff sand and cement mix and left for at least 24 hours to set.

Wet the wall prior to rendering to avoid excessive suction, which could cause the surface to crack. Wetting is especially important in hot weather: use a hose-pipe or watering can.

Rendering a wall

1. Keep the mixing area perfectly clean at all times. Use same-size buckets for measuring out the ingredients and mix them thoroughly. Make a hollow in the top of the pile and add clean water. Mix again until a smooth, lump-free consistency is achieved.

2. Scoop a load of render onto your trowel and spread it onto the wall. Press the lower edge of the trowel hard against the wall and push it upwards. With practise, you should be able to achieve a reasonably flat finish. Continue to spread the render (stucco) onto the wall to complete the base coat.

3. Scratch the base coat with one corner of your trowel to form a key for the finishing coat.

4. Apply the finishing coat working from the top of the wall and from left to right. Use lighter, sweeping strokes.

5. As soon as you have completd a substantial area use a straight-edged wooden batten to 'rule off' the rendering level with the surrounding

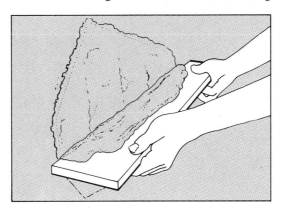

wall surface. Hold the batten horizontally and draw it up the wall, resting its ends on the hard render. Fill any hollows or cracks within the levelled area.

6. Smooth off the finished area, once it has stiffened, by drawing a wooden float or damp sponge acros.

Repairing pebbledash

When repairing a damaged area, you will not be able to make an 'invisible repair' on an unpainted wall. The rendering and stones are certain to be a different shade. The only way to conceal the patch is to make the repair using the same- or similar-size stones as in the surrounding wall, then to paint the entire wall. Throw chippings on to a soft cement rendering applied to the damaged area.

Fling new pebbles *onto the freshly applied render from a small shovel; most of the pebbles should stick, but you will have to press them in using a piece of board or a trowel*

Repairs to wood siding

Regular painting or staining of wood siding or shingles will avoid most of the problems which might occur. However, occasionally you may find that you have to repair or replace a damaged board. Neither is very time consuming and you will prevent the damage from spreading where the effects will be more serious.

Repairing cracks and splits

If the cracks or splits are minor then the treatment is simply a matter of filling the break with wood putty and sanding down the surface to prepare for repainting the damaged area. If, however, the crack is more serious, or a split is located at the end of a board, then the procedure is only slightly more involved.

First remove the nails from the lower section of the board at the appropriate end and lever the bottom section of the board away, taking care not to extend the split any further. Work some waterproof adhesive onto the two sides of the split and well into the crack. Remove the lever and nail the board back so that the gap is completely closed. Wipe away any excess glue which squeezes out before it dries. Finally, once the glue has had time to set, touch up the area with paint or stain.

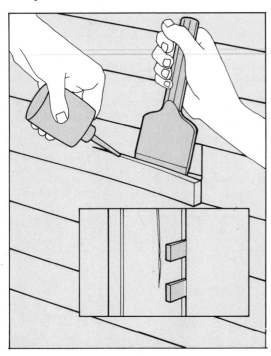

If your house is clad with board and batten siding and the split is fairly serious, first remove the batten nearest the split. Work some glue well into the gap and cut a couple of wedges to insert between the adjacent boards to close up the gap. Once the glue has set replace the batten over the joint.

Curing warped boards

If a board is warping because the fit is too tight then the remedy is simple. Remove the nails from the affected board and trim a little off one end using a plane. Drill pilot holes in the board so that the fixing nails do not split the board as you drive them in. Finally, fill any holes with wood putty and touch up the finish.

Replacing rotten wood

Occasionally the damage to a particular board is so bad that part of it must be replaced. The job is a little fiddly but not difficult. First make a vertical cut through the board at the end of the damaged section, allowing a little extra to ensure that you cut out all the rotten timber. Remove the nails in the exposed section of the wood and use a chisel to cut out the damaged wood. You will have to use a narrow chisel to cut out the section under the overlapping board. However, if you pry it up with a screwdriver you will find it easier to work under the upper board.

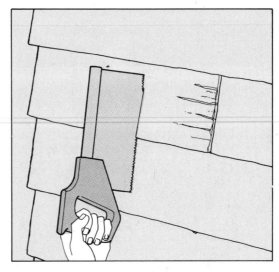

Once you have cleaned out the rotten wood, cut a patch from a matching length of siding to make a snug fit. Use a short length of board to knock against as you wedge the patch into position; that way the hammer blows will not damage the edge of the new wooden insert. When the patch is firmly in place, drive a few nails through the upper board to secure it. Drive the heads below the surface with a punch and fill the holes with wood putty.

Repairing board and batten siding

To replace a damaged or rotten section of board and batten siding the procedure is very straight-forward. First remove the battens adjacent to the damaged board and set them to one side. Then remove the entire affected board. Cut off the damaged end of the board at a 45° angle so that the top piece will overlap the lower section when returned to position on the wall. Now cut a replacement piece of wood using the old one as your guide.

Nail the lower section back into place on the wall and spread waterproof glue along the angled cut edge. Then nail the upper section back into place lining up the overlapping cut. Once the glue has dried, fill any small gaps with the wood putty and nail the two battens back into place over the joints. If the wall has been stained you will find it less messy to stain the new piece of wood before nailing it in place, leaving only a little touching up to do on the wall.

Replacing a shingle on a wall

The first part of the job is to remove the damaged shingle. To do this simply drive a chisel into the end of the shingle to splinter it and then pull out the sections as they become loose. This will leave the old fixing nails in position so you will have to cut slots to fit around

them. Mark the position of the slots by pushing the new shingle into place and then tapping it with a hammer so that the nails dent the edge of the shingle. Now cut a slot to fit around each of the nails.

Insert the shingle so that it is flush on the edge with the others. Secure it by driving in two new nails and punch the heads below the surface. Use wood putty to fill the holes and paint or stain the shingle to match its neighbors.

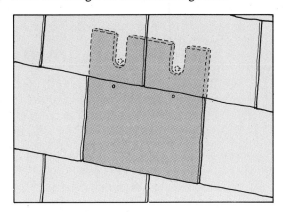

Fixing a dent in aluminum siding

Although aluminum siding is virtually mainte-nance-free, occasionally it does get dented, which can ruin the appearance of the entire wall. Luckily the repair is simple and does not require too much time.

Firstly drive a self-tapping screw into the center of the dent using a couple of washers to keep the head away from the surface. Then grip the head of the screw and pull until the dent pops out. Remove the screw and fill the hole with a little plastic aluminum. Once it has set, file it down and sand it flush with the surrounding surface. Finally touch up the paint to match the rest of the wall.

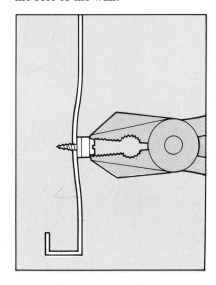
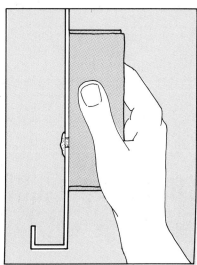

Repairs to flashings

Flashings seal joints in the house structure against penetrating damp – where the chimney stack meets the roof or where a roof meets a wall. The flashings may be made of metal (normally lead), cement mortar, or the more modern self-adhesive flashing strip.

The cement type is prone to cracking and parting from the brickwork, and when it does water will seep into the joint and reveal itself as a damp patch inside the house. A simple crack in a cement flashing can be sealed by using mastic (caulking compound). Mastic is supplied in a cartridge (either operated by twisting the base to force out the mastic or by inserting the cartridge in a special applicator gun) and applied as a bead run along the joint.

Where a cement flashing is in a bad state of repair it should be chipped away completely and replaced with a strip of self-adhesive, metal-faced flashing strip. This material is flexible enough to be moulded around unusual contours such as corrugated roofing.

Using self-adhesive flashing strip

1. Brush water-proofing primer onto the brick-work and adjoining surface to ensure good adhesion of the flashing strip.

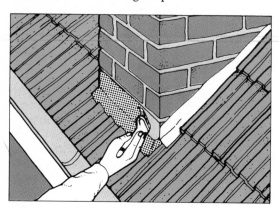

2. Cut the flashing strip to length then unpeel the backing paper.

3. Press the strip flat over the join and roll it smooth to dispel air bubbles with a wallpaper seam roller.

Worn metal flashings

Metal flashings are stronger and more durable than cement flashings. But if they wear badly or tear, simply cover them with self-adhesive flashing tape. If the flashing is in a very poor condition, remove it and replace it completely with flashing strip.

For minor cracks in metal flashings:
1. Press stiff mastic (caulking compound) into the damaged area.
2. Reinforce with strips of roofing felt.
3. Paint the area with two coats of bituminous waterproofing liquid.

If the metal flashing is sound but the top has parted from the mortar joint in brickwork, into which it was bedded, then repair as follows:
1. Rake out the mortar joint.
2. Tuck the edge of the flashing back into the joint and wedge it there with small pieces of rolled-up lead or wood offcuts.

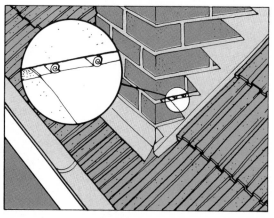

3. Fill the joint with a mortar mix of one part cement; five parts sharp sand and leave to set. Remove wedges and fill the holes with mortar.

3. Windows and doors_____

Window styles

Windows come in an enormous range of styles, shapes and sizes and, increasingly, in materials other than the traditional wood. Wooden windows come in three main types.

The double-hung sliding sash, usually called simply a 'sash window', and common in many older houses, has two sashes that slide vertically past one another in a specially designed frame. The sashes are counterbalanced by weights attached to each sash and running over pullies set at the top of the frame sides; these keep the sash in whatever open position is required. The obvious advantage of sliding sash windows over other types is that they give a large area of ventilation – up to half the window area – yet they do not take up any room when open. However, they can be awkward to maintain and decorate, and are easy for burglars to force unless extra security precautions are taken.

In modern sash windows, the old system of cords and weights has been replaced by springs, which are easier to fit and maintain and which also simplify the construction of the window.

You can also get horizontally sliding sash windows, which have two or more sliding sashes running past each other between top and bottom tracks, rather like miniature patio doors. These were occasionally made in timber, but modern versions usually use aluminium or rigid pvc frames. However, they are more commonly found as secondary glazing systems, fitted within an existing window frame.

The second window type is the casement window. The main frame is divided by vertical and horizontal cross-members (called mullions and transoms respectively), and fixed and hinged casements (or sashes) are fitted into each section. The opening sections, called lights, are usually hinged at the side, the top or (rarely) at the bottom. In most casements the main sashes are side-hung and the smaller lights at the top are top-hung. These small lights are often called top vents, and are intended to be left open at night to provide ventilation without being a security risk. Casement windows come in a huge range of permutations, enabling you to choose exactly the right mixture of fixed, hinged and top-hung lights in precisely the positions you want them.

As with sash windows, most casement windows are wooden. However, before and after the Second World War, metal windows were popular for a time until it became apparent that rust posed a bigger maintenance problem in the long term than did rot with wooden windows; they are seldom fitted nowadays. Instead, aluminium and rigid pvc have proved increasingly popular,

particularly as replacement windows (see page 27) since they offer the huge advantage of almost minimal maintenance. They do, however, tend to be considerably more expensive than their timber counterparts.

The third window type is the pivot window, so-called because the moving sash revolves on a horizontal (or occasionally vertical) axis. The advantages of this type are easy-to-control ventilation (the stay can be locked in various positions) and easy cleaning (the sash can be swung right round so that the outside is facing in). They can, however, interfere with curtains and blinds. They are available in wood, timber, aluminium and rigid pvc.

There are three types of pivot window. In the first, the casement is top-hung, but can be

A Colonial-style window of classic proportions

23

converted to a horizontal pivot window for easy cleaning. The second, called the moving-axis or canopy-action window, incorporates a special mechanism, which swings the sash outwards and downwards as it is opened. The third, the inward-opening tilt-and-turn window, is bottom-hung, but can be converted to a side-hung window for easy cleaning.

Bow windows are multiple windows assembled side by side to form a shallow curve. They are usually the casement type, incorporating main side-hung casements at each end and where they are easiest to reach, and a row of top lights – one in each section of the window.

Bay windows have angled corners instead of curves, and are usually made up from a series of standard windows (of any type), which are linked via corner joints.

Metal and plastic sash windows (above) are beginning to replace those constructed of wood. A traditional style casement window with leaded glass (above left). Centre pivot windows suit modern house designs and have the advantage that they can be rotated so that the outside can be cleaned from inside (left)

Repairs to windows

Problems with windows

Apart from the problem of replacing cracked or broken glass (page 26), the biggest single cause of trouble with wooden windows is rot; with metal-framed windows it is rust. Both are caused by water penetration.

In the case of wooden windows, keeping water out can be an enormous problem. The frame and its various opening lights or moving sashes consist of a large number of individual components, all expanding and contracting in different directions and subject to strain and stress in use. So it is little wonder that joints begin to open up and allow water in to start the process of rot, which can proceed unseen until severe damage is done. Water can also get in if the putty used to hold the panes of glass in place begins to crack.

In addition to these problems, hinged casement windows suffer from many of the same problems as doors – binding, warping, and even strained hinges caused by windows blowing backwards and forwards in the wind. Furthermore, their hardware – stays and catches – may be damaged or broken. Sash windows suffer most of all from a unique problem – broken sash cords, which prevent the sashes from staying where they are put.

Curing window problems

• If you find flaking paintwork and opening joints on the exterior of a window frame, strip the paint then fill all the cracks thoroughly with an exterior quality wood filler before priming and painting the woodwork again.

• Where rot has begun to take hold, you may be able to patch small areas but larger ones will have to be cut away and replaced with new wood. Where you are cutting in new wood, try to cut the ends of the patch at an oblique angle to increase the glueing area and hence the strength of the repair.

• Where putty has cracked or shrunk away from the glass, hack it out using a hacking knife or old chisel and replace it with new putty. Form the sloping profile of the putty using a putty knife. Undercoat and paint the new putty within 14 days, taking the paint line 3 mm (⅛ in) onto the glass surface to seal the joint.

• Where hinged casements have distorted frames, you may be able to clamp the frame back square after unscrewing the hinges. Take care not to crack the glass, though: it may be wise to remove this before clamping, and replace it later. Reinforce weak corner joints with L-shaped screw-on repair plates. If hinged casements bind and stick, check that top and bottom edges are thoroughly painted. Remove paint build-up from leading edges, as described under doors.

Repairing sash cords

1. To replace broken sash cords on sliding sash windows, you will have to remove the affected sash from its frame. The sashes slide in tracks separated by pinned-on beads, and you will have to prise off first the sash bead (A), then the parting bead to allow each sash to swing free.

2. Cut the cords (B), lift out the sashes and set aside. Then open the small removable pockets at each side and retrieve the sash weights. Use a length of string and a small weight to feed in new sash cord over each pulley (C), and attach the weights. Then place the outer sash in position at the top of the frame and mark the cord ready for cutting and nailing to the sash at each end side (D); the weight should be at the bottom of the pocket when this sash is raised.

3. Repeat the process with the inner sash; in this case the weight should be at the top of the pocket when the sash is lowered into its correct position, so holding the sash at the top of the track with the weights at the bottom of the pocket will give you the correct cord length. Nail the cords to the sides of the sashes, then pin the parting and sash beads back into place.

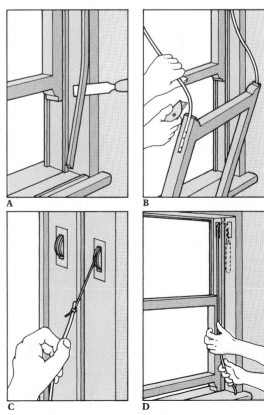

A   B

C   D

Replacing a pane of glass

When a window is cracked or broken, a temporary repair with tape, polythene (polyethylene) or hardboard will help keep the weather out in the short term, but fitting new glass should be undertaken at the earliest possible opportunity.

Accurate measurement for the new pane is all-important. You may be able to measure the rebate size before removing the old pane, but it is generally best to take it out and clean up the rebate first.

1. Lift out broken pieces of glass carefully, then, using an old chisel or a hacking knife (special glazier's tool), chop out all the old, hard putty. Pull out any old fixing sprigs or clips you find, too. With a cracked pane it is often quicker to break the glass rather than to try to remove the pane; cover one side first with adhesive tape and then break the glass with carefully aimed hammer blows. Lift out the fragments and proceed as before. Wear old leather gloves when handling broken glass. Dispose of the glass immediately.

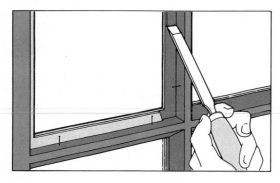

2. When all the glass and putty is removed from the frame, brush out the dust and debris and measure the rebate height and width along each side. Write down the smaller measurement in each case; if they differ the frame is slightly out of square. Note which way the pattern runs on patterned glass, and take a fragment of the old glass with you when you go to order the new glass so you get the right type. The new glass should be about 2 mm (1/16 in) smaller in each direction than the dimensions across the rebates. This is to allow for any expansion which may occur when the glass is in the frame.

3. To fix the new pane you will need some putty (most putty is now general-purpose, and will fix glass in wood or metal frames; otherwise, you need linseed oil putty for wood frames, metal casement putty for metal ones) and glazing sprigs (for wood windows) or clips (for metal ones).

4. Before fitting the new pane, check the condition of the rebate, priming bare wood and

treating rusty metal as necessary. Then bed in a thin layer of putty all round the rebate (A) and offer up the new pane, pressing it in at the edges, not the centre, until the bedding putty can be seen to form a continuous line all round (B).

A

B

5. Insert sprigs or clips to hold the pane in place (sprigs usually go at about 300 mm/1 ft intervals, while clips have to fit in the pre-drilled holes in the frame). Then press in the facing putty and finish it off to a neat 45° mitre using a putty knife. To help the putty form a watertight seal to the glass, run a moistened finger or a small paint brush (used dry) over the putty surface. Finally, trim away the excess bedding putty on the inside.

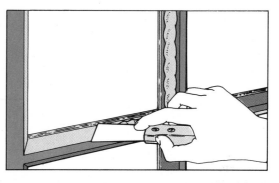

6. Leave the putty to harden for about two weeks. Then paint over it, taking the paint line onto the glass by about 3 mm (1/8 in), especially along the lower edge of the pane where water is most likely to get in. Lastly, clean off all the putty marks.

Replacing windows

You may decide that your windows need replacing purely for cosmetic reasons, but it is more likely to be an essential job made necessary by the state of your existing windows – deterioration caused by rot or rust, or general deterioration caused by years of neglect. If replacement is called for, the first decision you have to make is which type of new windows to fit, and whether to fit them yourself.

Your first thoughts are likely to turn to wooden windows, which are the most widely available type. They come in the largest range of styles and standard sizes, and are quite straightforward to install. But if long-term maintenance is an important factor, it may pay you to consider choosing metal (aluminium) or plastic (upvc) frames instead. They may cost more initially, but you will then be free from future worry about maintenance. They are widely offered by window replacement contractors, but can also be installed by the do-it-yourselfer.

It is also worth thinking at this stage about the style of window you choose. You may fancy picture windows or the segmented multi-paned look, but before you take the plunge look at other houses in your area to see whether the wrong choice might spoil the look of your home and its neighbours. Nothing looks worse than windows completely out of keeping with local architectural styles.

There is one last point: double glazing. These days it is foolish not to take the opportunity to double-glaze windows wherever possible, and the replacement of your window frames offers the perfect opportunity of having factory-made sealed units fitted. They come in plain, small-paned and even leaded-light versions, and will not add a vast amount to the cost; after all, you would have to buy glass anyway to single-glaze your new windows, so that expense will have been saved.

The job of replacing windows starts with the measuring up. You may be able to obtain new frames that match your opening size exactly, but if you cannot, your choice is either to widen the opening slightly or to make it smaller. In the first case you can remove only a couple of inches from the masonry at each side; knock out any more, and the lintel over the opening will no longer be properly supported. In the second case your problem will be to match the existing outside wall with new work – easy enough if it is rendered (stuccoed), but harder with brickwork.

How to replace a window

1. Once you have your new frames, you can remove the existing frames: to do this, saw through timber ones and hacksaw through the fixing screws of metal ones. Clean up the

Aluminium-framed windows (above) make the ideal replacement for old ones that suffer from extensive deterioration (below)

opening and modify its width (and height, too, if necessary, by raising or lowering the sill: never be tempted to tamper with the lintel unless you are prepared for major building work).

2. What you do next depends on the type of window you are installing. Timber windows are fitted direct to the masonry, so offer up the frame, wedge it in place absolutely square and drill through the frame into the masonry at each side. Plug the holes and screw the frame into place; then repair the surround indoors and outside, sealing exterior gaps with mastic to make them waterproof. It is a good idea to prime and paint the frame before you install it; unless it is a large window or a ground floor one, you will also save time if you glaze it first.

3. Aluminium windows are usually fitted in a hardwood subframe, which must be installed absolutely square and must obviously be the precise size to receive the new aluminium frame. Windows of upvc are sometimes fitted direct to masonry, sometimes in a hardwood frame.

Door styles

Doors come in two main types, called flush and panel. The panel door is the traditional type, and consists of a solid timber frame (vertical stiles joined by two or more horizontal rails), subdivided in some cases by vertical muntins into four, six or more panels. The spaces between these frame members were usually filled with thinly cut solid wood, but may also have plywood or glass instead. The frame itself may be of hardwood, or a good-quality softwood, such as hemlock or western red cedar.

If the panels are wooden, they usually fit in grooves in the inside edges of the frame members. Glass panels are usually fitted into rebates and are held in place with lengths of beading. If there are a large number of glass panes, glazing bars may be fitted between the frame members, as in windows. If there are just one or two large panes of glass, it is usual to use some sort of safety glass – toughened, laminated or wired. When you buy a panel door, you will generally find that the stiles have been left over-long; these 'horns' are designed to protect the door in transit, but must be cut off before it is hung (see page 29).

Flush doors are the more modern type, and are so-called because they have flush surfaces. The heart of the door is a relatively lightweight frame clad on both sides with a thin sheet of material such as hardboard or plywood. These give the door its rigidity, but extra support is provided by filling the core of the door with a cardboard 'egg-box' lattice (on the cheapest types), flaxboard or lengths of solid timber (glued side by side on the best doors, like the core of blockboard). As the frame members are not substantial, extra blocks are usually fitted between the stiles to provide a firm fixing for the door handle and lock; occasionally further blocks are also added at the hinge stile, so it is important to fit such doors the right way round.

Flush doors faced with hardboard or plain plywood are intended for painting, but more expensive types have decorative hardwood veneers (and edge lippings) that can be varnished or waxed to enhance their appearance. You can also get flush doors with moulded resin facings that actually resemble panelled doors yet cost considerably less.

Both types of door come in a range of standard sizes and in two common thicknesses – 35 mm (1⅜ in) for internal use, and 45 mm (1¾ in) for external use.

You may also come across ledged-and-braced doors, consisting of a number of closely fitting tongued-and-grooved boards held together by horizontal and diagonal battens on one face. These are nowadays usually used only on outbuildings, but were popular on many cot-

Many styles of timber front doors are available in solid or glazed construction

tage-style older properties.

Aluminium and rigid pvc are also used nowadays to make doors – usually modern-style front doors and sliding patio doors, which are now extremely popular as a replacement for old French windows. They are usually fitted with double-glazed sealed units, and offer advantages of long life and low maintenance.

Hanging a door

Once you have chosen the style of door, measure the frame and choose a door that is the same size (standard door sizes have been around for a long time now) or, if necessary, slightly bigger. Remember that you can cut down a panelled door by removing wood from the stiles and rails, but with a flush door the inner frame may be only 25 mm or 50 mm (1 in or 2 in) thick and removing more than a little timber could seriously weaken the door. Remember, too, that internal doors are 35 mm (1⅜ in) thick.

To hang your door you will need a pair of hinges (three on heavy external doors) and a latch or lock set (you may want to use the existing door hardware to match other doors nearby, of course). You can choose ordinary butt hinges, rising butts (useful where thick carpets are fitted) or lift-off hinges (these and rising butts allow you to lift the door off its hinges – helpful when moving furniture about, and when you are redecorating).

How to hang a door

1. Begin the job by removing the old door. You may have to cope with stuck or painted-up screw heads, which can often be loosened by striking them with a screwdriver and mallet, or by pressing a hot soldering iron against each screw head to make it expand and so loosen its grip on the wood. If you intend to reuse the existing hinge recesses on the frame, insert glued dowels in the old screw holes to provide a good fixing for the new hinges; the screw holes never match up precisely, so you will have to make new screw holes anyway.

2. Offer up the new door, and mark how much has to be removed (A); you can also do this by using the old door as a template, provided it was a good fit originally. Saw or plane off the required amount equally from top/bottom or each side as appropriate.

3. Hold the door in place, wedging it up with a slim offcut, and mark the hinge positions on the door edge. Stand the door on edge, draw round the hinge leaf at the required positions (B) and use a mortise or marking gauge to mark the depth of the recess to match the leaf thickness. Chisel out the recesses on the door edge (C) and screw the hinges in place. Stand the door in place again, wedged up as before, and mark the new screw positions in the existing hinge recesses on the frame. Drill pilot holes, fix the door with one screw top and bottom (D) and check that it swings freely and closes properly. If it does not, chisel out or pack out the recess as appropriate; when you are happy with the door's action, drive in the other screws.

4. When you fit the door hardware depends on whether you are simply fitting knobs and a ball catch, or a more substantial mortised-in latch or lock mechanism. Fit the latter at the same time as you attach the hinges; then you can mark and cut the frame to take the latch keep when the door is hung.

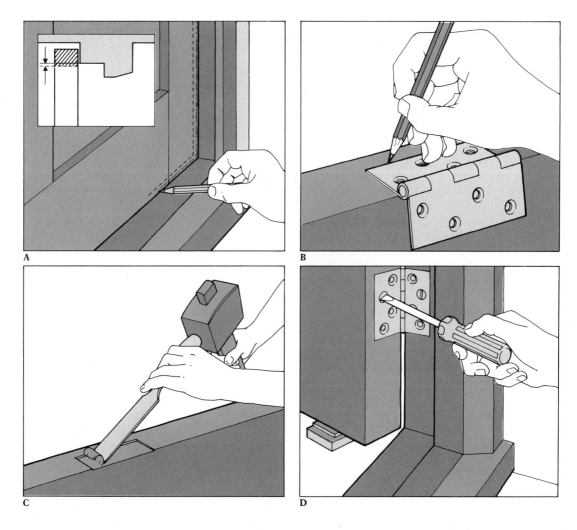

A

B

C

D

Repairs to doors

Problems with doors

Exterior doors usually cause more problems than internal ones because they are exposed to the elements. Moisture penetrating the timber can cause it to swell and will make the door stick in its frame. Eventually it will lead to rot, especially along the foot of the door and in the lower parts of the door frame. It can also cause the door to warp so that it no longer fits snugly in the frame nor closes squarely against it.

Panelled doors, whether internal or external, can suffer if their joints begin to open up due to strain; internal panel doors, particularly in centrally heated houses, are prone to shrinkage in the dry atmosphere, and this may cause the panels themselves to split or become loose. Joints may begin to open up, too.

The other common problem with doors of all types is a build-up of paint on their edges. Whenever a door is painted, a thicker-than-usual film of paint accumulates along the door edges, and after several redecorations this can build up to such a degree that the edges bind on the door frame, making it hard to open and close.

Curing door problems

• If an external door binds, especially along the bottom edge, the cause is moisture being absorbed by the unsealed wood along the bottom (and sometimes the top) edge of the door. Remove the door from its hinges after a spell of dry weather and prime and paint the normally inaccessible bare wood.

• To cure edge binding caused by a build-up of coats of paint, strip the paint off – either chemically with a paint stripper, or mechanically with a blowtorch and scraper or even with a rasp-like shaping tool (do not use a plane; you could damage the blade). Take off a further 1 mm or 2 mm (about 1/16 in) of wood with a sharp plane when you have stripped the paint to avoid the risk that repainting could cause the trouble to recur. Then sand, prime and repaint the edge to match the existing paintwork.

• Where rot has taken hold, you may be able to cut away small areas and patch them with wood filler, but if the rot has really taken hold there is no alternative to cutting away the rotten wood and inserting new wood in its place. Where the foot of the door has been attacked, take the door off its hinges and saw right across the foot of the door to remove the affected timber. Then cut a new section to length, glue and screw it in place and plane it down to the right shape.

• If the bottom of a panelled door is rotten, you

may have to renew the whole bottom rail: dismantle the joints carefully and use the old piece as a pattern for the new piece. On flush doors, replace the bottom frame member and renew the cladding as far as necessary, fixing extra horizontals between the stiles to support the new piece.

A

• Correcting warped doors is difficult to do successfully. A better short-term solution is to reposition the door stop beads instead to match the profile of the door. If they are pinned on, prise them off carefully with an old chisel and reposition them with the door in the closed position. If they were planed out of the door frame timber, you may be able to pin in new wood: use filler otherwise, or a double layer of draughtproofing strip if the discrepancy is small.

• Where door joints have opened up, glue and clamp them back into place, adding timber wedges to the ends of the tenons to prevent them from pulling apart again (A). As an extra precaution, drill a hole carefully through each stile into the tenons and out through the other side; tap in a length of glued dowel. Trim off the dowel flush with the face of the stile (B). You can use this method to close up cracks in the panels, too.

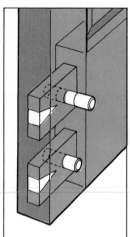

B

• If door hinges are giving trouble, check first that the screws attaching them are secure. If they are loose, unscrew them and tap in a piece of glued dowel to provide a firmer fixing. If the door swings open or closed by itself, the hinges are not set vertically above each other: move one of them backwards or forwards accordingly (C). Hinges set too deep in their recesses will strain and force the hinge knuckle as the door is closed; pack the recesses out with card or hardboard and replace the hinges (D). If the screw heads protrude or the hinge recesses are not deep enough, the door will be hard to close. Drive the screw heads deeper to cure the first problem, chisel out the recesses slightly to put the second right.

C

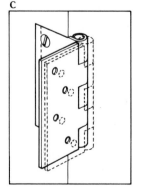

D

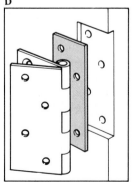

4. Home security

The risk of break-in seems to increase every year, so home security must be very carefully considered. It is obviously important to be able to securely lock the vulnerable points of entry, and it is also a good idea to take steps to deter a potential intruder by making the house look occupied, with lights on time switches for example, or by making a burglary look difficult by having a prominent burglar alarm box fixed to the outside of the house.

Most burglaries are carried out by young, opportunist thieves, on the look-out for easy pickings by entering through poorly secured, or even open, doors and windows. The last thing this type of thief wants to do is spend time forcing a door or window, so fitting extra locks to these entry points will probably be enough to send him elsewhere.

The most vulnerable points of entry are shown here, and these are the areas to which particular attention should be paid by fitting locks and other security devices.

The front of the house
Likely points of entry for determined burglars are:
1. Window over a flat roof
2. Communicating door from garage
3. Open top-hung casement
4. Front door, especially with porch
5. Unsecured ladder

The back of the house
Usually more secluded, the back of the house is particularly vulnerable:
1. Sliding patio doors
2. Back door (often glazed)
3. Drainpipe provides access to upper floor windows
4. Louvre windows
5. Bushes screening door
6. Garage entry door
7. Skylight

Securing the doors

Doors are particularly vulnerable to being forced because even if an intruder enters through a window he will probably want to make a quick getaway with his haul through a door.

Obviously, good locks and bolts are required, but it is no good relying on these alone if the door itself is weak and easily smashed. So take a good look at all the exterior doors and make sure that they are in good condition, rot free, and that they are at least 45 mm (1¾ in) thick, which means that they are exterior-quality doors (interior-quality doors are thinner).

Many exterior doors have glass panels which may be easy to smash, giving a burglar easy access to the locks and bolts on the inside. To make the break-in more difficult it is a good idea to change the glass for laminated or toughened panes, or to fix clear security film over the glass on the inside to make it harder to smash.

The door by which you leave the house, normally the front door, needs a particularly secure lock because it cannot be given the additional protection of bolts at top and bottom, except at night when the house is occupied and less likely to be burgled.

Side and back doors need a lock that will prevent a burglar using these doors as a means of easy escape and they should also have bolts at top and bottom to prevent the door being smashed-in from outside.

If any of your doors open outwards – often found on back or side doors – you should fit a hinge lock to prevent forcing from this side.

Choice of locks

The basic choice is between mortise locks and rim locks. Mortise locks are fitted into a slot in the edge of the door, which gives a secure fixing so long as the door is thick enough to be suitable for a mortise lock. Because the lock is neatly out of harm's way it cannot be easily tampered with by a burglar. Rim locks are screwed to the surface of the door; they tend not to be as secure as mortise locks, as they may be easier for burglars to remove.

However, it is as well to remember that there are both secure and insecure locks of both kinds. What affects security is not only the quality of the case and the method of fixing, but also the quality of the lock mechanism.

To give a high degree of security on a front door it is a good idea to have two locks – a rim latch to hold the door closed automatically when it is pulled shut, and a mortise lock with a key-operated deadbolt to prevent the door from being forced once the key has been turned. For side and back doors, two-bolt mortise locks are the usual choice. You can choose rim locks, but mortise locks are more secure. These two-bolt

locks have an automatic springbolt operated by a handle or knob from either side of the door and a deadbolt, which is operated by turning a key. A deadbolt is one which cannot be pushed back once the door's closed. The springbolt enables the door to be opened from either side without a key, whereas with a rim latch (as fitted to a front door), the door can be opened by means of a lever or knob from inside, while a key is needed to gain entry from outside.

A problem with the traditional cylinder rim nightlatch is that it cannot be deadlocked with a key. It is easy for a burglar to gain entry by pushing a strip of plastic – such as a credit card – between the door and the frame to push back the lock. So, when buying a rim lock, choose one with an automatically deadlocking springbolt, and with a key-operated deadlocking internal handle. Alternatively, choose a rim lock with a deadlockable latch: the lock and internal handle is deadlocked by an extra turn of the key.

Installing locks

If the door stile is less than 45 mm (1¾ in) thick and 63 mm (2½ in) wide, fit a rim latch; otherwise, choose a mortise lock. There are special narrow versions of these for fitting to glass-panelled doors with narrow stiles.

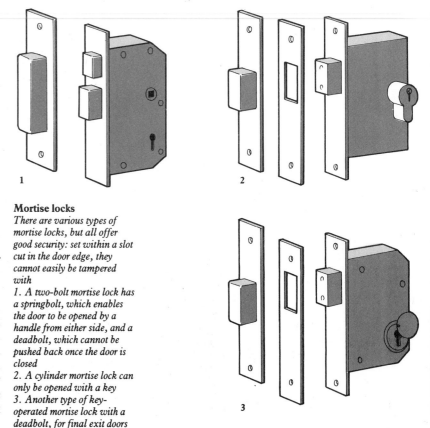

Mortise locks
There are various types of mortise locks, but all offer good security: set within a slot cut in the door edge, they cannot easily be tampered with
1. A two-bolt mortise lock has a springbolt, which enables the door to be opened by a handle from either side, and a deadbolt, which cannot be pushed back once the door is closed
2. A cylinder mortise lock can only be opened with a key
3. Another type of key-operated mortise lock with a deadbolt, for final exit doors

Rim locks

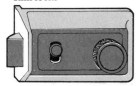

The cylinder rim nightlatch offers little protection against intruders; the lock can be pushed back easily

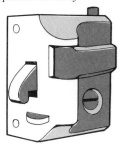

A more secure form of rim latch is the type with a hook bolt, which makes forced entry more difficult

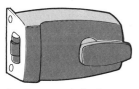

Another secure rim latch, this lock features a deadlockable roller bolt, which cannot be forced back

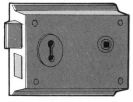

This lightweight rim lock has a springbolt to enable handle operation from both sides and a key-operated deadbolt, but it is not suitable for final exit doors

Fitting a mortise lock

1. To ascertain the size of the mortise (slot) required, hold the lock on the inside face of the door (A). Mark the centre line of the mortise on the edge of the door and drill out the mortise to the width and depth of the body of the lock (B). Complete the mortise using a chisel to smooth the sides of the slot.

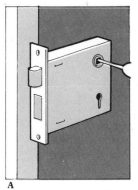
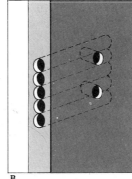

A   B

2. Push the lock into the mortise and mark the shape of the 'forend' (rectangular plate) on the edge of the door. Turn out the bolt to give a means of withdrawing the lock. Chisel out a recess for the forend, which will allow it to lie flush with the edge of the door. Before fitting the lock, hold it against the door once more and mark the centre point of the keyhole, then drill a hole for it. Complete the keyhole shape using a padsaw. Fit the lock, handle and the cover plates over the keyhole on each side of the door (C).

3. Operate the bolt and mark the position of the bolt and springbolt, if fitted, on the door jamb (frame). Working from the door stop on the jamb, mark the distance from the face side of the door to the centre line of the bolt. Cut mortises for the bolts at this position and check that the door closes properly without rattling. Finally, fit the striking plate in a recess cut in the door jamb (D). Operate the lock in the closed position to make sure it turns freely in its mortise and does not bind; if it does, cut a deeper mortise.

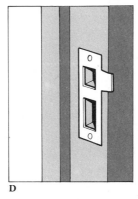

C   D

Fitting a rim latch

1. The first stage of fitting a rim latch is to mark the position of the key cylinder on the door stile using either the template supplied with the lock, or the lock mounting plate (A). Either one large hole will be required (B), or a specially shaped hole made by drilling first two smaller holes followed by a larger hole. Ideally, use a large flat bit to make the hole for the cylinder, but if one of these is not available then drill a number of smaller holes around edge of the hole for the cylinder and use a chisel to remove the waste.

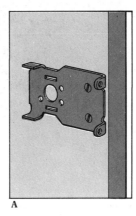
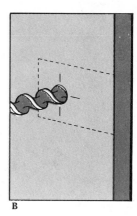

A   B

2. It will probably be necessary to cut a recess in the edge of the door for the forend of the lock; when you have done this screw the lock mounting plate to the inside face of the door stile (C). Position the key cylinder and cut the connecting bar to length to suit the thickness of the door. Hold the cylinder in place by passing the fixing screws through the mounting plate. Engage the body of the lock in the cylinder connecting bar, then secure the plate with the screws provided.

3. Use the keys to check that the bolt works and mark where the striking plate/keep is required on the door jamb. Cut a recess for the plate in the jamb then screw it into place (D). Finally check that the lock operates properly and holds the door tightly closed. Sometimes it is necessary to sink the keep slightly deeper into the door jamb.

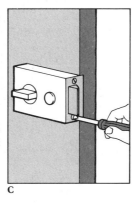

C   D

Fitting bolts, chains and viewers

Door security is completed by fitting bolts at the top and bottom of each door, plus a door chain and door viewer to the front door, or to side doors which may be used for callers.

Traditional surface-mounting bolts offer very little security because they are fairly easy to force (the thin steel staple is usually fixed to the door jamb/frame by only two screws) and they are readily accessible to a burglar, who may be able to reach them once an adjacent window has been broken.

The best type of bolt to fit is the security mortise bolt (also called a rack bolt). These are fitted into holes drilled in the edge of a door and the bolt is wound out by means of a special key. Therefore, the bolt is difficult to tamper with and because the bolt shoots some distance into the edge of the frame it is difficult to break in by force without almost destroying the door.

● To fit a mortise bolt, first drill a 16 mm (⅝ in) diameter hole in the edge of the door, then drill a smaller hole through the inside face of the door for the key. Cut a recess for the faceplate of the bolt, which is secured with two screws.

● When you have fitted the bolt, close the door and wind out the bolt to mark the door jamb. Drill an engagement hole at this mark and fix on the recessed locking plate.

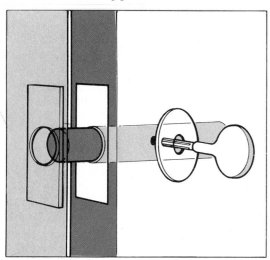

A mortise (rack) bolt can only be operated by a key from inside. It is a simple bolt rebated into the door, which is shot into a bolt box or cover plate fixed to the jamb

● Door chains must be of good quality to ensure that they are strong enough to resist forcing. Screw the chain anchor to the door jamb and fix the metal channel, in which the other end of the chain slides, to the face of the door. The fittings must be attached with the longest screws possible to ensure that they cannot be wrenched from the door by force.

● A door viewer is a special lens fixed to the door at eye level which gives a very wide angle of view, allowing you to see who is standing at the door before it is opened. The viewer comes in two parts, which screw together from each side of the door. They are suitable for doors from 38 mm to 50 mm (1½ in to 2 in) thick. Drill a hole of about 12 mm (½ in) diameter through the door, hold one part of the viewer against the inside face of the door and screw on the other section from the other side.

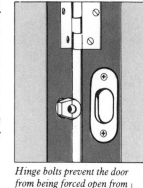

Hinge bolts prevent the door from being forced open from the hinge side

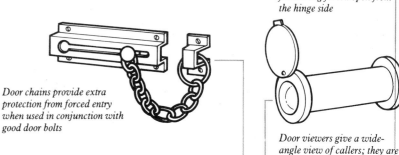

Door chains provide extra protection from forced entry when used in conjunction with good door bolts

Door viewers give a wide-angle view of callers; they are usually screw-together types for doors 40 mm (1½ in) to 60 mm (2½ in) thick

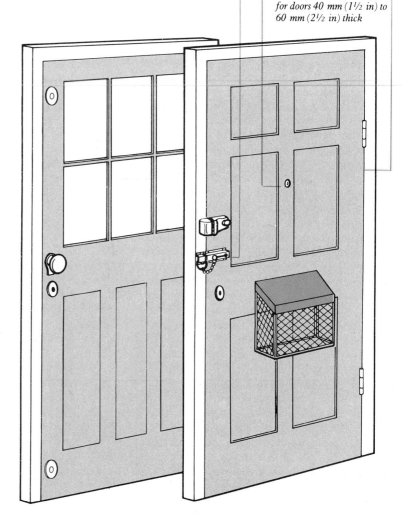

Securing the windows

In the majority of cases burglars get in through windows, so these must be secured carefully, especially those which are vulnerable – see page 31. Generally, for timber windows, the most secure locks fit in mortises in the wood rather than being simply screwed to the surface, where they can be tampered with and may be prised off. With metal windows fitting is harder because generally it is necessary to cut screw threads in the metal. So long as the correct size hole is drilled, in most cases the screws themselves cut the thread as they are inserted (self-tapping screws).

Casement windows

For timber hinged windows mortise rack bolts (similar to door rack bolts) give high security combined with a neat appearance. Surface-mounted dual screws are easier to fit, but are not so neat. For speedier locking of casement windows key-operated casement window locks are available, or for an even neater job the cockspur handle can be changed for an integral locking version. Casement stay locks are useful as easily fitted supplementary locks.

A very neat lock for metal casements is the sliding wedge lock which fits inside the channel within the metal frame. There are also various clamps, which are very easy to fit, and these lock the casement stay on to its rest. Another alternative is to screw a cockspur handle lock to the frame. This device has a sliding or pivoting bolt, which, when locked in position, prevents the handle from being operated.

You can also obtain a lockable cockspur handle, with which you replace the original; a key will secure the window closed, or slightly open for ventilation.

Sliding windows

Sash windows are the most common sliding timber windows and there are various locks for securing these. Key-operated sash locks have the quickest action and provide good security because a special key is needed to operate them. Cheaper to buy is the screw-operated locking stop, in which a stop can be screwed to a metal plate by means of a special key to prevent the sashes from sliding. Both the key-operated and screw stops can be fitted to allow the top sash to be lowered a little for ventilation.

A neater device for locking sash windows together is the dual screw, in which a bolt fixed to the inner sash can be screwed out by a special key to engage in a hole in the outer sash.

The best way to improve security with metal sash windows is to fit a key-operated sliding window lock. Alternatively a clamp-on lock can be fitted to the sliding window track.

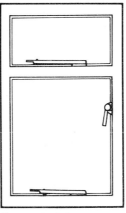

Casement windows *Wooden casement windows can be secured with an assortment of lockable stays, frame locks and handle catches – each quick and easy to undo from inside, and unobtrusive*

Sash windows *The best way to prevent a sash window from being forced is to fasten the two frames together: there are many devices that will do this*

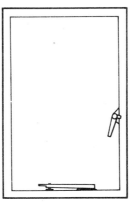

Metal casement *Opening metal-framed windows can be locked by securing the stays and cockspur handles, or by clamping the opening frame to the fixed frame*

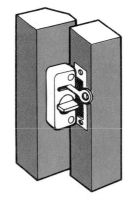

Locking bolt *Rim-mounted lock, which secures the casement or fanlight to a bolt box in the outer frame*

Screwlock *A neat, strong fixing which screws a wooden casement window or fanlight to the outer frame*

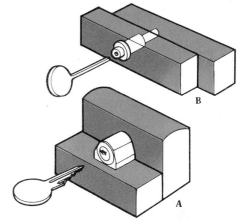

Sash lock *Key-operated cylinder lock, which drives a small bolt into a reinforced bolt hole (A).*

Dual screw *This is mortised within the inner frame to shoot out a bolt that connects with a plate on the upper sash (B).*

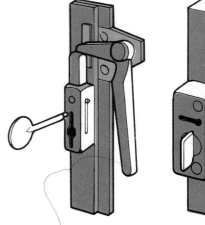

Cockspur handle lock *Fits onto the metal frame and is locked to prevent the handle from being released*

Frame lock *The lock is fixed to the opening part of the frame and a bolt hooks onto the fixed frame*

5.Exterior decorating

Planning a colour scheme

Exterior decorating serves two useful functions; it improves (and can alter) the look of the house and protects the structure from the weather by keeping it sound and dry. The first thing to remember is that there are no short cuts to achieving a good and lasting finish. You must spend time preparing all surfaces carefully before you can apply the final, finishing, coat.

Choosing a good colour scheme is important: it should express your individuality, but not in a way that makes the house look too overpowering compared to its neighbours. If your house is one of a row, be particularly careful when choosing the colours so that the house is given a character of its own without detracting from the overall appearance of the whole row. Although you can paint in colours that contrast with neighbouring houses it is best to retain some uniformity by keeping all the woodwork – door and window frames, for instance – white, or some other neutral shade. With a semi-detached house a similar problem exists – the scheme should harmonize with the colours used on the adjoining property.

The ideal situation where colour can be used to good effect is where the road has houses of different ages and various architectural styles, which gives you a free hand to pick any colour you choose. But try not to be too flamboyant in your choice of colours: many people are quite conservative in their taste and a house that is considered garish may not only be difficult to sell but also could decrease in value. In general, the 'safe' colours are the neutrals such as white, grey and beige, which can be a good background to stronger colours, perhaps used on doors and windows.

If you are unsure as to whether a new colour scheme will work it is a good idea to test it out first by selecting a photograph of your house from which you can make a number of tracings. Use watercolours, crayons or felt-tip pens to experiment with various colour schemes to see how they will look. Take the tracings outside to check that any likely schemes will blend with their surroundings and with neighbouring properties.

Of course, exterior decorating can involve more than applying a new coat of paint. Remember that you can also improve the appearance and weathering properties of a house by fixing on various cladding materials (see page 48) or by changing the front door hardware (see page 50).

Providing a new look for the outside of your house may involve patience and a lot of hard work, but, properly done, it will make your house one to be proud of for a number of years.

Left: *a colonial-style house in Williamsburg, Virginia. The timber clad walls have been painted in a neutral sand colour and windows and porch, in white, harmonizing with the picket fencing*

Far left (top): *a very individual house built by the owner. Because it is situated in open country the colours do not need to blend in with other houses. Note the dramatic use of contrasting colours*

Left: *a detached house typical of many British city suburbs. Neutral colour rendering (stucco) and white window frames contrast with the deep natural colours of the front door and imitation half timbering*

Far left (bottom): *the exterior decoration of period terraced cottages should be treated sympathetically. Certain areas have regional colour schemes which have developed over the years. Where possible these should be followed*

Equipment and materials

In order to carry out even the most straight-forward exterior decorating job you will need a selection of tools and materials – plus the necessary equipment to enable you to reach the job and work safely.

Choosing access equipment

● **Ladder:** The extending type is best, so that you can reach up to eaves height without overstretching. The top should extend at least three rungs above the highest point you wish to reach. Aluminium ladders are lighter and feel more secure than timber ladders – and they will not rot. Choose a ladder with wide treads that will be comfortable to stand on for long periods. If your house has plastic gutters you will also need a ladder stay, which holds the top of the ladder out from the wall, clear of the gutters.

There are a number of vital safety precautions you should follow when using ladders. They are:
1. Tie the ladder securely to the building with rope passed round the top rung and through a stout screw eye fixed directly to the wall, or screwed into the eaves timbers.
2. Place the ladder at the correct angle to prevent it toppling or slipping. It should be placed 1 m (3 ft 3 in) out from the wall for every 3 m (10 ft) up the wall.
3. Stand the ladder on firm ground, or placed on a wide board if the ground is soft.
4. Anchor the base of the ladder to a stake driven into the ground or wedge its feet with a sand bag so that the ladder cannot slip.
● **Step ladders:** Platform steps are ideal for painting ground floor windows and walls at lower levels, and if painting a bungalow.
● **Scaffold tower:** This costs more to hire than a

ladder, but gives a safe, flat, working platform. A tower is invaluable if repairs have to be carried out. They cannot be erected or moved as quickly as a ladder and must be securely tied to the building or fitted with outriggers if over 5 m (16 ft 6 in) high.

The decorating tool kit

● **Brushes:** For gloss-painting woodwork you will need 25 mm, 50 mm and 75 mm (1 in, 2 in and 3 in) brushes, plus a 19 mm (¾ in) angled-bristled cutting-in brush for painting window frames. For painting walls a 100 mm (4 in) or 125 mm (5 in) wall brush will be required.
● **Paint roller:** You may prefer to use a roller for painting walls if you find holding a large paintbrush tiring. Choose a long, shaggy pile roller for highly-textured surfaces and a medium-pile roller for smoother surfaces.
● **Flat scraper:** Use a scraper with a 50 mm (2 in) blade for removing paint from wood.
● **Shave hooks:** Triangular – or curved – bladed scrapers are used for scraping paint from door architraves and window frames.
● **Scrubbing brush:** An ordinary household scrubbing brush is ideal for washing down walls and removing loose, flaky paint.
● **Wire brush:** This is needed for removing rust from metal surfaces and for preparing walls.
● **Plastic bucket and S-hook:** The bucket is

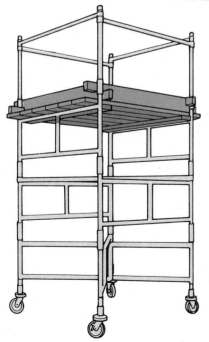

A scaffold tower gives a secure, flat, working platform (left) – it is especially useful if you have extensive repair work to carry out prior to decorating, as there is plenty of space for all the tools and equipment you are likely to need. If the amount of work does not warrant a tower, choose an extending ladder (right) and fit a stay to hold the top away from the gutters; tie it to a screw eye fixed to the fascia or wall. Wedge the feet of the ladder with a sand bag, or tie the base to a stake driven into the ground, so there is no danger of it slipping

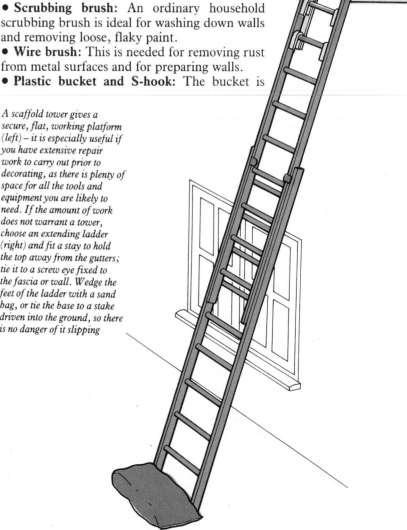

used when washing down and the S-hook allows you to hang the bucket (and paint tins) from the rungs of a ladder.

● **Filling knife:** A flexible-bladed knife is used to apply filler to wood and masonry.

● **Abrasive paper:** Use wet-and-dry paper in coarse, medium and fine grades for preparing woodwork for repainting. You can also buy a pumice block and abrasive stripping blocks.

● **Safety goggles:** Wear these when rubbing down walls to prevent dust and flying fragments getting into your eyes.

● **Blowtorch/hot air stripper:** Use either of these tools for removing paint from woodwork.

● **Dust sheets:** Place polythene (polyethylene) dust sheets below your working area to protect paths, low roofs and garden areas.

● **Sponge:** A good, strong sponge is useful for washing down walls and paintwork.

● **Tacky rag:** For wiping the prepared surface just before painting, to remove dust.

Essential materials

● **Knotting:** A shellac-based material applied to knots in wood before finishing to prevent resin from the wood seeping out and spoiling the surface of the paint.

● **Fillers:** Use an all-purpose exterior filler for cracks in woodwork and masonry, and a fine surface filler for smoothing chipped paintwork.

● **Wood stopping (Plastic wood):** This useful, long-established wood filler is available in a

number of wood shades. Useful for filling wood that is to be finished with clear varnish.

● **Epoxy resin-based fillers:** Two-part, quick-setting fillers used for repairing decayed wood.

● **Mastic (caulking compound):** This flexible, non-setting filler is used for sealing gaps around frames for which a non-rigid seal is required.

● **Fungicide:** Use this in solution with water for killing mould and algae growth on walls.

● **Primers:** For most jobs, use an all-purpose primer. But use an aluminium wood primer over previously bitumen-painted surfaces, on seasoned hardwood, and resinous timber. Zinc chromate or zinc phosphate primers are suitable for all bare metals except new galvanized steel, for which calcium plumbate primer should be used. Use an alkali-resistant primer for painting asbestos cement.

● **Stabilizing solution:** Use over chalky wall surfaces before applying masonry paint.

● **Oil-based undercoat:** Use after primer as a base for most gloss paints. Some non-drip gloss paints do not need an undercoat.

● **Gloss paint:** Outdoors you should apply two coats of gloss over undercoat. Do not use matt or silk finish paints outdoors as these attract dirt.

● **Masonry paints:** Cheaper cement-based types are useful for initially sealing pebbledashed (stuccoed) walls, otherwise use a specialized wall paint reinforced with mica or resins. Exterior grade emulsion (latex) paint can also be used, but this will not seal fine cracks.

Equip yourself with a kit of good quality tools for decorating your house. You will need:
1. *25 mm (1 in) brush*
2. *50 mm (2 in) brush*
3. *75 mm (3 in) brush*
4. *19 mm (¾ in) cutting-in brush*
5. *125 mm (5 in) brush*
6. *Scrubbing brush*
7. *25 mm (1 in) filling knife*
8. *50 mm (2 in) scraper*
9. *Combination-blade shavehook*
10. *Triangular-blade shavehook*
11. *Plastic bucket*
12. *Paint kettle*
13. *Paint tray for roller*
14. *Deep pile roller*
15. *Protective goggles*
16. *S-hook*
17. *Sponge for washing-down*
18. *Abrasive paper and block*
19. *Hot air stripper*
20. *Electric sander*

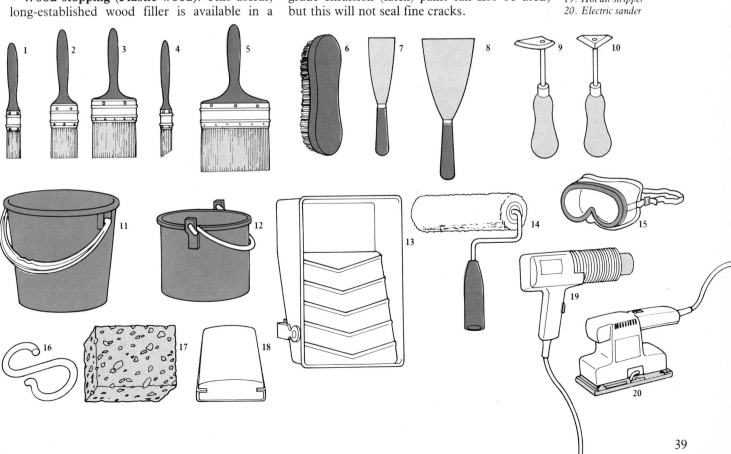

Preparation for wood

In all forms of preparation before decorating, and particularly for wood, it is vital that you produce a sound surface; if you do not take meticulous care at this stage the resulting finish will be poor and after a short time will crack, peel and generally disintegrate.

Before you start to paint, make sure you complete *all* the preparatory work – stripping, rubbing down and so on – so that dust, dirt and flakes of paint will not land on surfaces you have just decorated. Start work in dry weather on a calm day, working downwards from the top of the house.

Apart from keeping prepared surfaces clean, you will also be able to treat bare wood with primer before the end of the day, while it is still dry. The amount of preparation you do depends on the condition of the existing surfaces: sound, painted surfaces which only need brightening up can simply be washed down and keyed for the new paint.

It is more likely, however, that outdoor paintwork will be in bad condition, with flaking, peeling, chipped or split paintwork over a wide area. In this case you should strip it back to bare wood so that a new paint system – primer, undercoat and top coats – can be built up on a sound surface.

When you are examining the paintwork, look for signs of undulations in an otherwise flat surface. These can be a sign that the wood is rotting, even though the paint surface may be unbroken. Probe the surface with the edge of a filling knife or penknife blade: you may find that the wood is soft and spongy, in which case it must be repaired or replaced.

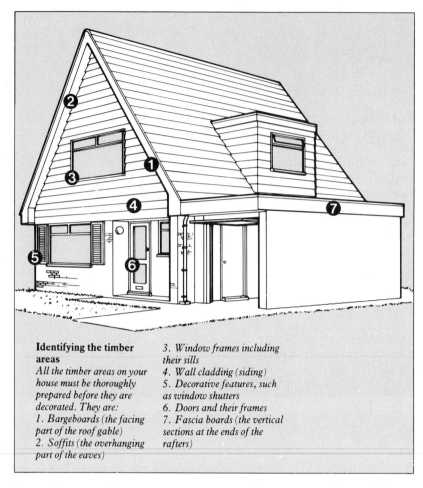

Identifying the timber areas
All the timber areas on your house must be thoroughly prepared before they are decorated. They are:
1. Bargeboards (the facing part of the roof gable)
2. Soffits (the overhanging part of the eaves)
3. Window frames including their sills
4. Wall cladding (siding)
5. Decorative features, such as window shutters
6. Doors and their frames
7. Fascia boards (the vertical sections at the ends of the rafters)

Preparing wood for repainting

If painted wood surfaces are sound, simply wash down the paintwork using a solution of sugar soap and warm water. While the surface is still wet rub it with a pumice or stripping block, or with wet-and-dry abrasive paper, used dry, which will remove deep-seated dirt and take the gloss off the surface to produce a good key for the new paint. Rinse the surface with clean water and allow it to dry.

Filling defects

If, despite a few chips or blisters in a painted surface, the overall condition of the paintwork is basically sound, it is unnecessary to strip the entire surface. Scrape and rub down the surfaces around the chipped or blistered area then fill the indentation with a fine surface filler, after priming the bare wood. When the filler has hardened, rub down the surface until smooth, then apply undercoat in the normal way.

Using a blowtorch

Heat will soften paint quickly, allowing large areas to be stripped easily. A gas blowtorch offers a fast method of stripping paint. Use the

Left: *a timber window frame showing extreme signs of deterioration. The blistered, flaking paint film would have to be stripped back to bare wood, and the surface treated to prevent rot, before you could apply a new paint system*

torch carefully: allowing the flame to rest on one surface for too long can scorch the wood. Play the flame over the entire area you are stripping. Be particularly wary, when using it under the eaves, that you do not set light to any birds' nests and cause a serious fire.

Because it is generally safer you may prefer to use an electric paint stripper. It works on the principle of a ferocious hair dryer with a fan sending a blast of hot air from the nozzle, which softens the paint and allows it to be scraped off. It has the advantage in windy weather of not blowing out as a gas flame can, although its heat will be dissipated in these conditions. Be careful not to let hot, softened paint fall on to your hand. When stripping paint from a window frame, remove the curtains first in case they should catch alight, and do not play the heat onto the glass: it will crack. Flaking paint on putty is best removed by dry scraping or, if this fails, chemical stripping.

Using dry scrapers
Sharp-bladed scrapers with renewable blades are available for stripping dry paint. They work quite effectively, but are slow and quite laborious to use. Confine dry stripping to areas where it is difficult or impossible to use a hot-air stripper or blowtorch, and be careful you do not gouge the wood.

Stripping with chemicals
Chemical stripping is an expensive method of removing outdoor paintwork and therefore best used only for paintwork close to glass or in intricate mouldings (such as on panelled doors). Use it also where the woodwork is to be given a clear finish and it is important not to scorch the wood. Chemical stripping is much slower than other methods. Dab on the chemical liberally with an old paintbrush and leave for about ten

minutes for it to soften and bubble the paint, then scrape off using a flat-bladed scraper or shave hook. Be careful not to splash your eyes with stripper, or get any on your skin – it will burn. If this does happen, wash immediately with plenty of water.

Repairing decayed wood
When preparing outdoor woodwork for re-decoration it is likely that areas of softened and crumbling wood will be found due to the effects of wetness, perhaps caused by a leaking gutter. To make a repair you will either have to replace the rotted wood completely (perhaps – in the worst cases – by fitting a new window or door frame), or cut away the rotted section and replace it with a new piece of wood. An easy method can be chosen which is to attempt a repair using a modern wood repair system. The best of these consist of three parts – a wood hardener to give a firm basis for the repair, a two-part high-performance wood filler (based on glass fibre resin), which gives a hard, durable repair that will expand and contract naturally with the wood, and special pellets, which are inserted into holes bored into the timber around the damaged areas. The pellets release wood preservative into the timber as soon as the moisture content of the wood reaches a level at which rot can start.

Use a shavehook to strip defective paintwork from door frames: the triangular or pear-shaped blade can reach the smallest of crevices without damaging the wood. Combination shavehooks have curved and angular blades to deal with flat and moulded sections

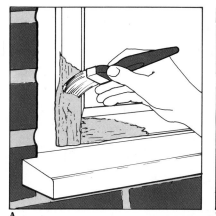

A

Stop the spread of wet rot with a proprietary treatment which begins with the application of a chemical wood hardener (A)

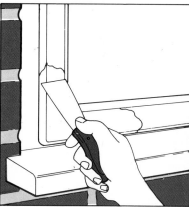

B

Fill the damaged area with an all-purpose wood filler applied by filling knife, and smooth it to the shape of the original wood (B)

Complete the treatment by inserting special wood preservative 'tablets' into pre-drilled holes to stop the spread of decay (C)

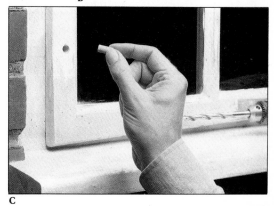

C

Preparation for walls

Algae and mould growth should be killed off by scrubbing with a fungicide solution (far left). Scraping will remove flaking paint and loose surface particles

Preparation should always start at the highest point and you should work downwards so that previously prepared or painted surfaces are not contaminated by subsequent work. It is also a good idea to cover areas surrounding the working site to make clearing up easier and to stop paths and roofs at lower levels being spattered by paint. Heavy-duty plastic sheets or old curtains or bed sheets weighted at the edges with bricks or pieces of timber are ideal for this purpose.

Brick walls

If they are not to be painted the most brick walls will need is a wash down with a hose and a rub over with a scrubbing brush to remove loose dirt. Do not add detergent to the water, as this can leave a whitish stain, which may be difficult to remove. Also, do not attempt to wash down bricks that may be covered with a whitish powdery residue, known as efflorescence. The powder is caused by salts in the brickwork or mortar being brought to the surface as the wall dries out – a fault usually found in fairly new walls. After a time the problem will disappear, so simply brush off the worst of the powder with a dry brush. Do not wet the wall: this will only bring fresh salts to the surface.

● If decorative facing bricks are marked, the best way to remove the marks and bring out the colour is to rub over the surface using a brick of similar type and colour while washing down with water.

● If green algae is growing on a wall, this is a sure sign that the wall is damp. Remedy the real cause of the dampness then kill off all the algae and mould growth by scrubbing the wall with a fungicide solution diluted according to the manufacturer's instructions. Do not forget to wear rubber gloves when doing this

job. Leave the fungicide on the wall for 24 hours, then wash it off using a hose and hand brush.

● If you are not going to paint the wall, brush on a colourless silicone water-repellent treatment, which will prevent rain penetration without affecting the appearance of the wall.

● If the surface of a previously painted brick, stone or cement-rendered wall is sound it is sufficient to clean it with a stiff brush. If it is very dirty, scrub it with a solution of sugar soap and water, then rinse it down thoroughly using a hose.

● If there is moss or mould growth on the surface, scrape or brush this off, using a stiff-bristled brush. Do not use a wire brush: it will leave grey marks on the surface, which could mean that an extra coat of paint is needed to obliterate them. After scraping and brushing,

Undercut the edges of large cracks using a chisel to give a better grip for the filler material. Spread on the filler with a filling knife and allow it to stand proud of the wall surface; when it is dry, sand smooth with glasspaper

apply a fungicide and rinse off, as previously described.

● Cracks in the surface are best filled with an exterior-grade filler. Fill any larger cracks and bare patches with cement mortar, which is cheaper. Rake out and undercut the edges of the crack or missing rendering with a cold chisel, to give a key for the new material. Brush away dust and paint the damaged area with a pva bonding agent. To improve adhesion, also mix some pva adhesive into the mortar, which should consist of one part cement to four parts sand. Press the mortar well into the crack or damaged area and leave the surface smooth by polishing it with a builder's trowel or steel float. If the rendering (stucco) is more than about 12 mm (½ in) thick you may need to apply two coats of mortar. Apply the first coat about 10 mm (⅜ in) thick, scratch the surface with the trowel blade, then allow to harden before applying the second coat.

● If, after preparing the surface, you find that a powdery dust is left on your hands when you touch the wall, you must paint the surface with a stabilizing solution. This should be applied generously and left for 24 hours before the first coat of paint is applied.

● Water stains are occasionally seen in previously painted walls and these can indicate defective gutters or downpipes, which should be repaired immediately (see page 84). Allow the stain to dry out, and then brush on alkali-resistant primer so that there is no risk of the stain bleeding through to the surface of the wall paint.

● If areas of pebbledash (stucco) are missing, cut back and repair the hole with mortar, then, while the surface coat is still soft, throw handfuls of pebbles of similar size and shape to the existing ones on to the rendering and press in lightly with a piece of wood. If you plan to paint the wall, the colour of the pebbles is not important.

● If there is a fairly large area of missing pebbledash (stucco) to repair use a keying liquid mixed with a cement-based paint and plastering sand as filler, then stipple the surface to produce

an effect similar to the surrounding pebbledash, using a household banister brush. The same brush, partially loaded with the mix, can be used after about 15 minutes to tap back any sharp points on the surface.

● Wash down unpainted rendering and pebbledash (stucco) with water and a stiff brush to remove grime. Treat mould as already described and fill holes and cracks; masonry paint will fill hair-line cracks only.

● Plastic cladding and gutters need only washing down with water and detergent. Do not use abrasive cleaners and do not let the dirty water run onto brickwork. Plastic gutters are not meant to be painted, but if you do not like their colour, leave them until they are at least one year old. Primer and undercoat are not required; just apply two coats of gloss paint.

● Thoroughly scrape and wire-brush metal surfaces, to remove loose, flaking rust, ideally using a wire cup brush in an electric drill. Wipe the surface with a dry cloth and apply a rust-inhibiting primer. Prime metal windows with cold galvanizing paint. If you want to paint aluminium, rub it down first with fine emery paper, then wipe over with a clean rag soaked in white spirit (methyl hydrate). Finally, prime with an all-surface or metal primer.

Brush down metal gutters with a wire brush to remove rust and other debris. Treat with a primer before repainting

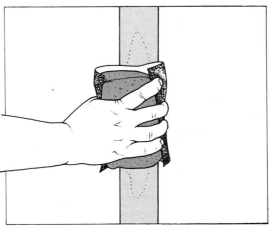

Wrap wet-and-dry abrasive paper round a sponge and use to rub down downpipes: the sponge accommodates the curve of the pipe

Painting and varnishing

When to decorate

Once you have thoroughly prepared the surfaces you plan to decorate you can start to paint. But it is important to choose the correct time if your results are to be successful. Follow these guidelines as to your exterior decorating timetable:

• The basic structure of the house should be as dry as possible, so aim to complete your exterior decorating between late spring and early autumn.

• Always paint on a dry, calm day when there is little risk of rain spoiling a freshly-painted surface.

• On a bright day, follow the sun. Allow the sun to drive away dew and leave the surface to be painted in a warm condition, but paint in the shade, where it will be easier to see what you are doing without glare (especially if you are using white paint).

• Avoid painting on a windy day. Dust will be blown onto the freshly painted surface, which will mar the finish. If this does happen, rub down the surface when dry and paint it again.

• Do not paint later than about two hours before sunset. This will give the paint time to harden before dew can settle on the surface; it will also allow the paint to form a skin before any flies can stick to and spoil the finish.

Order of painting

Start by painting the barge boards (on the face of the gable), then paint the fascia boards (at the end of the rafters), followed by the gutters and the undersides of the eaves (called the soffits).

After this you can tackle the walls. If possible it is best to divide these into sections where natural breaks occur, such as at bay windows, gutter downpipes, and soil pipes. In this way the joins between painted areas should not be so noticeable. Right-handed people will find it best to paint a wall working from right to left from the top first, followed by the middle section and finally the lower part.

After the walls have been completed the pipes can be tackled. Push a sheet of hardboard or card behind the pipes to shield the wall from the paint and be careful not to allow drips to fall onto the wall lower down. To finish, paint the upstairs windows, the downstairs windows and finally the doors.

Estimating quantities

For wall paints, most manufacturers quote spreading rates for brush-applied coats on a smooth rendered surface. For roughcast or pebbledashed surfaces, allow at least 50% more paint. Extra paint will also be required if the wall has not previously been painted. Apart from the fact that the paint may be covering a dark colour, a new wall may be porous, which will absorb more paint. In the latter case follow the manufacturer's instructions regarding the application of a primer or thinned-down first coat to seal a porous wall.

When pricing various paints remember that cheaper, inferior brands may not spread or cover as well as the more expensive, better-quality paints. Therefore, at the end of the job there may be little to choose between the cost of applying good-quality or inferior paint, but the better-quality brand may retain its appearance and give better weather protection for longer.

With wall paints, the number of coats required depends on the colour of the existing surface and the colour of the new paint, as well as on the condition of the surface. If the surface is in good condition and the colour is the same as the one previously used, then one coat should be sufficient. If you are changing the colour from light to dark, or vice versa, or if the surface was in bad condition and needed stabilizing or priming, two or three coats will be required.

For undercoats and gloss paints, simply work out the approximate area to be covered, multiply this by the number of coats required, and compare this area with the covering power of the chosen paint (which will be stated on the tin).

WHICH PAINT?

It is important that you apply the correct paint system to your house, both for protection from the weather and as decoration. Consult this ready reference guide to choosing:

Woodwork (painted)
Preservative Choose a colourless liquid that can be painted over as initial protection for exterior woodwork such as doors, window frames and weatherboarding (siding)
Primer Use an all-purpose or ordinary wood primer to help the paint to adhere better to the wood. Use an aluminium wood primer on resinous timber
Undercoat Most top coats (except some non-drip gloss (enamel) types) need an undercoat to give a key for the finish; each top coat requires a particular type of undercoat, specified by the maker
Gloss (enamel) Solvent-based top coats typically have a gloss or semi-gloss finish. In most cases you will probably have to apply two coats over one undercoat to obliterate previous colours

Woodwork (exposed)
Stains Use coloured stains to protect and decorate hardwood (often used for sub-frames for aluminium windows and some high quality window sills) where you want to display the wood grain
Varnish Again used for protecting attractive wood where you want to display the grain. Oil-based (not polyurethane) varnishes are best for sealing with a gloss, semi-gloss or matt finish

Masonry
Stabilizing primer Use to seal dusty surfaces prior to painting (not for resin-based masonry paint: use an all-surface primer instead)
Cement paint This is the cheapest. It comes in a limited range of colours
Stone paint A durable finish for any type of masonry and will conceal minor cracks

Exterior grade emulsion (latex) This is a more durable type of paint than its interior counterpart and comes in a wide selection of colours
Masonry paint A resin-based paint with a tough, semi-gloss finish

Metalwork
Primer Use an all-purpose or metal primer to prepare metal window frames, gutters and railings for repainting; or a calcium plumbate primer on iron and steel
Undercoat As for woodwork, metalwork must have a layer (sometimes two) of undercoat to give a key for the finish
Gloss (enamel) Again, use a solvent-based, gloss finishing coat on metalwork
Bituminous paint Use this on gutters and downpipes that have been previously painted with bituminous paint: do not use ordinary gloss without applying a sealer or the old finish will 'bleed' through

Start to paint on a calm, dry day between late spring and early autumn; begin in the morning when any dew has evaporated. Aim to follow the sun but paint in the shade so it is easier to see what you are doing without any glare

MIDDAY

Stop painting about two hours before sunset so that the paint has plenty of time to harden before the next morning's dew can mar the finish

9.00AM
prepare in sun

5.00PM
paint in shade

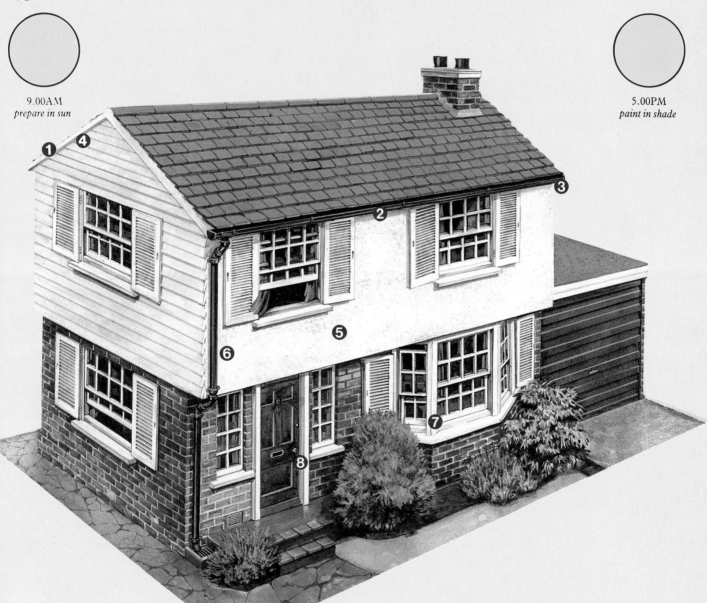

1. Bargeboards
Start at the highest part of the house with primer, undercoat and gloss paint

2. Fascias
Working down, the fascia boards are the next parts to tackle, using the same paint system

3. Gutters
Paint the gutters with an all-surface primer, followed by undercoat and two top coats

4. Soffits
If the soffits are wood, treat as for other woodwork; if they are asbestos you will need to be especially careful in the preparatory stages

5. Walls
Divide the walls into easily manageable sections and treat with exterior emulsion (latex) or other masonry paint

6. Downpipes
After the walls come the downpipes; protect the surface of the walls as you apply the paint

7. Windows
Tackle the upstairs and downstairs windows using primer, undercoat and two top coats of gloss (enamel)

8. Doors
Finally, you can paint the doors and their frames with the normal paint system for woodwork

Windy weather
Do not paint on a really windy day or you will find that dust will be blown onto your freshly painted surface, ruining the finish

45

Painting techniques

Preparation is vital for a smooth, long-lasting finish, but equally important is the application of the paint. When you are painting woodwork, always brush *with* the grain, not across it, to avoid streaking. Finish each area with light, sweeping strokes to even out brush marks. Brush into corners and edges, not from them, to avoid an unsightly ridge of paint.

Barge boards and fascias

These are the first items to decorate because they are the highest – and least accessible – parts of the house. Prepare the surface then apply primer to dry, bare wood. When this has dried, apply undercoat.

When dry, lightly sand the surface by hand, using fine-grade glasspaper, to remove any particles stuck to the paint, then brush the surface to remove loose dust and wipe over with a tacky rag or a rag dampened with white spirit (methyl hydrate) to ensure the surface is clean. Apply the first coat of gloss paint. You can apply a second coat 12 to 24 hours later.

Gutters

Gutters are the next items to paint. Prepare them thoroughly (see page 43), then give the inside of metal gutters a liberal coat of weatherproofing paint or gloss paint. Paint the outsides of the gutters with all-surface primer, aluminium primer, or a zinc-based metal primer. When dry, apply undercoat followed by two coats of gloss paint. You can use up old, nearly empty tins of gloss paint by painting the insides of gutters with the contents. Any mix of colours will not be noticeable from ground level.

Soffits

These should be painted after the gutters and fascias have been decorated. If the soffits are made of wood, preparation and painting is as for barge boards. However, sometimes they are made from asbestos cement and in this case preparation must be done with care because asbestos dust is dangerous. Wear a dust mask and to be on the safe side just clean and key the surface of the existing paintwork rather than try to get back to the bare asbestos. If the paint has flaked to reveal any bare areas these should be painted with an alkali-resistant primer. Finish with undercoat and two coats of gloss paint.

Walls

Larger areas such as walls can be painted using a brush, but the size you are likely to need – at least 100 mm (4 in) – would be very tiring to hold for long periods. You will probably find it easier to use a roller, except on the most textured surfaces.

Load the roller from a paint tray and apply to the wall in crisscross motions, finishing an area with straight strokes before moving on.

Start at the highest point and work from right to left (if you are right-handed), across and down, finishing at the bottom left-hand corner. Even if you are using a roller you will still need a brush – 75 mm (3 in) is ideal – to paint a band of paint close to soffit boards, downpipes and window frames.

Paint smooth walls with normal brush or roller strokes, but tackle rough rendered and pebbledashed (stuccoed) walls with a stippling action for even coverage – special stippling brushes are available. New pebbledashing (stucco) is particularly difficult to paint because it is so absorbent: apply a first coat of slightly thinned cement-based paint and, to help this coat to spread better, dampen the wall slightly.

If you have very large areas of wall to paint, consider hiring pressure spraying equipment to apply both stone-based paints and exterior grade emulsions (latex). The advantage of spraying is that it is quick and by angling the nozzle it is possible to get the paint into all the nooks and crannies. However, it is most important to spend time masking off with brown paper all the surfaces you do not want to paint. Also you must only spray on a calm day to avoid 'spray drift', which could result in you painting more than you intended.

Opening casement windows
Follow this sequence for painting an opening casement window: rebate (1); edge of frames (2); glazing bars and putty (3); top and bottom rails (4); vertical stiles (5); centre frame bar (6); top and bottom rails (7); side bars (8); window sill (9).
Use a 50 mm (2 in) brush, and an angle-bristled cutting-in brush for the glazing bars. If you do not have a steady enough hand use a paint shield or stick masking tape around the edge of the glass

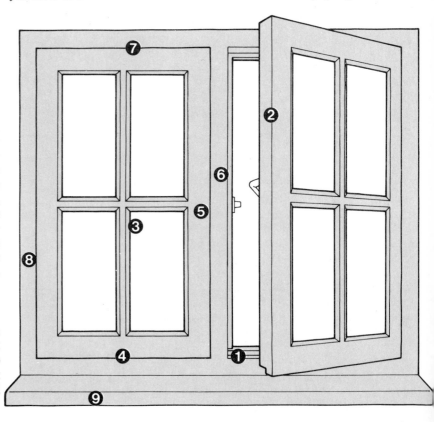

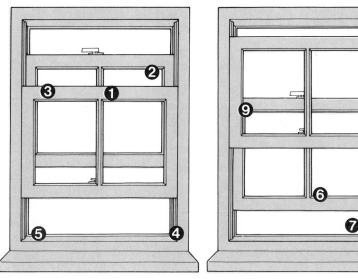

Sliding sash windows
Follow this sequence for painting a vertically sliding sash window:

Raise bottom (inner) sash to centre of the frame. Pull the top (outer) sash below bottom one. Paint top of bottom sash

Windows

You can apply paint to window frames with an ordinary 25 mm (1 in) or 50 mm (2 in) brush, but use a cutting-in brush, which has bristles cut at an angle, to take the paint up to the glass and along the glazing bars. The gloss coats can be taken 1.5 mm (1/16 in) onto the glass to form a seal, which prevents rain water from running between the glass and the putty. If you do not have a steady enough hand to do this use a metal or plastic shield, made for the purpose.

To protect the rest of the glass pane when painting, stick masking tape around the edge. Remove the tape before the paint has dried or you may peel paint off with the tape.

The order of painting hinged casement and sliding sash windows is shown in the diagrams. Windows are not easy to paint, especially if they contain a lot of small panes separated by thin glazing bars. Because you have to paint all the meeting faces with primer, undercoat and top coat – and have to allow drying time between coats – you must follow a strict routine.

There are two important points you should note regarding window sills. First, make sure that the groove in the underside of the sill is not clogged with paint. It is needed to ensure that any water that runs off the sill drips well clear of the wall, and does not seep under the sill, where dampness could result. The second point concerns oak and other hardwood sills. These have an open grain, which is very difficult to fill and paint successfully. It is best to treat these sills with clear preservative (see page 40), but if you prefer to paint them then, after stripping any existing paint, the entire surface should be filled

centre rail (1); bottom sash top rail (2); top of bottom sash side rails (3); top sash runners (4); bottom sash runners (5). When dry, almost close both sashes then paint bottom sash centre rail (6); bottom sash bottom rail (7); bottom sash side rails (8); all of the top sash outer frame (9) and glazing bars. Paint the inner face of the window at the same time, but in reverse order

with fine surface filler worked well into the cracks. When the filler has hardened, smooth it down with abrasive paper (worked in line with the grain), then prime and undercoat the sill and finish with gloss paint.

Apart from initial preparation metal windows can be painted in exactly the same way as timber windows.

Doors

Doors are the last items you should paint. Remove all metalwork, except hinges, before starting. The painting system is as for other woodwork; the order in which to paint a panelled door is shown in the diagram below.

On a door with glass panels, check to see whether the putty is cracked or loose. If so, it must be removed and the wood under the putty primed and allowed to dry, before fresh putty is pressed into place, and finished with a neat bevel (the same applies to loose window panes). On metal doors and windows it is important to use metal casement putty for glazing.

Panelled doors
Follow this sequence for painting a panelled exterior door:
Paint the panels and mouldings (1); the centre vertical sections (2); the top, centre and bottom horizontal rails (3); the door edge (4); the side verticals, or stiles (5). Lastly, paint the frame (6)

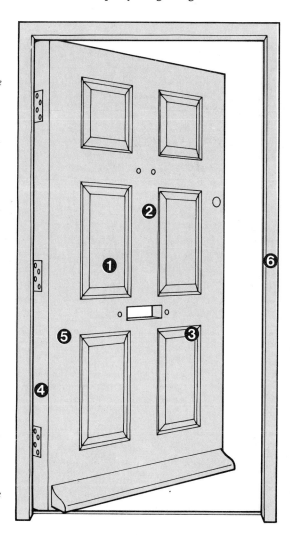

Seals and stains

Rather than covering up timber with paint you may prefer to apply a clear finish, which will highlight the colour and natural beauty of the wood grain. Hardwood doors, door frames and window frames and sills are particularly attractive if treated in this way.

1. Before the new finish can be applied the old finish must be stripped back to bare wood. This needs to be done carefully to avoid scorching or marking the surface. If you are using a blowtorch to remove old paint, handle the tool very carefully. If you are not used to using a blowtorch you would be wise to remove the old finish with a hot-air stripper or a chemical paint stripper. If the old surface was varnished, use a proprietary varnish remover – in the same way as a chemical paint stripper – to strip off the old finish.

2. When the old surface has been cleaned off, rub down the timber with abrasive paper, working in line with the grain and not across it. If possible carry out only a minimal amount of filling holes and cracks: there is a risk that the filler will not take any subsequent stains that you may apply and will stand out as unsightly marks. If you intend to bring up the colour of the wood with a stain, use an oil- or spirit-based type and fill the wood with waterproof stopping (plastic wood) of a suitable colour.

3. A good way to finish timber cladding and window frames is to apply two coats of a water-repellent preservative stain (below). This is an excellent treatment for oak sills, which tend to expand in hot weather, quickly destroying most paint surfaces. For red cedar cladding special cedar-coloured preservative stains are available to bring back the original colour.

When a gloss finish is required, apply two coats of exterior-quality varnish. Many types are based on polyurethane, while the more traditional yacht varnish gives a durable finish outdoors.

Cladding the walls

Timber cladding (siding), *used to line the exterior walls of a house, makes a striking decorative treatment, especially when painted in a contrasting colour to the window and door frames*

Exterior decorating can mean a lot more than just repainting a house. You can change its whole appearance, for example by fixing decorative cladding to part or all of the exterior. In addition this will waterproof the walls and, apart from giving a degree of insulation in its own right, cladding will also enable the walls to be insulated with glass fibre quilt.

Before cladding the whole or part of a house it is important to consider the end result in relation to the effect the cladding may have on neighbouring properties. In a row, for example, your house might stand out unattractively, while with a detached house you have much more freedom: even here it is still worth bearing in mind local building styles.

The basic choice of cladding materials is between wood, plastic and metal, all of which are normally fixed horizontally, giving a plank-like effect. You can also obtain concrete and clay tiles for vertical hanging and it is best if these are chosen to match the colour of the roof tiles. Slates are sometimes used for vertical cladding where the roof is slated.

Fixing the cladding

Before fixing cladding materials, cover the wall with heavy polythene (polyethylene) sheeting or roofing felt fixed horizontally with 75 mm (3 in) wide laps between adjacent sheets and 150 mm (6 in) vertical overlaps at the ends of adjacent sheets, to prevent moisture penetration.

Fix the cladding materials to vertical battens nailed to the wall surface. The battens should be preservative-treated and preferably tanalized, or pressure impregnated. Battens should be 38 mm × 19 mm (1½ in × ¾ in) and fixed to the wall with masonry nails. For timber cladding the battens usually have to be fixed at a maximum of 450 mm (1 ft 6 in) apart, and for plastic cladding this is usually reduced to 400 mm (1 ft 4 in).

With all types of exterior cladding, the thermal insulation of the wall can be boosted by increasing the thickness of the fixing battens, which will allow you to fix polythene- (polyethylene-) backed glass fibre insulating quilt between the battens, polythene side out, before you fix the cladding.

Timber cladding is commonly a shiplap moulding and may be ordinary softwood, western red cedar, or a hardwood. Elm is a popular waney-edge cladding material. Treat the cladding with clear wood preservative before fixing, or use a wood preservative water-repellent stain, or with paint (which is best applied over dry clear wood preservative). Fix the boards to the battens with galvanized nails and drive the heads below the surface using a nail punch. Fill the indentations with filler before applying a final coat of paint or preservative.

Plastic cladding comes in two basic types – a simple extruded upvc hollow moulding and a upvc-clad cellular extrusion, which can be sawn, screwed and nailed just like wood but gives better thermal insulation. These extrusions are usually available only in white, but they have the major advantage of being virtually maintenance-free. Most types of plastic cladding are inter-locking and are held by metal clips or galvanized nails through the fixing tongue so that the fixings are hidden once all the cladding strips are in place. Plastic cladding tends to expand and contract a good deal, so it is important to leave expansion gaps of about 6 mm (¼ in) at the ends of adjacent planks.

Metal cladding is usually white-finished aluminium, which is maintenance-free and fixed in the same way as plastic cladding. It does not, however, have the same insulation value as either wood or plastic cladding.

Concrete and clay vertical-hung tiles are available in a range of colours and in plain and decorative styles. Attach an underlay of roofing felt over the wall surface and fix preservative-treated tiling battens horizontally to the wall surface at about 112 mm (4½ in) spacings (depending on the size of the tiles – the manufacturer will specify the actual spacing in his literature). For finishing at the end of a run of tiling, use special tile-and-a-half tiles. There are also special angle tiles for ensuring that both internal and external corners can be covered.

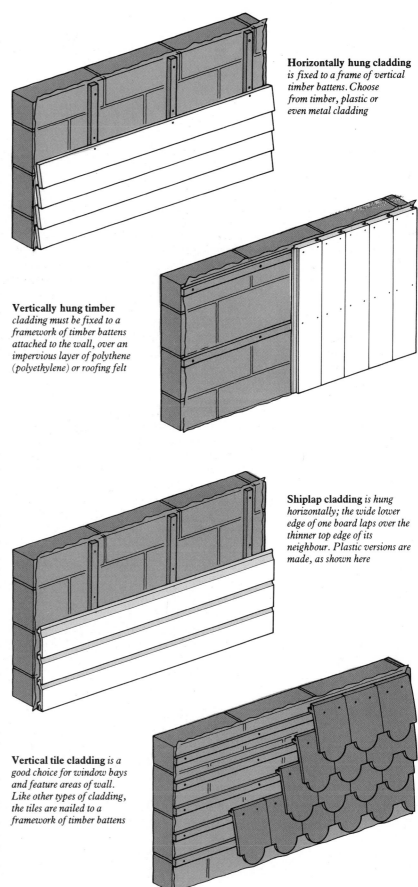

Horizontally hung cladding *is fixed to a frame of vertical timber battens. Choose from timber, plastic or even metal cladding*

Vertically hung timber *cladding must be fixed to a framework of timber battens attached to the wall, over an impervious layer of polythene (polyethylene) or roofing felt*

Shiplap cladding *is hung horizontally; the wide lower edge of one board laps over the thinner top edge of its neighbour. Plastic versions are made, as shown here*

Vertical tile cladding *is a good choice for window bays and feature areas of wall. Like other types of cladding, the tiles are nailed to a framework of timber battens*

Fitting door hardware

First impressions count, so after perhaps noting the general condition of the house it is the front door that will set the scene and perhaps make a lasting impression for most visitors to your home. Therefore it is important that this door in particular looks suitably cared for. Make a point of dressing it with attractive door hardware. A range of items is available, including door knockers, letterplate covers, house numbers, knobs and handles, bell pushes and keyhole cover plates.

The traditional door hardware sets are in polished brass and black iron, but there are also modern styles in stainless steel, polished aluminium and chrome. Try to choose a style in keeping with the style of door and type of house. Black iron sets look perfect on cottage-style oak doors and cottage-style houses. Brass sets look in place on varnished panelled hardwood doors and on older-style town houses. Steel and aluminium need a modern setting. Once you have settled on a type, keep all hardware the same style.

In most cases the fittings can be fixed simply with screws to the door or frame. But it is important to get the positioning right, so measure up carefully to get the items square; temporarily fix small pieces, such as numbers, in place with adhesive tape until you are satisfied that they are visually correct. Then mark the screw fixing points with a bradawl and drill the pilot holes for the screws. Make sure that the fixing screws match the fitting; a brass fitting needs brass screws, for example.

As door knockers tend to be heavier than other items of door hardware they are usually fixed with screw bolts, which pass right through the door. Select the position you want for the knocker and measure the distance between the screw bolts; mark the drilling positions on the face of the door. Drill the bolt holes squarely through the door using an electric drill with a suitable size wood drill bit. Get a helper to hold a block of scrap timber on the other side of the door to prevent the drill bit from bursting through the door and splintering the surface. Slot on the bolts and secure.

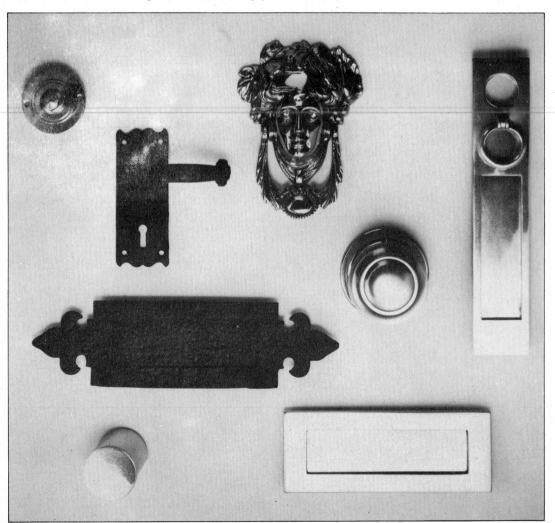

Handles *may be ornate brass or black iron types, or the more modern styles in chromium-plated or stainless steel finish; your choice should depend on the style of your door*

Knockers *also come in old and new designs; the more ornate types typically feature a lion's head, the plainest versions a simple ring and strike plate*

Letterboxes *are made in a diverse range of designs, from plain and practical to ornately moulded featuring embossed lettering and scroll patterns*

Doorbells *may be bold and ornate, perhaps with plastic or porcelain buttons, or plain and unobtrusive plastic types*

6. Porches

A porch is defined, in architectural terms at least, as an exterior structure forming a covered approach to the entrance of a building. In practice, the word is used to cover anything from a roofed recess in front of the house's main entrance to a fully enclosed lobby built out from the front of the house. Many house styles over the past 150 years have included the former, the purpose of which was twofold; to provide a modicum of protection to callers waiting on the doorstep and to draw the eye to the front door as the major feature of the building. The recess might be provided by setting the door itself back from the front wall of the house or by placing the door next to a protruding bay window and continuing the bay roof across the doorway.

However, such a porch provides only partial protection, especially against wind-blown rain

Porches can be large or small, enclosed or open. This American house of period style has an open porch and veranda (left). The factory-made porch (below), fully glazed, suits the house style

51

and snow, and whenever the front door is opened the weather simply whips into the house. This is unpleasant enough, but in these days of energy conservation it means that expensive warmth can also escape from the house whenever the front door is opened. So a fully enclosed porch has become a desirable feature because it acts as a kind of airlock between the house and the outside. The inner door can be opened to callers in the porch without allowing undue heat loss; provided the outer door is closed only the air in the porch will be admitted.

Such a porch has other advantages, too, apart from energy conservation. The extra door in the porch will make your home that much more secure against burglars. The enclosed porch can provide valuable extra storage space – for bikes and so on if it is big enough, or as somewhere to leave boots, coats and umbrellas in wet weather.

If you decide not to keep your porch locked, it can serve as an undercover place for deliveries to be left out of sight of the road. And if you glaze it all round, it can even do double duty as a small conservatory for plants – an attractive feature in itself. Such porches are an increasingly popular feature of many modern homes.

Choosing a porch

If you have no porch, or you have only some sort of canopy over your front door, then adding one will be a worthwhile improvement to your house. However, it is important that your new porch does not alter the character of your house too drastically. It all depends on the style of the house – and in some cases on the restrictions the site may pose. For example, if you have an older house with the recessed entrance or bay window canopy described earlier, the simplest solution will be to fill in the front of the recess with flank walls – solid or incorporating windows – on each side of a second door. This in-fill should fit in with the style of the rest of the house; for example, if there is a bay window alongside it the sill line should be maintained and the windows flanking the door should be in the same style as the existing ones; nothing looks more out of place than a modern aluminium door fixed across the porch of an older-style terrace house, for example. The door, too, should match the house style; one solution is to use the existing front door in the new in-fill wall, and to fit a simple glazed door leading from the porch to the house.

If your house does not have this type of recessed porch already, you will have to consider building outwards to form the new porch. Space will be the first consideration – the porch needs to be at least deep enough to allow the new outer door to open, although this can be avoided by

A purpose-built porch combined with a room extension

having the door opening outwards, or by fitting narrower-than-usual double doors instead of one wide one.

In the UK, plans for building may be restricted; you can add a porch without applying for planning permission so long as its frontage is more than 2 m (6 ft 6 in) from the boundary of the property, as long as the floor area is less than 2 sq m (22 sq ft), and so long as no part of the structure is over 3 m (10 ft) in height. Exceed any of these criteria and planning permission will be needed.

Next you have to consider what type of building you want to erect, and how much effort you are going to take to make it blend in and look like part of the original house. Consider whether the porch walls are to be glazed from floor to ceiling, or only from sill height upwards, and find out whether any masonry can be made to match the house walls. Decide whether the porch is to have a flat, lean-to or pitched roof, whether the floor levels need building up and consider whether the porch will restrict access round the house. Once you have answers to these questions, you can tackle the next problem – who is going to build the porch, and whether it is to be custom-built or bought as a kit.

Erecting a kit porch

If you decide to put up a kit porch, you will have quite a wide range of building styles and finishes to choose from. Collect as many catalogues as you can to get the best idea of what is available, and if possible visit manufacturers' show sites (or ask them to put you in touch with someone local who has already built one) so you can see the porches on your shortlist in the flesh.

Once you have decided which one you want, the next stage is to measure up exactly so the kit components can be ordered. Porch kits used to come only in standard sizes, but the manufacturers (who often make home extensions, too) can now tailor-make a porch to suit your exact requirements. You may be able to get help with this stage from the company's sales force, who will often visit your home to make up the order for you.

1. All you have to do is prepare a suitable concrete base for the porch to be built on (see page 130). When the kit arrives, the first stage is to lay a special damp-proof strip round the perimeter of the base. Then the first wall panel is held up to the edge of the base next to the house wall, and is screwed in place.

2. The next section is held up alongside it, and the two are screwed together. Corner posts and door frames are added to complete the walls, and the roof (usually a lean-to type) is assembled by fitting rafters between a wallplate on the house wall and the front wall of the porch. The roof may be of corrugated plastic or of roofing felt over plywood decking.

3. Once the structure is complete, all that remains is to weatherproof the join between the house wall and porch roof with flashing strip, seal the porch walls to the house with mastic and add the finishing touches such as cladding strips and gutters, lighting and a new house number.

Small kit porch provides excellent weatherproofing for an exposed outside door

Building your own porch

If you prefer to build your own porch, you can either construct the whole thing from scratch or make use of prefabricated components such as window and vestibule frames (which combine door and window openings) to speed up the construction. It all depends on the finish you want to achieve, and on whether you are simply filling in a recessed porch or building a complete three-sided structure. If the former you will either be filling the mouth of a 'tunnel' already formed in the front wall of the house or using an existing canopy roof (and possibly a side wall or corner post) as part of the construction. In the first case you will probably have enough width only to fit a door frame, and possibly a narrow glazed or solid panel at each side.

Recessed porch

1. Start by fixing vertical and horizontal frame members all round the opening, checking that they are square and true. Add verticals to form the door opening and a door head, too. Notch these into the side and top frame.

2. Next, add battens to form rebates for glazed areas and stop beads (door stops) round the door opening, and fill in the side and top panels with glass or exterior-quality plywood, timber cladding or whatever finish is appropriate. Finally, hang the new door.

3. Under canopy roofs, or where the tunnel opening is wider, you can build up brickwork flank walls to sill height and fit a set of off-the-shelf window frames on top of them with a door frame between them; alternatively you can instal a vestibule frame in the opening. If you cannot get one the right size and your carpentry is reasonably competent, it is a simple matter to build up a framework within the opening, especially if the side of the porch recess is already filled in. If it is not, you simply use the existing corner post as a fixture and fill in the side and front panels separately. Notch horizontals into this post and where appropriate into the bay window uprights at the other side. Add uprights to form the door frame, and proceed as described under tunnel openings earlier.

4. If you are building brickwork up to form the walls of your porch, it is important that apart from matching the existing brickwork if possible, you also tooth the new work into the existing brickwork. Otherwise the join will surely crack in the future. Do not forget to include a damp-proof course (d.p.c.) linked to that in any adjoining walls. Timber frames should also be set on d.p.c. strip if they are built up off the existing porch floor, since this may not include a damp-proof membrane. It is a good idea to use preservative-treated timber throughout.

Freestanding porch

A freestanding porch follows similar principles. Walls will either be built-up masonry or floor-to-ceiling glazed panels; bond in brickwork, and

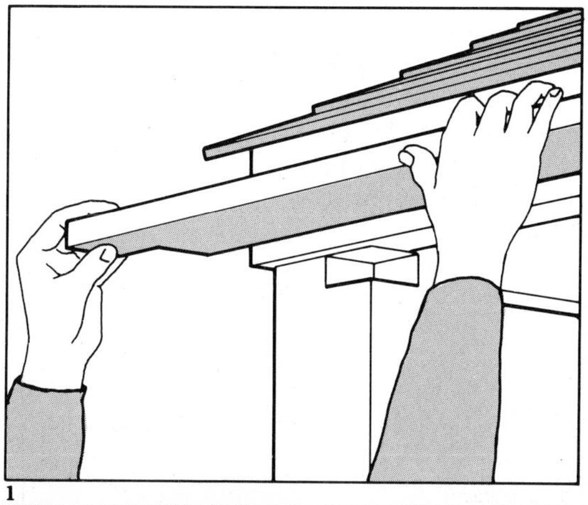

1

2

ERECTING A PORCH
Notch horizontal frame members into the vertical bearers of a recessed canopy (1), then fit frames for the door opening and head, plus any hinged lights (2). Tooth new brickwork into the house walls and build up to sill height (3) then incorporate a sloping sill on top and fit outer frames for windows (4). Build up the entire frame ready to accept home-made or off-the-shelf windows and doors (5). Hang a door within the opening to complete the porch (6)

3

4

5

6

seal frames to existing walls with non-setting mastic. At corners, use square timber posts to link window frames and add a wall plate on top of the windows and door frame to carry the rafters. Whatever roof cover you propose to use, make sure that any 'flat' roof actually has a slight fall away from the house to a gutter fixed along the front edge of the porch.

You may prefer to build up a pitched-and-tiled roof to match the main roof of the house. In this case, build up the walls as before and link

them with joists to carry the porch ceiling. Then fit pairs of rafters, cut a ridge board and assemble the porch roof structure, skew-nailing the components together like a full-scale roof. Add felt and battens, tile the roof and use lead or self-adhesive flashing to seal the gap between the porch and the house wall. Finish off by adding fascia boards and fill in the gable end with exterior-quality plywood, timber cladding or vertical tiles. Fix gutters to the fascia board, then decorate with a standard paint system.

7. Patios

Designing a patio

There is a lot more to successful patio planning than is immediately evident. It is vital to consider every aspect of the construction and design of the project before starting work since you cannot easily rearrange things once work is under way.

A patio should be designed so that it receives maximum use throughout the year. Ideally it should be partially sunny and partially shaded for most of the day. This gives you the option of choosing preferred conditions for sitting out.

Practical design

Patios are often used for outdoor meals on warm days, so a shaded area will be welcome for those who prefer to dine in cooler conditions. If it is not possible to site a patio where it will naturally get the best of both worlds, you can create shade by building a high screen wall, planting tall conifers or building a small pergola. A sunblind (awning) fixed to the house wall or a sun umbrella used in conjunction with a table will also provide ample shade.

Privacy is another important factor in patio design. Most people will want at least part of the area to be shielded from neighbours or passers-by. Whether or not this is possible depends to a large extent on the location of the house in relation to those surrounding it. Usually there are more possibilities with a detached or a semi-detached property, where, if necessary, an L-shaped patio can be taken around the side of the house. The alternatives would be a strategically placed fence, wall, trellis or high hedge.

Shelter from the wind is an important aspect: it can make the patio much more pleasant on breezy days. The same options specified above for creating privacy on the patio can be applied in this area, too.

Calculating size

The size of the project will be governed by the site, economy and its intended use. Here you should be certain not to make the patio too small, especially from front to back. Anything less than about 2.5 m (7 ft 6 in) will be very cramped and awkward to position chairs, sun-loungers and a table and still leave sufficient space for movement around them. The side-to-side width of the patio is not so important.

The larger the patio, the more it will cost you to build, so keep your budget in mind when you work out the design. Plan the project with an eye to the future if possible, so that you can extend the patio as and when needs and finances allow. Bear in mind, however, that matching materials – slabs and decorative blocks, for example – may not be available if the extension to the patio is

left for more than a few years: apart from unavailability of materials, weathering will have changed the appearance of the original materials.

The simplest patio is a conventional rectangular strip laid along the back of the house. Be careful not to make the patio look too formal. Avoid square slabs of the same colour; create interest with materials of differing sizes, colours and textures: bricks are ideal in an ornate design whereas crazy paving (flagstone pattern) suggests a less formal effect.

Creating special features

There are practical advantages to a straightforward design, however. The project will be much easier to plan if its size is geared to available materials: cutting slabs and pavers can be wasteful and time-consuming. But, with a little forethought it is still possible to avoid an ordinary, uninteresting patio without involving a great amount of expense or effort. Three examples are shown below.

Interest can be added to a patio by introducing features such as steps, low walls, planting areas, or even a pond or waterfall. If you plan to use the garden in the evenings, outdoor lighting is both attractive and practical.

Steps can be introduced more easily on a site which slopes either towards or away from the house. On a flat site you can excavate so that steps can be built on the perimeter of the patio to lead up to the lawn.

It is not so easy to have steps leading down to a lawn since this could mean having to set the patio too close to the house d.p.c. level in order to gain the required height. The alternative would be to set the patio on two levels by excavating deeply for one half and using the soil to build up the other half – the cut-and-fill technique. Steps could then be made to link the two levels.

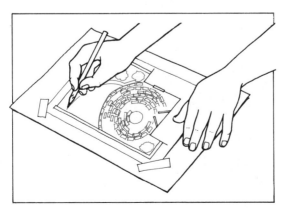

Sketch out some ideas for your patio, defining your basic requirements: the four plans, right, give examples of the many designs that are possible for the same garden

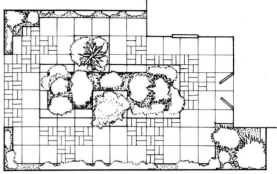

The grid layout, *where everything is neatly ordered: the rectangular patio fits in with the various segments of the garden, and square concrete slabs complement the geometry*

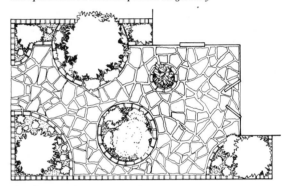

The freestyle layout *is quite the opposite: here the patio covers a curved, irregular area using random-shaped paving materials and blending with the 'wild' freeform garden*

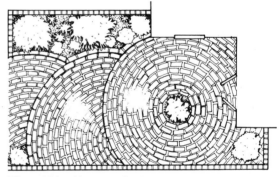

The multi-level layout *again adopts a freeform pattern, using small-scale paving materials; steps and changes of level create a gradual terraced effect for areas of interest*

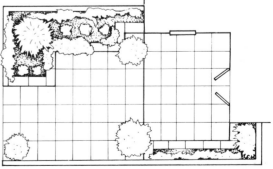

The paved layout *is the ideal design for a small garden. The entire surface has been given over to paving, with only small concessions to planting areas*

Construction materials

Concrete paving slabs, crazy paving, bricks and concrete paving blocks are the favourites for patios: they are hardwearing, easy to clean and available in a range of colours and textures.

Paving slabs

The cheapest slabs are cast in concrete 50 mm (2 in) thick. They are tough and durable, but if there is any likelihood of the paving having to bear the weight of a car, then use hydraulically pressed concrete slabs instead. These are only 38 mm (1½ in) thick and lighter in weight, but they are much stronger.

Slabs come in a selection of colours – usually greens, reds, greys, yellows, white and buff tones – and in various shapes and surface finishes. The more expensive slabs use crushed stone for the aggregate, while the cheaper types are made of coloured concrete.

There are four basic surface finishes:
• smooth with a non-slip surface
• textured, where the surface is in relief and the aggregate in the concrete is exposed
• riven, having the appearance of split stone
• patterned, where the surface is cast to create a decorative brick, tile or cobblestone effect. Some square-edged slabs have different finishes on each side and can be used either way up.

Square and rectangular slabs are the most commonly available. Some can be used in a single coloured design or combination of colours, perhaps for a chequerboard pattern. Other slabs come in co-ordinated rectangular sizes so that you can build up a design using four different shapes to make a repeat pattern. Hexagonal slabs range in size from about 225 mm sq (9 in sq) up to 675 mm × 450 mm (27 in × 18 in). You can also buy circular slabs of similar diameters.

Larger slabs are heavy and awkward to handle, so the most popular size is 450 mm × 450 mm (18 in × 18 in). Be careful if you want to mix ranges from different manufacturers. Some are made to metric dimensions and others to imperial. The small difference in size is not great with one slab but can escalate when multiplied over a large area.

Crazy paving

Broken concrete or stone slabs are sold as crazy paving. You can obtain many different sizes, shapes, colours and textures to use as a hard-wearing surface with a highly decorative pattern.

Crazy paving is sold by the square metre or square yard, or by the ton; when ordering remember that one ton equals about 3 sq metres (3.5 sq yd). If you have the transport, it is worth paying a visit to a local builder's yard to select your own paving pieces. You are then able to

choose a good balance of colours (pink, grey and white are the most common); if delivered, you have to accept pot luck, although most suppliers will give you a balanced load.

Crazy paving tends to fit well into any setting due to its informal, colourful appearance. It is also far easier to lay than formal paving since accuracy is less important, curved shapes are more easily formed and there is little likelihood of you having to cut any pieces. Even if you have to make cuts, breakages in the wrong place are hardly likely to be critical.

Bricks

Bricks blend well into any setting, especially old second-hand bricks, which have an immediate weathered appearance. Be sure that the bricks you select are suitable to use as paving – some are soft, porous and easily damaged by frost.

There is a huge variety of coloured and textured bricks available, although many will have to be specially ordered.

Concrete paving blocks

These tough, individual units – about the size of a brick – are laid on a sand bed, without mortar, in an interlocking pattern. They are either rectangular or decoratively shaped and available in thicknesses typically 35 mm (1½ in) to 65 mm (2½ in) and face dimensions 200 mm × 100 mm (8 in × 4 in).

Various colours are available – reds, yellows and multi-coloured 'old brick' effects being the most popular – and some incorporate a bevel around the top edge for an attractive recessed appearance. You can lay them – like bricks – in a number of patterns.

One advantage of these units is that, should it be necessary to gain access to underground pipe runs, you can simply break out a section of paving and replace it once the repair has been made.

Gravel

Although not particularly suitable for a complete patio, gravel combines well in small amounts with other materials – perhaps as an edging strip or an occasional square to relieve and soften formal paving. It also harmonizes with brick.

Cobbles

Again not suitable for a complete patio because they are difficult to walk on, but they combine beautifully with paving slabs and bricks if used in small feature areas.

Paving sets are also available, which give the appearance of a brick. They are, in fact, a solid unit with the surface quartered into four false joints.

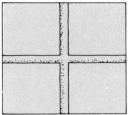

Paving slabs, *square or shaped, in various colours*

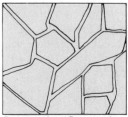

Crazy paving *(flagstone) is made from broken slabs*

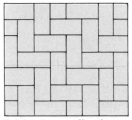

Bricks *give a small-scale patterned effect*

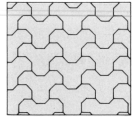

Concrete pavers *come in various interlocking shapes*

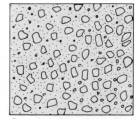

Gravel *can be used to make a small feature area in paving*

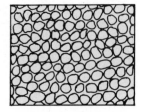

Cobblestones; *large and rounded for feature areas*

Foundations for a patio

A patio will receive a lot of wear – especially from people and furniture – so it is important that you lay your choice of paving on a sound, firm base. Levels, proximity to the house and drainage are vital aspects of making suitable foundations. If you work carefully and methodically the job is quite straightforward – even for a substantial patio.

Set out the perimeter of the patio using string stretched between pegs. Dig out 100 mm to 150 mm (4 in to 6 in) of topsoil until you reach fairly firm soil. Take out the greater depth on soft clay or fibrous soils, and the shallower depth on stony or sandy soils. Retain the fertile topsoil for topping up raised flower beds, planted walls, and other planting areas.

Make a note of the d.p.c. level of the house (if it has one: not always so with older buildings). The finished surface level of the patio must be at least 150 mm (6 in) below this level to prevent rainwater splashing above it and bridging the barrier.

If there is a concrete pathway around the house this often can be left as it makes an excellent base for the paving so long as the finished surface level will be the correct distance below the d.p.c. If the concrete is too low, build it up with hardcore (broken rubble); if it is too high break it up with a sledge hammer (or an electric hammer breaker, which you can hire). The broken concrete makes excellent hardcore.

With the concrete out of the way the soil can be dug out to the required level.

Sometimes airbricks in the house wall are well below d.p.c. level and it is possible that when the patio is completed it will cover them. To maintain an air supply to the air bricks, lay air ducts from the airbrick positions to the perimeter of the patio. The ducts can be a minimum of 100 mm (4 in) diameter pipes suitable for underground drainage. The pipes are stocked by builders' merchants and may be made from plastic, clay, pitch fibre or concrete.

At the house wall use a cold chisel and club hammer to remove the air brick and insert the ducting pipe into the hole to give an unrestricted air supply – make sure the pipe slopes away from the house wall. The opposite end of the pipe can be built into the outer retaining wall of the patio and can be sealed with a new air brick, which will keep out rodents. Any ducting system is bound to restrict the air flow to a certain extent, so it is a good idea to compensate for this by inserting additional air bricks in those parts of the house wall not covered by the patio, or by laying extra ducts under the patio.

Replace a conventional drain inspection cover with an inset type designed to accept paving slabs. Alternatively, hide the cover with a movable flower tub or leave a soil pocket beside the drain cover and plant a horizontal-growing conifer to cover it.

Preparing patio foundations often requires the removal of considerable amounts of top soil. Ensure you organize yourself adequately to cope

Laying the paving

Preparing the base

1. Ram the base really firm using a sledge hammer or heavy garden roller. If you do not own either, improvise with a length of stout fence post – remember to wear stout gloves to prevent splinters.

2. Prepare the site for foundations of 75 mm to 125 mm (3 in to 5 in) of hardcore. Accuracy here will make laying the paving easier. Drive in stout timber pegs at about 1.5 m (4 ft 6 in) intervals over the entire area so that 100 mm to 150 mm (4 in to 6 in) of each peg – the total depth of the foundations including the ballast layer – is proud of the base level.

3. The tops of the pegs must be level with each other across the width of the patio, although they should slope slightly from front to back to give a drainage fall (12 mm in 1.5 m – ½ in in 4 ft 6 in) away from the house. Insert a peg at one corner of the site close to the house, and use a spirit level on a long straight-edged length of timber to level the peg tops across the width of the plot. Place a small wedge of wood under the lower edge to give the required fall.

4. Next, shovel the hardcore into the excavation, with the largest pieces at the base, so that it comes within about 25 mm (1 in) of the tops of the pegs after it has been rammed down, again

using a roller, sledge hammer or fence post. Finally, spread a layer of ballast (a mixture of sand and gravel) over the hardcore to fill any voids and give a smooth surface level with the peg tops. Lightly water the ballast to settle it before compacting with the roller.

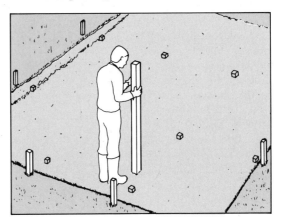

Setting out the base

Paving slabs are usually laid to a symmetrical pattern, so it is important that you mark out the base accurately with string guidelines stretched between wooden pegs as a guide to correctly positioning them, especially at the perimeter of the patio. A stringline would not be suitable, of course, where the perimeter of the patio is to be curved. Instead you could use a garden hose pipe to mark out the shape of the area you plan to pave.

Where there are two walls at right angles to each other, for example the house and garden wall, you have ready-made guidelines. But you will still need a line set to the required drainage fall of the patio away from the house so that the surface level of the slabs will slope correctly. If the two walls are not at right angles, set up a string line parallel with one wall – ideally the house wall – and another one slab width in from the other wall. The space left at the edge can be filled later with cut slabs.

Lay the slabs on a mortar mix of one part cement to five parts sharp sand. Aim for a dryish mix – if it is too sloppy it will not support the weight of the slab.

The slabs can be laid on five dabs of mortar – one at each corner and one in the middle – or with a complete band of mortar to support the edges of a slab, with one complete band through the middle. Both of these beds allow a slab to be tapped down easily to the correct level and fall and improves the bond. Omit the central band or dab with small slabs. A complete mortar bed under each slab is essential where a drive is being laid. This makes a far stronger construction, but you will find it much more difficult to tap down the slabs; each bed must be initially laid to the correct thickness of 30 mm to 38 mm (1¼ in to 1½ in) with a trowel.

Laying the paving slabs

1. Stretch strings between pegs to mark out the perimeter of the patio. Check that corners are at right angles with a builder's square (which you can make). You could also use a large sheet of paper or card which you know is square.

2. It is essential that the edge slabs are laid correctly since these will be the guide for the remainder. Trowel mortar on to the base and lower the first slab on top: be careful, even small slabs are very heavy. Slide the slab into position, using your stringlines as a guide.

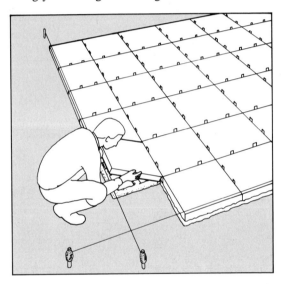

3. Tap down the slab gently with the shaft of a club hammer until it is level with the 'fall' guidelines. The slab must not rock in any direction. Place a spirit level on top of the slab to check its level in both directions – this confirms the accuracy of the stringlines.

4. Lay the second slab in the same way – with equal size square slabs just align the edges and allow for a 10 mm (⅜ in) mortar joint. You can accurately gauge the joint thickness by inserting wood spacers between the slabs. Where a patterned patio, comprising different sized slabs is being laid, keep a constant check on the accurate positioning of each slab to ensure the pattern is followed.

5. Check each slab for alignment with the neighbouring slabs by laying a long timber straight-edge across the paved surface. Make sure it sits perfectly flush in all directions: no daylight should be visible below. Tap down each

slab as necessary to achieve this. If any slabs are too low, remove them, add more mortar, then replace them.

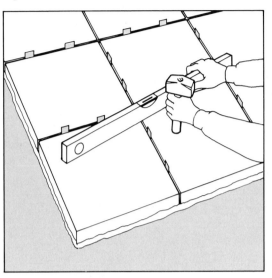

6. With a large patio, it is best to lay the corner slabs after completing the perimeter of the area. Lay about three or four slabs in each corner then check for their correct alignment with intermediate stringlines. You can then fill in the middle of the patio.

7. Some cut slabs will probably be necessary, especially at the edges. To cut a slab use a bolster chisel and club hammer. First, score a cutting line with the edge of the bolster. Use a length of wood as a guide to squaring the line around both faces and edges of the slab. Place the slab on soft sand or soil to prevent it shattering and chop around the scored lines with the bolster and club hammer. Deepen the groove on all faces until the slab breaks cleanly along the line.

A much less strenuous and more accurate method is to fit a masonry disc into a circular saw and use this to score a deep groove in the slab, which can then be split easily with the bolster and club hammer. Remember to wear goggles to protect your eyes from flying particles when cutting slabs.

8. Cut edges are rarely smooth so try to place these where they will be concealed against a wall or lawn edge. When fitting slabs into a tight space, cut them about 6 mm (¼ in) undersize for an easier fit. Fill the joints between the slabs after a couple of days, using a dry mortar mix forced well into the joints. Clean any smears off the slab surface immediately with a damp sponge: if you allow the mortar to set it could cause an ugly stain.

Laying the paving

Bricks and paving blocks

Bricks and paving blocks can be laid either flat or on edge. If you lay them flat, allow for 40 bricks per square metre (per sq yd); if on edge 50 bricks per square metre (sq yd) will be needed. An attractive pattern is important and with bricks many arrangements are possible, from a standard stretcher bond to herringbone or a personalized geometric design (see diagrams). The outline of an area can be square or curved. Bricks or blocks can be trimmed using a bolster chisel and club hammer to shape them. Set the individual units either on a solid bed of mortar (as for paving) or, without mortar, on a bed of 25 mm (1 in) of sand. Some blocks are intended for laying only on a sand bed.

Leave a 10 mm (⅜ in) joint between bricks laid on mortar and point the joints as for brick walls (see page 99). Bricks and blocks laid on sand can be butted up closely and the joints left open or filled by brushing sand or dry mortar into them.

Solid support is needed to restrain the bricks or blocks at the edge of the area. This can be provided by excavating the ground so that the edges will be automatically supported by a lawn, although for greater strength you should line the excavation with concrete edging strips or a strip of concrete.

Bricks or blocks being laid proud of the existing surface will need an edge restraint of concrete edging strips, or bricks themselves set on edge in concrete. If they butt up to a permanent fixture such as a house wall you will not need any further restraint at this point.

Laying bricks and blocks
1. For a really firm edge restraint set concrete edging stones (or blocks on edge) in concrete so their top edges will be level with the paving.
2. Make sure the base is firm and lay 50 mm (2 in) of sand inside the edge restraints. Level this off using a straight-edged plank; check falls with a spirit level. Place the blocks in your chosen pattern. Lay all the whole blocks first then fill in with cut ones.

3. Compact the entire paved area using a machine called a plate compactor, which you can hire. Try to get a machine with a rubber sole plate, which will not damage or scuff the paving; if one is not available, use the compactor over a strip of old carpet or rubber matting.

Parquet design

Herringbone

Stretcher bond

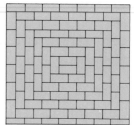

Perimeter squares

Interlocking bond

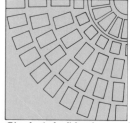

Circular 'wheel' bond

4. After the initial compaction, brush sand over the entire surface, working it into the joints between blocks. Run over the area once more with the plate compactor and finally brush more sand into the joints.

5. If you cannot obtain a plate compactor you can compact the blocks by hand. Rest a length of stout timber on the paving and use a heavy club hammer to ram the blocks into the sand bed – be very careful not to shatter any of the blocks by hammering too hard. Use the timber parallel to, and then diagonally across, the run of blocks for even compaction. This, however, is really tough work and suitable only for smaller areas.

6. Bricks can be laid dry on a sand bed, like concrete blocks, or you can bed them in mortar for a permanent, rigid paving. Trowel mortar on to the base of the foundations then arrange each brick in your chosen pattern, tapping down with the handle of a club hammer and checking the level across the top. Leave 10 mm (⅜ in) joints between each brick for pointing with a stiff mortar mix. Alternatively, simply brush dry mortar – mixed with a little sand – into the joints and water the surface with a watering can or a fine spray from a garden hose.

Patterns with crazy paving

The method for laying and bedding down crazy paving is essentially the same as for formal paving slabs, although you do need to pay special attention at the planning stage. Even though the overall design is random you must choose individual stones carefully to give the best balanced effect.

Crazy paving is usually delivered as a random pile of pieces, which you must first sort out into piles of the same colour and approximate size. Check the thickness of the slabs – this can vary. Keep the thinner ones in one pile – these will require a thicker bed of mortar to build them up to the required level. For the borders of the patio select pieces which have a fairly long straight edge. Smaller pieces of paving are useful for filling in, but in general medium and large-size stones look better.

First of all, set up stringlines for the perimeter of the patio and for a crossfall guide.

Laying crazy paving
1. Bed down the largest straight-edged pieces around the perimeter; use a full layer of mortar under each and tap them down gently until they are firm and level with each other. Fill in the corners then check for alignment and crossfall with intermediate stringlines and a long straight-edged plank.

2. As you select stones bear in mind the colour arrangement. Also, lay the pieces to avoid continuous joints or too formal a pattern. In general, keep the joints between the edges to no more than 25 mm (1 in) or so – the thinner the joints, the less mortar you will need to fill them. Because of the irregular shapes of the stones, this will not always be possible – a few wider joints will even enhance the overall appearance of the paving. Small pieces of stone can be used occasionally to fill really wide joints.

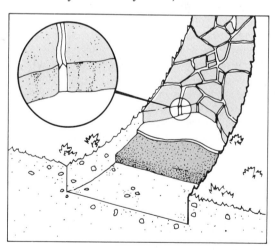

3. When you have laid all the slabs allow a couple of days before filling the joints. Use a dryish mortar mix and pack it firmly down to fill all gaps. For an attractive decorative effect – which is also good for drainage – draw the tip of the trowel through the mortar around the outline of each slab to leave a shallow groove.

8.Roofs and chimneys

There are few areas of the home as important as the roof over your head. The roof takes the full brunt of exposure to the elements and if you neglect its maintenance not only will rainwater get in to cause serious, possibly extensive, damage but also there could be a danger to anyone walking nearby from falling debris.

If you are not observant, the first sign of trouble from a neglected roof could be a damp patch on a ceiling and ruined decorations – and by then the damage is done. Ideally, you should carry out regular inspections of the roof, either from a ladder or roof crawling boards, or from the ground using binoculars. In this way, as soon as the first signs of trouble become apparent – a broken tile, a slipped slate or a corroded metal flashing strip at the base of the chimney – you will be able to carry out the repairs before major renovation or a complete re-roofing is necessary.

Safety

Whether you are likely to replace only the odd broken tile, or renew large sections of your roof covering, you must provide a safe working platform. For most jobs working from a conventional ladder will not be suitable; instead you will need specialist equipment to enable you to reach all areas of the roof.

Obviously you are going to be working aloft, so if you do not like heights, do not attempt roof repairs: call in specialist help at an early stage, when only minor work is required and charges can be kept to the minimum.

If you are going to tackle the work yourself, stick to the following safety rules:

● Never take chances with suspect equipment and never try to cut corners to save time.
● Build a scaffold tower to give a safe working platform at roof level. These sectional, slot-together towers can be hired (see telephone directories), but if you are likely to do a lot of maintenance on the outside of your house it may be worth buying a tower. Use a strong rope to tie the tower to the house; an eye-bolt screwed into the brickwork just below the eaves is an ideal anchor.
● Apart from flat, boarded, felt-covered roofs, never walk directly on a roof surface. Always work from a roof ladder; this is usually made from lightweight aluminium and has small wheels that enable the ladder to be pushed up the roof to the ridge (or apex), where it is turned over to locate the large hook at the top over the ridge tiles to prevent the ladder from slipping down. Roof ladders can be hired, although a bolt-on conversion set is available to turn an ordinary ladder into a roof ladder.
● Always use a scaffold tower when carrying out

repairs on a chimney stack set at the side of a roof. If it is not too large, repair of a chimney stack set within a roof can be tackled from a pair of roof ladders. To repair tall chimney stacks you will need an arrangement of scaffolding. Special chimney scaffold kits are available and it may be possible to hire one. If not, erect ordinary scaffolding so it hooks right around the chimney stack. Should this be necessary it will probably be better to have the work done by a chimney specialist.

Major roof work

When a roof shows signs of overall deterioration, with loose or missing slates or tiles over a wide area, with flaking, cracked or crumbling slates or tiles and corroded and loose metal flashings and valleys, patching up will not be sufficient and you should call in a roofing contractor to lay a new roof. Before you do this, check with your

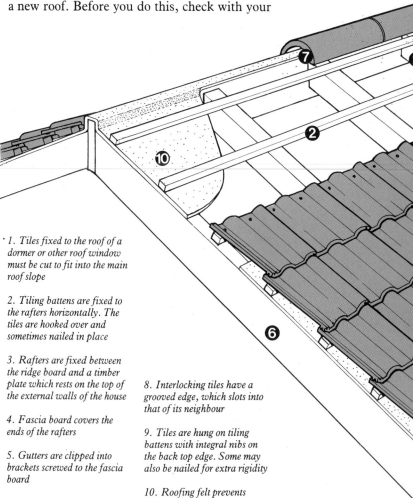

1. Tiles fixed to the roof of a dormer or other roof window must be cut to fit into the main roof slope

2. Tiling battens are fixed to the rafters horizontally. The tiles are hooked over and sometimes nailed in place

3. Rafters are fixed between the ridge board and a timber plate which rests on the top of the external walls of the house

4. Fascia board covers the ends of the rafters

5. Gutters are clipped into brackets screwed to the fascia board

6. Bargeboards fill the gap between the roof and the top of the house wall

7. Half-round ridge tiles are bedded in mortar on top of the last row of tiles

8. Interlocking tiles have a grooved edge, which slots into that of its neighbour

9. Tiles are hung on tiling battens with integral nibs on the back top edge. Some may also be nailed for extra rigidity

10. Roofing felt prevents moisture seeping into the roof space and causing a damp problem. If moisture does bypass the tiles themselves it will trickle harmlessly down the felt and discharge at the eaves

11. The chimney may protrude through the roofing. Where it exits, it is sealed with flashings, either stepped lead seals or modern self-adhesive strips which cover the join

local authority in case you are eligible for a grant.

Types of roofs

The method of tackling roof repairs depends on the type of structure and its covering. There are many different constructions and it is important that you can identify which you are dealing with.

For the main roof, plain tiles, single-lap or interlocking tiles, and slates (see overleaf) are the usual types of covering and these are fixed to the roof structure in a variety of ways. It is also common to find flat, bitumen-felt roofs on outbuildings, glass roofs on lean-tos and other, less popular types, such as corrugated steel, asbestos-cement and shingle roofs.

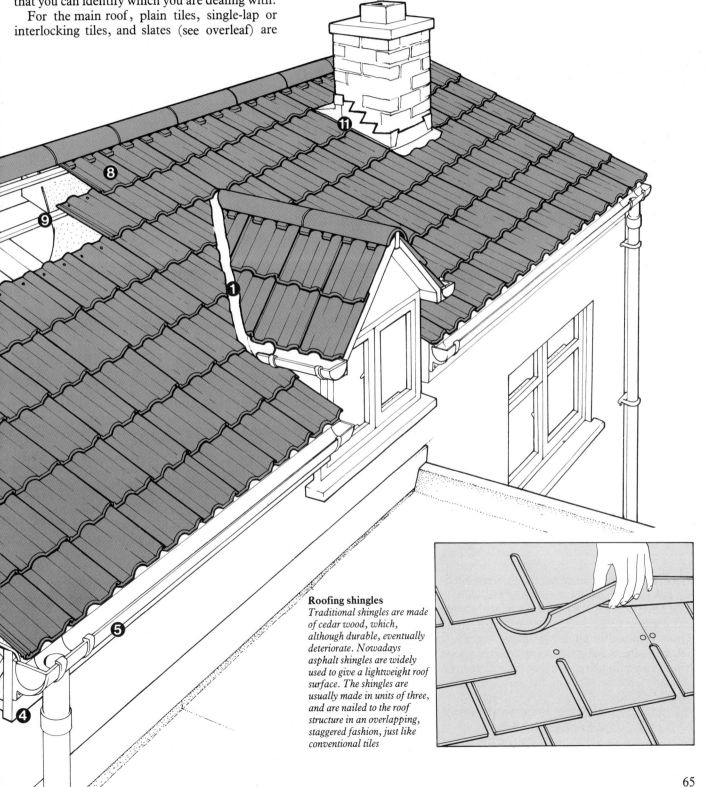

Roofing shingles
Traditional shingles are made of cedar wood, which, although durable, eventually deteriorate. Nowadays asphalt shingles are widely used to give a lightweight roof surface. The shingles are usually made in units of three, and are nailed to the roof structure in an overlapping, staggered fashion, just like conventional tiles

Repairs to tiled roofs

Plain tiles are the most common type. They have a slightly curved surface, two holes at the top for the fixing nails and usually two projections (called nibs) on the underside at the top edge, to hook over the tiling battens, which are fixed horizontally across the roof. Tiles may be made from clay, the traditional material, or concrete with a rough sand face. There are many types and colours, so take a sample as a pattern when buying replacements. Plain tiles usually measure 265 mm × 165 mm (10½ in × 6½ in), although there are other sizes available. In addition there are special shaped tiles, used to maintain the correct lap and weatherproof the roof at the verge (side of the roof), eaves (gutter level) and ridge (apex of the roof). These are typically a wide tile-and-a-half tile for the verge, and short tiles for the eaves and ridges. Special curved tiles are also produced to weatherproof the ridge, hips (external corners) and valleys (internal corners) of a plain tiled roof.

Single-lap, or interlocking, tiles are used mainly on new houses and for roof replacement. Clay single-lap tiles, such as the distinctive 'S'-shaped pantiles, have been used for many years, but the cheaper interlocking concrete tiles, which are available in a wide range of colours and designs, are largely superseding them. Sizes vary, but basic types measure about 430 mm × 380 mm (17 in × 15 in).

Unlike plain tiles, which are laid in a double thickness, interlocking tiles are laid in a single layer with overlapping and interlocking head, tail and side joints to give a weatherproof finish. They can be used on low-pitched (sloping) roofs down to 15°, while for plain tiles the minimum pitch is 35°. Most types have a range of specially made matching ridge, hip and valley tiles to finish the roof neatly.

Plain tiles and interlocking tiles are usually laid with vertical joints staggered, but some unusually shaped tiles – notably pantiles – are laid one on top of the other, with only their sides linked.

Identifying faults

Although a sure sign of a defective roof is a damp stain on the ceiling of a room below, this is not always the case if the roof has, as is modern pratice, an underfelt lining beneath the battens: the underfelt channels rainwater back to the eaves. However, the felt is only a second line of defence, so keep an eye on the roof, ideally using binoculars from time to time if you cannot make regular checks, and put right defects as soon as you notice them.

Tiled roofs should also be examined for cracks between the ridge and hip tiles. Again these can result in rainwater seeping into the roof void and, if neglected, can cause tiles to become dislodged or rot the structural timbers.

Another problem area is where a tiled roof butts against a wall – the house wall, a parapet wall or a chimney stack, for example. If the seal between the two structures fails, rainwater can trickle down the wall to appear as a damp patch, which can ruin decorations. These repairs are dealt with on pages 70 and 80.

Repairing defective tiles

Damaged tiles should be replaced with new ones of a similar type. The job is not difficult, even if you have to replace several tiles, and requires no special tools. If for some reason there is a delay in obtaining replacements you can make a temporary repair to keep the roof weatherproof.

Replacement of single-lap or interlocking tiles and plain tiles is similar, although sometimes the sides of interlocking tiles are held by metal clips. If an isolated tile is being replaced you will not be able to replace the clip, but if an area of tiling is being renewed then the clips should be refitted.

With all types of roof tiles, when an area is being replaced, start at the lowest point and work up the roof, replacing the last tile as described below.

Cracked and loose ridge and hip tiles should be removed, repaired or replaced, then rebedded on mortar.

Plain tile

Interlocking tile

Plain tiles *come in a vast selection of colours, and typically measure 265 mm × 165 mm (10½ in × 6½ in). They have a slight curve along their length and at the lower corners to ensure they are bedded firmly. Nibs on the back top edge hook over tiling battens and the tiles are secured with nails. Tiles are hung in double thicknesses: there are short versions for use at eaves and ridges and wide types for verges*

Interlocking tiles *are now widely used for new roofs and in re-roofing. They typically measure 430 mm × 380 mm (17 in × 15 in) and are hung in a single layer; grooves on their opposite edges interlock with those of their neighbours. Nibs hold the tiles in place and some are secured with nails, too. Others feature special clips, which hook onto the tile and are pinned to the tile battens*

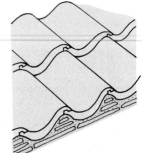

S-shaped pantiles *are found on older roofs. Like modern interlocking tiles, these single-lap tiles link with their neighbours via grooved edges*

Valley tiles *are used to seal the join between two meeting roofs on a plain tiled roof. They are basically wedge-shaped and curved to match the tiles: nails are fixed in holes at each side of the tiles*

Making a temporary repair

To make a temporary repair to a cracked or broken tile, wire-brush the surface of the tile to clean it then coat the top face with flashing strip primer. When the primer has dried, stick a patch of self-adhesive flashing strip over the tile, lifting the tile in the row above so you can tuck the top of the flashing strip underneath. The repair may not look attractive, but it is an effective stop-gap measure and will not make it any harder to remove the broken tile once a replacement has been obtained.

Replacing a plain tile

To replace a plain tile, cut two small wooden wedges and push them under the two tiles in the row above the broken tile to raise them. Slide a bricklayer's trowel under the broken tile and lift the top edge of the tile to release the nibs from the batten. If the tile is nailed to the batten as well, you may be able to work it loose by wiggling it from side to side while lifting it with the trowel. If this does not work, cut the nails using a tool called a slate ripper (see slate repairs overleaf).

To fit the replacement tile, place it on the builder's trowel and use the trowel to offer it up to the batten so that its nibs hook over the top edge. Withdraw the trowel and remove the wedges holding up the adjacent tiles.

Replacing interlocking tiles

To replace an area of interlocking tiles that use clips to hold them against the battens, work up from the lowest tile within the area; hook the tile's nibs over a batten and attach a clip to the interlocking edge. Position the clip so that its nail can be driven into the top edge of the next batten down. The next tile along in the row conceals the clip.

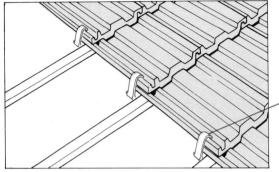

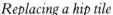

Replacing a damaged ridge tile

To replace a loose or damaged ridge tile, remove the tile and clean up the old mortar bed on which it sat by chipping off loose, rough pieces with a cold chisel and club hammer. Clean off the hardened mortar from the removed tile, or buy a replacement. Soak the tile in water to aid adhesion then trowel mortar (1 part cement; 4 parts sharp sand) onto its edges and end – leave the cavity under the tile free of mortar for air to circulate. Bed the tile on the ridge, butting it up to its neighbour.

When you rebed a ridge tile on a roof with curved tiles, such as pantiles, set specially made pieces of tiles, called 'dentil slips' in mortar to fill the hollows between the base of the ridge tiles and the hollows in the roof surface.

Replacing a hip tile

Hip tiles can be replaced similarly to ridge tiles, except that they are prevented from slipping down the roof by angled lengths of wrought iron or galvanized steel called 'hip irons', which are screwed to the foot of the hip rafter using zinc-plated screws before the hip tiles are rebedded.

Renewing a bonnet hip

Bonnet hip tiles are difficult to replace singly as each one is nailed at the top to the hip rafter and the tail (exposed part) of the tile above is bedded on mortar, concealing the fixing. Try to chop out the damaged tile with a chisel and mortar in a replacement, without nailing, using a mix of 1 part cement; 4 parts sharp sand.

Sealing cracks

At the verges and eaves the tiles may be bedded on mortar to seal the edges of the roof. If the old mortar is slightly cracked, seal the cracks with non-setting mastic (caulking compound), which is available in a cement colour in cartridges for application by mastic gun. Where the damage is severe, rake out the old mortar with a club hammer and cold chisel and repoint the tiles with 1 part cement; 4 parts sharp sand.

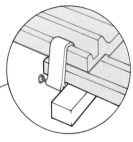

Interlocking tiles (*above*) *are sometimes fixed to the battens with small clips, which hook over the interlocking groove and are pinned to the batten*

Ridge tiles, *which seal the apex of a roof, are either pointed or rounded. They are bedded in mortar on top of the last row of tiles*

Hip tiles *are used on an external corner of a tiled roof. Basically triangular, they have a single fixing hole at the top, and incorporate a curve across their width*

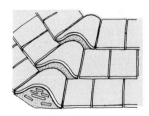

Bonnet hips *are formed by nailing the hip tiles to the hip rafter and filling the curved recess with mortar. Tile pieces are slotted into the recess to strengthen the mix.*

Repairs to slate roofs

Slate is an excellent, long-lasting roof covering, but it is expensive if you need to replace more than a small area. As a result many slate roofs are neglected and consequently they have reached the end of their useful life. Because of the high price of slate there is a tendency to replace old slate roofs with modern, cheaper, interlocking concrete tiles, but in doing so the character of the house is often spoilt. Whenever possible try to renovate a slate roof rather than replacing it with some other type of roof covering. The cost of replacements can be kept down if second-hand slates are used, and these are widely available from roofing contractors and demolition sites. When buying replacements check that slates are the correct size, thickness and colour, and ensure also that the new slates are not cracked or delaminating, which shows as flaking of the surface.

Identifying faults

Unlike tiles, which have projecting nibs to hook over the tiling battens, slates are smooth and flat and rely on nails to hold them in place. Even though the slates are perfectly sound it is likely that the nails have corroded – a defect called 'nail sickness' – and this causes the slates to become dislodged. Slipped or missing slates, in fact, are the most common problems with a slate roof, and the cause of leaks.

The slates may also be cracked, usually the result of someone clambering over the roof to carry out other repair work. Delamination is the worst fault in slates; if widespread, the affected slates must be replaced – they cannot be restored.

Slate roofs also suffer from the faults that afflict all roofs, namely leaks caused by problems with the metal and cement flashings and valleys, which waterproof the junctions where slate roofs butt on to walls, or where two roofs meet. There can also be problems with cracking along ridge and hip slates.

If there is a frequent need to repair cracked, leaking, loose and flaking slates, this is a sign that a major overhaul and perhaps a new roof is required. However, it is possible to give such a roof about 10 years' additional life by applying an overall membrane treatment. A snag is that such treatment spoils any slates that could be reused on the new roof. Treatments are plastic-based and bitumen-based. Bitumen treatments usually involve painting the roof with a bituminous solution in which a reinforcing membrane is embedded; this is followed by another two or three coats of bitumen emulsion. Plastic treatments are similar, except that the reinforcement is usually confined to the joints. In both cases the manufacturer's installation instructions must be followed carefully.

Repairs for slate roofs

To replace a single slipped slate, first remove the slate and put it to one side. This will expose two slates in the row below the missing slate; you will see the nails holding these slates to a batten, or timber boarding. If the slate has slipped out of place, general 'nail sickness' must be suspected, so it is worth inserting two new nails beside those holding the two lower slates to prevent them slipping out of place in the future. The best nails to use are 38 mm (1½ in) long aluminium alloy nails, but if these are difficult to obtain use 38 mm (1½ in) large-head galvanized clout nails instead. Refixing the slate is quite straightforward, if a little fiddly. It involves the use of home-made lead strips or proprietary metal clips.

If you have to repair a large area of slates you can fix all the slates with nails except those in the top row, which again must be fixed with lead strips or metal clips. Work up the roof, fixing each slate with two aluminium alloy or galvanized nails. In most cases the slates will be fixed through their centres, but sometimes the fixing

Slates are nailed *to wooden battens through holes in their centre (left). Alternate rows of slates are staggered, and each row overlaps the lower one by over half*

Cutting slates *is easy if you use a special slate cutting tool; it works like a pair of scissors to chew its way through the slate. Alternatively, you may be able to chop off sections of slate using a sharp pointing trowel*

nails are driven through the tops of the slates. Follow the technique used on the rest of the roof when making a repair.

Replacing defective slates

● Cut a strip of lead about 200 mm (8 in) long by 25 mm (1 in) wide. Use a clout nail to fix one end of the lead strip to the batten, which should be just visible between the two exposed slates. Replace the slipped slate, pushing it up so that its lower edge lines up with the other slates in the row. To do this you may have to work the slate from side to side until its top edge rests on the batten holding the row above. In this way the slate will be held tightly against the roof by the weight of the other slates and the wind will not be able to lift its lower edge.

Bend the protruding end of the lead strip up and over the bottom edge of the slate (below left) to prevent it from slipping out again. It is a good idea also to fold the end of the lead strip over on itself (below right) so that, should the clip be lifted by snowfalls slipping down the roof, the double-thickness tail will help to prevent the clip from being flattened out completely, releasing the slate. If you have to fit too many strips you should consider renewing the whole roof.

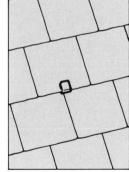

● An alternative way of holding slipped slates in place is to use proprietary hinged metal clips made specially for the job, which you can fit from inside the roof. Attach the clips to the underside of the slate at about its mid-point, then fold them against the slate, which is then slipped up into place. Once the clips clear the batten to which the slate would normally be nailed, they swing down to hold the slate.

● Replacement of a broken or flaking slate is similar once the old slate has been removed. If the fixing nails are corroded it may be possible to lever the old slate out of place without too much difficulty, but you will probably need the assistance of a tool called a slate ripper, which you can hire. Push the slate ripper underneath the damaged slate, then move it to one side so that one of the barbs on the head of the tool hooks around the fixing nail. A sharp downward tug on the slate ripper will either cut through the nail or pull it out of place. If this proves difficult, strike the raised handle of the ripper sharply with a hammer. Repeat this procedure for the other nails, and remove the slate.

● Ridge slates are bedded on cement mortar and sometimes the joints between them crack. The best way to repair these is to inject a bead of non-setting mastic (caulking compound) into the crack from a special gun. Or you can press thick bitumen mastic into the cracks with a trowel.

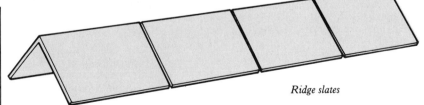

Ridge slates

● If examination shows the ridge slates to be loose, lift them off and chip away the old mortar, then rebed them on new mortar. A suitable mix is 1 part cement; 4 parts sharp washed sand. Dampen the ridge slates then trowel mortar around their edges, leaving a cavity under the main part of each tile, which allows air to circulate and helps to keep them dry. Set flat pieces of tile into the mortar at each open end of the ridge to close the cavity.

Sealing roof joins

Patching valleys

Where two roofs meet at an angle the joint is waterproofed with a metal lining called a valley. Lead, zinc and aluminium alloy sheets are commonly used and each is susceptible to corrosion. You may not have to renew the entire valley: small holes and cracks can be successfully patched.

● Clean the area around the defect by wire-brushing, then rub with abrasive paper. Cut a patch from a roll of self-adhesive metal-backed flashing strip large enough to cover the damage by at least 50 mm (2 in) all round then apply a coat of flashing strip primer before positioning the patch.

● Although it does not make such a long-lasting repair, when flashing strip is not available, press thick bitumen mastic into the crack and over the surrounding surface to a depth of about 1.5 mm (1/16 in). Press a patch of aluminium cooking foil or thin roofing felt over the repair and trowel on another 1.5 mm (1/16 in) thick coating of mastic. Finally coat the entire valley with liquid bitumen proofing, applied by brush.

● If the valley is severely corroded, remove the slates (or tiles) on each side of the valley, remove the old lining and re-line the valley with new strips of lead or zinc, nailed at the sides. Cut the sheet to size using tinsnips. Allow 50 mm (2 in) overlaps all round.

● If the old lining is corroded, but not wrinkled, simply re-line the valley with wide self-adhesive flashing strip instead. Coat the surface with flashing strip primer about 30 minutes before sticking down the strip.

Renewing flashings

These metal strips are designed to waterproof the junction where a roof butts on to a wall. (For flashings around chimney stacks see page 80.)

Stains on the wall beneath a flashing are signs that the top edge of the flashing has parted from the mortar joint into which it should be tucked. Push it back and repoint the joint as described on page 81. Tears, cracks and holes in flashings are repaired as described for valley repairs using self-adhesive strips.

1. Badly corroded flashing is best replaced with a self-adhesive flashing strip. Remove the old flashing and discard, then repoint the mortar joints in the wall.

2. When the mortar has set, wire-brush the wall, then paint flashing strip primer in a band 150 mm (6 in) wide along the wall where the flashing strip will be applied.

3. When the primer has dried, peel off the backing from the flashing strip and press the strip into place, ensuring that it overlaps the roof by at least 100 mm (4 in).

4. There will probably be only about 50 mm (2 in) of strip turning up the wall, so apply a second strip of flashing along the wall to overlap the turn-up of the first strip. Use a wallpaper seam roller to flatten the flashing strip and dispel any air bubbles.

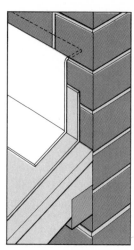

The original flashing strip (above) will most likely have been mortared into a joint between bricks. If the flashing is badly corroded, do not try to replace it – renew it instead with a self-adhesive strip

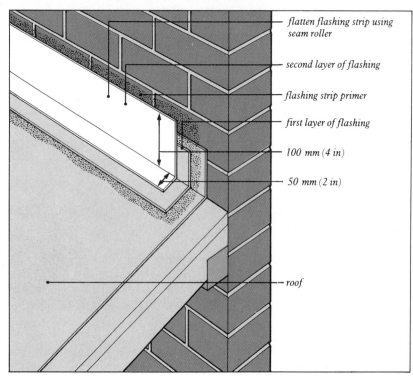

flatten flashing strip using seam roller

second layer of flashing

flashing strip primer

first layer of flashing

100 mm (4 in)

50 mm (2 in)

roof

Repairing a flat roof

When a flat, felt-covered roof gives trouble the first sign will probably be a damp patch on the ceiling of the room below. But when you go on to the roof to find the source of the trouble it is often difficult to locate the actual spot: the water can enter at one point and travel some distance under the roof covering before appearing inside as a damp patch.

If examination shows that the roof is in good condition except for minor cracks or blisters that have caused leaks, these defects can be repaired without having to resort to an overall treatment.

If there are no obvious defects – tears in the roof covering, water lying in patches – the roof may just be suffering from old age and it is quite easy to give the roof a second lease of life by applying an overall membrane treatment. Such a treatment should only last about five years, but will give you time to plan for re-felting (see overleaf).

Applying a bitumen membrane

1. There are various membrane kits available and you apply these according to the instructions. Start by removing any stone chippings that have been applied to the roof, by skimming them off with a sharp spade or scraper – be careful not to damage the roof covering.

2. Once you have removed the chippings you can prepare the surface to accept the membrane. Sweep the roof, fill cracks with mastic (caulking compound) then apply a bitumen solvent primer coating to the roof and leave overnight.

3. The next day brush bitumen over the roof –

use an old stiff-bristled broom for this – and while this is wet unroll an open-weave glass-fibre membrane on to the surface and press it in. Then apply a second coat of bitumen and allow it to dry.

4. Finally, apply two more coats of bitumen, followed by the chippings bedded on a coat of chipping compound to give a reflective surface that will help to keep the roof cool.

Patching cracks and blisters

● To repair a crack in a felt-covered roof, scrape any chippings away from the region of each crack, then play a blowtorch flame over the area of the crack to dry out moisture under the roof covering – be careful not to set the roof alight.
● The heat will also melt the bitumen underneath the felt: press it down using a cloth. Next, cut a strip of foil-backed self-adhesive flashing strip to cover the crack. Prime the area with flashing strip primer, then remove the backing paper and press the flashing strip into place using a wooden wallpaper seam roller to dispel air bubbles.
● Blisters and bubbles (A) can be repaired similarly. Make two cuts with a sharp knife across the blister and fold back the segments of felt to make it easier to dry out the underside with the blowtorch (B).
● When the adhesive has melted, or by using cold felt adhesive, press down the segments of the blister again (C). They will cover the hole, but they will not fit exactly; complete the repair by sticking a patch of self-adhesive flashing strip over the defect (D).

Use an old brush to apply a coat of bitumen over the prepared roof surface and, while this is still wet, unroll a sheet of glass-fibre membrane over the film

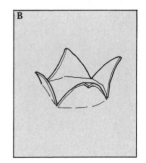

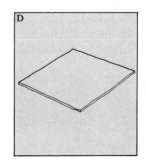

Refelting a flat roof

If a flat roof is seriously damaged, with severe cracks, loose sections, bubbles and bad wrinkles over a wide area, it is best to strip and replace it. If the roof has an asphalt covering (it looks just like the smooth, black finish of some pavements and paths) then the job should be left to an asphalt and felt roofing specialist.

Flat roofs covered with bituminous roofing felt, however, are straightforward to strip and replace. If the roof is covering an extension or garage there will usually be two or three layers of felt fixed down over a deck made up of timber boards or particle board sheets over timber joists. If the roof has been professionally laid the layers of felt will be welded into a single membrane by using hot bitumen to bond the various sheets. This technique is very dangerous for the inexperienced, so you would be wise to use only cold adhesives specially made for the do-it-yourselfer.

With cold adhesives you do not get the instant bonding that is achieved with hot bitumen, so you should use one of the new 'torching grade' bitumen felts; the roll has to be heated with a gas torch as it is unrolled and this melts the backing and gives instant bonding without the need to spread hot bitumen or adhesive beforehand.

Whichever type of felt is to be used for the roof covering the first step is to strip off the old felt if this is possible. If it is well fixed it may be possible to leave it, although it is vital to remove blisters, creases and loose patches. Make sure that old fixing nails are removed wherever possible or punch their heads well below the surface. Sweep the surface clean and check at the same time that it is smooth. High points can be removed using a coarse abrasive disc fitted in an electric drill or angle grinder.

Depressions should be levelled with a filler paste. Make sure the roof decking is firm and sound: it should not deflect when you walk on it. Also, it should have an adequate fall to ensure reasonably quick drainage of water to the gutters. The minimum fall is 1° (18 mm per metre – ¾ in per 3 ft).

To ensure that rainwater drips well clear of the walls, nail a 50 mm × 25 mm (2 in × 1 in) timber batten to form a drip rail around the edges of the roof. At the eaves, the drip batten ensures that water will run into the gutters. At the verges the drip rail should be raised by about 50 mm (2 in) against an angled timber fillet fixed to the inside of the fascia board, which will stop rainwater from driving over the edge of the roof, channelling the water down to the gutters.

It is usual to use asbestos-based felt or glass fibre-based felt for the first two layers of roofing with the top layer being a mineral-surfaced felt, or a mineral-surfaced felt covered with chippings where the roof slope is less than 10°.

Lay the roofing felt with the lengths parallel with the fall of the roof. It is helpful to take the wrappers off the rolls to allow them to relax before use, and, where possible, cut the felt roughly to length beforehand and leave it flat for 24 hours before fixing. This will minimize the subsequent effects of curling and stretching. Cut all the lengths of felt before you start work.

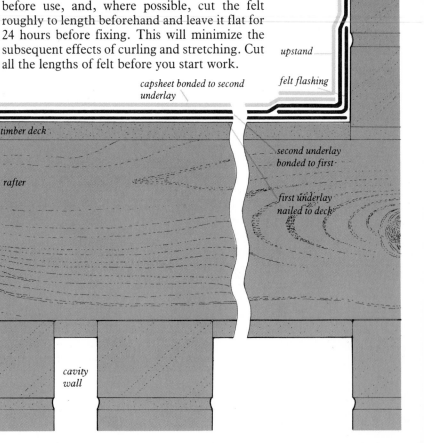

A welted drip is used at the verge of a flat roof to prevent rainwater driving over the edge. A triangular batten is fixed to the inner face of the fascia and the two underlay felts taken over this. A drip batten is fixed to the outer face of the fascia and a strip of felt is nailed to it. It is then folded over to cover the underlay felt and the capsheet for a waterproof join

felt flashing slotted into mortar joint

upstand

felt flashing

welted apron at eaves

capsheet bonded to second underlay

drip batten

timber deck

second underlay bonded to first

rafter

first underlay nailed to deck

gutter

fascia board

soffit

house wall

cavity wall

Recovering a timber deck

1. On timber and particle board roof decks, fix the first layer of felt by nailing with 20 mm (¾ in) long galvanized large-head clout nails inserted at 150 mm (6 in) intervals in both directions. Fix each sheet starting from the centre and working outwards so that wrinkles cannot form. Overlap adjacent sheets by 50 mm (2 in) and nail the overlaps at 50 mm (2 in) centres. When you reach the end of a roll overlap the new roll by 100 mm (4 in).

4. In both cases, when the second layer is fixed, make sure that the joints do not coincide with the joints on the first layer. Set the second layer back about 150 mm (6 in) from the edge of the roof to give room for the weatherproofing drip strip to be formed along the edge of the roof. Again, allow for side laps 50 mm (2 in) wide and end laps 100 mm (4 in) wide. If you find when using the cold adhesive that the side laps do not stick very well, peel them back and stick them down using lap cement.

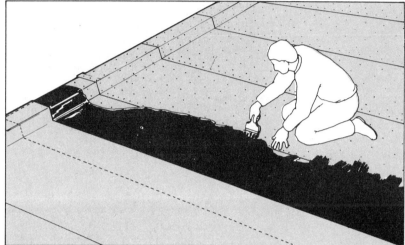

2. Fix the second layer of roofing felt next. If you are using cold adhesive mastic to fix the sheets, brush or trowel this on to the roof and leave it for about 30 minutes to become tacky before applying the second layer of felt. Unroll the felt along the roof and press it into the adhesive. Take care to expel all the air bubbles.

3. If you are using torching grade felt, separate adhesive is not necessary; all you have to do is to play the flame of an industrial-type gas blowtorch with separate gas canister (this can be hired) on the low point where the roofing meets the underlayer. As the release film of bitumen on the back of the roll melts, roll the material forward, ensuring that it is well pressed down.

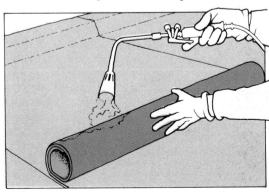

5. At the eaves form a 'drip' from a strip of mineral-surfaced felt. It must fold onto the roof, butting up against the second layer of felt. Form the drip after the second layer of felt has been laid: cut the strip along the roll in a lengthwise direction. Nail one edge of the strip to the face of the drip batten with the top surface of the felt against the batten. Score the felt and warm it about 20 mm (¾ in) below the fixing nails, using the blowtorch. Turn back the felt and stick it down onto the roof.

6. Stick the final layer of felt (called the capsheet) over the main roof area, finished to within about 25 mm (1 in) of the drip. Verges are finished similarly; the drip is folded over after the capsheet has been laid.

7. Finishing the roof against an adjacent wall requires different treatment (see diagram opposite). The first layer of felt is taken up to the wall, then the angle between wall and roof sealed with another strip of felt flashing. The second layer of felt is taken about 150 mm (6 in) up the wall and tucked into a slot cut in a brick joint. The capsheet is added, then a second felt upstand is fixed into the mortar joint and carried down over the angle between wall and roof. The felt is finally mortared into place.

A welted drip is used at the verge of the flat roof to prevent rainwater driving over the edge. A triangular batten is fixed to the inner face of the fascia and the two underlay felts taken over this; a drip batten is fixed to the outer face of the fascia and a strip of felt nailed to it then folded over to cover the underlay felt and the capsheet for a waterproof join

Glass roof maintenance

Because of their relatively flimsy construction, it is not surprising that glass roofs are particularly prone to deterioration and accidental damage. Typical signs that a roof needs attention include cracked panes of glass, leaks along the glazing bars, and wood rot in the main timbers. If the roof butts on to the wall of the house, you may also see rainwater running down the wall – a sign that the flashing strip has deteriorated. This can easily be cured by fitting a self-adhesive flashing strip (see page 70). Other problems with glazed roofs demand special treatment.

For mending cracks in glass, clear self-adhesive glass sealing tape is available, and this is simply pressed down onto the glass surface, which should be clean and dry. Make up a solution of warm water and caustic soda and wipe over the glass. It is essential that you wear rubber gloves to protect your hands from the solution, and protective goggles in case you should accidentally splash any in your eyes.

Stick on the tape and press it down firmly; to ensure a completely waterproof seal, stick a length of tape to the underside of the crack.

If the crack is forked there is a danger of dagger-like pieces of glass eventually falling from the roof: in this case the pane should be replaced. Ideally use wired or laminated glass for roofwork as these types will not shatter if anything – a slate or tile – drops onto the roof from above.

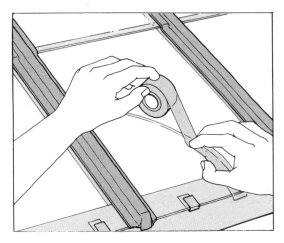

For the permanent repair of leaks along wooden glazing bars, it is best to lift the glass and re-bed it on mastic glazing strips, which are preferable to putty because they never completely harden. When the glass has been removed, rub down the glazing bars with glasspaper – or strip them back to bare wood – prime and repaint them. Any glazing bars that have rotted should be replaced – timber suppliers usually have a number of different glazing bar mouldings to choose from.

Replacing a pane of glass

1. Remove any existing mastic tape from the glazing bars to give access to the edge of the damaged glass. Put on some tough gloves and remove the broken pane of glass. Hack off any old putty from the glazing bars using an old chisel or putty knife and remove any glazing pins that might have been left in place. Check the condition of the timber.

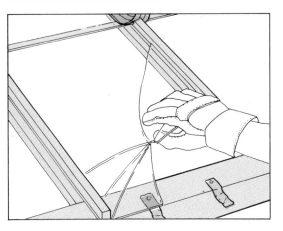

2. Treat the timber with a suitable wood preservative and make good any areas of rot. Pin a couple of aluminium or copper strips to the verge timber to ensure that the new pane of glass will not slip down. Apply a thick bead of non-setting mastic (caulking compound) to the rebate, using a cartridge gun.

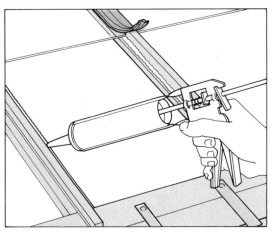

3. Slide the new pane of glass under the end of the pane above so there is an overlap of about 12 mm (½ in) to prevent water penetration. Press the glass firmly but carefully onto the bead of mastic around the edges, not in the centre. Fold the metal strips over the edge of the new pane to hold it in place, then tap in glazing spigs or coppered hardboard pins to retain it securely. Remove excess mastic that is squeezed out, using a putty knife.

Resealing glass roofs

1. If the overlap between adjacent glass sheets is not sufficiently large it is possible for rainwater to seep between the panes, drawn by capillary action, and cause leaks. You can, however, seal this gap with the special clear glass sealing tape or, even better, by squeezing a bead of clear silicone sealant (as used for sealing leaking car windows) between the panes.

2. Seal leaks along the glazing bars using foil-backed mastic waterproofing tape. Choose a width of tape that will overlap the glass by at least 12 mm (½ in) on each side. Make sure the exposed part of the glazing bars and glass is clean and dry. Start at the high point of the roof and lay the tape over the glazing bar, pressing it down at each side. At glass overlaps double the tape on itself as this helps to form a watertight joint. If you have to join two lengths of tape, overlap the upper tape on the lower one by at least 75 mm (3 in) for a good seal.

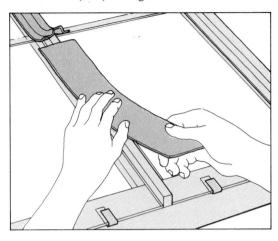

Where a chimney stack *or wall projects from the glass roof, seal the join with a strip of self-adhesive foil-backed waterproof tape, pressing it into the angle and smoothing with a seam roller to dispel air bubbles*

SNOWGUARDS

An avalanche of snow sliding off a pitched roof above a glass roof will shatter the glass and may even smash the glazing bars. To prevent this from happening, snowguards consisting of galvanized steel mesh or metal strips attached to support brackets are fixed to the sides of the rafters, or to the fascia board to which the gutters are fixed.

If the mesh has come loose, refix it to the brackets using twists of copper or galvanized steel wire. Corroded mesh can be replaced with a strip of new galvanized steel mesh of the appropriate thickness, or with galvanized steel strips bolted horizontally to the brackets and fixed about 38 mm (1½ in) apart. The brackets themselves may need to be replaced, and this will involve making your own brackets from strips of galvanized steel. Try to alter the fixing positions of the new brackets so that the screws can grip into new wood. Fill the old screw holes with filler.

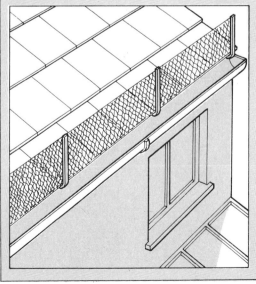

Installing a roof window

Rooms built in a converted roof space commonly have a dormer-type window – a standard window is set into a hole formed in the roof and the sides or 'cheeks' of this dormer are weatherproofed either to match the tile or slate roof covering or they are clad with a weatherproofing sheet of lead, zinc or even roofing felt or timber boards. The roofs of most dormers are flat, with perhaps a very slight forward slope to a gutter fixed above the window frame. Occasionally, when the roof is sufficiently high, the dormer may have a pitched roof to match the main roof.

Basically, faults that are likely to occur are rotting of the window frame, leaks due to deterioration of the roof covering, the weatherproofing of the sides or cheeks, and the breakdown of the flashings and back gutters. For repairs see the appropriate sections dealing with window, roof and flashing repairs.

Types of roof window

Dormer windows have the advantage of giving extra headroom in a loft (attic), but fitting one involves making major structural alterations in the roof space and as far as d-i-y installation is concerned there can be no doubt that the best way to get light into the roof space is to fit a pivoting roof window. There are several types of these modern versions of skylights. Pivoting roof lights are double glazed, lockable and can be swung through 180° to enable both sides of the glass to be cleaned from the inside. They are supplied in kit form with comprehensive instructions.

In some cases it is possible to do the entire installation from inside the roof space, although usually it is easiest to go up on to the roof and remove the initial slates or tiles from outside in the area where the roof window is to be sited. Once a hole has been made in the roof covering it is easier to confirm the exact positioning of the roof window, which can be marked on the rafters. Remove the roof covering to slightly beyond the extent of the window.

Installation will be easier if you can site the window against a rafter, but even so it will still

Pivot roof window

Roof covering and structural timbers are cut away to form the roof window

Maintenance-free aluminium cladding

Laminated pine frame pre-treated with preservative for a durable, attractive finish

Sealed double-glazed pane

Pivot action ensures adequate ventilation in the loft room and makes cleaning much easier

Lead flashing strip seals the frame from moisture penetration

be necessary to saw through other rafters that cross the window position. Before these are cut they must be propped on the inside with strong lengths of timber, which will support the weight of the roof until 'trimmer' joists are fixed – these are horizontal lengths of timber, which are nailed between the uncut rafters at each side and to which the ends of the cut rafters are fixed. Fix another length of rafter between the trimmers to complete a box framing into which the frame of the roof window can be positioned.

The roof window frame is fixed on to the rafters with special brackets, but before fixing all the screws check that the window frame is square (the diagonals should be equal) and level at the base. At this stage the slates or tiles at the bottom of the window can be replaced and then the bottom section of flashing is fitted to the frame. The side flashing sections clip on next, followed by the top section of flashing. Finally the tiles at the sides and top of the frame are refitted before the opening light is fitted and held with screws.

A

B

C

The opening for the roof window can be formed from the inside. A tile is pushed out and unhooked from its nibs and the others follow easily (A). Once the main roof timbers have been suitably supported from inside, the rafters can be cut away within the perimeter of the proposed window (B). Trimmers are used to frame the opening and the window outer frame is screwed in place (C). The metal inner frame and flashing seals are fixed to the outer frame (D) and finally the pivoting pane itself is screwed into place, and the roof tiles refitted around the unit (E)

D

E

Chimney repairs

The first signs of trouble with a chimney stack or the chimney pots will probably be damp patches on the chimney breast or on the ceiling of an upper floor room. Rain may start to trickle down the chimney and you may notice that the fire is not drawing properly. If you use coal or wood as fuel you may even notice smoke coming out of cracks in the stack as well as from the chimney pot. If you ignore these symptons you could be faced with some expensive major repairs should part of the chimney fall, not to mention the danger that this would cause to people passing below.

It is a good idea to inspect the chimney stack through binoculars from time to time, although if you are carrying out other roof repairs this is an excellent opportunity to examine the chimney at first hand. The faults to watch for are cracked, leaning and loose chimney pots, cracked cementwork (called flaunching) around the base of the chimney pots, cracks in the brickwork and decaying and crumbling mortar joints. If the chimney is rendered (stuccoed), look for cracks and bulging on the surface.

Replacing a cracked pot

Do not attempt to repair a cracked chimney pot: such repairs never last for long and it would be extremely dangerous if a pot was to come loose – they are much larger than they appear from the ground. The only cure for a cracked pot is replacement with a new pot of the same type.

Before you start work, make sure you are working from a secure platform and can reach the top of the chimney stack comfortably. Also make sure you have a sturdy, thick plastic builder's bucket in which pieces of debris can be placed and carried down to ground level, or lowered on a rope to an assistant. Do not let pieces slide off the roof – they will not only damage the roof covering and block gutters, but also they could seriously injure anyone below should they fall.

1. Place any loose bits of chimney pot into the bucket, then loop a rope around the pot and tie the ends around the top of the chimney stack to prevent the pot from falling into the flue when you remove the cement flaunching. Even if you work very carefully it is likely that debris will fall down the flue, so hang sheets over the fireplaces of rooms below to prevent dust from spreading.

2. Now, wearing stout gloves and goggles to protect your eyes from flying fragments, use a hammer and cold chisel to carefully chip away the cement flaunching from around the base of the chimney pot. It does not matter if the pot

breaks up even more, but do not allow too much debris to fall into the flue.

3. Once the pot and flaunching have been removed, brush away dust from the top of the stack and if further repairs to the stack are necessary, carry out these next.

Measure the size of the flue opening and if possible buy a new chimney pot with a square base that will fit exactly over this opening. If you are working on an old house, you may find that the base of the pot is far too small to rest over the flue: lay strips of slates to straddle the flue opening to restrict its size to a width that will support the base of the pot.

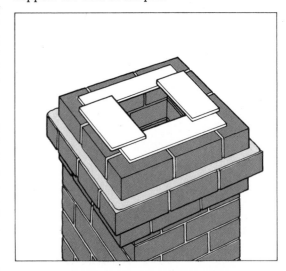

4. Dampen the brickwork at the top of the chimney by splashing on water from a brush, then bed the slates on cement mortar (using a mix of 1 part cement; 4 parts sharp sand).

Position the pot centrally over the flue and make sure that any gaps that would allow the flaunching mortar to fall into the flue are sealed with pieces of slate.

5. Thoroughly wet the base of the pot and the surface of the chimney stack brickwork, then trowel the flaunching mortar over the top of the chimney stack and spread it around the base of the pot. Smooth the mortar so that it is about 60 mm (2½ in) thick against the base of the chimney pot, sloping down to about 20 mm (¾ in) thick around the edge of the stack. The slope is to shed water, so make sure that there is a smooth, even slope in all directions.

Leaning and loose chimney pots
Due to settlement, chimney pots on old houses may develop a lean to one side and you may find that the pots are actually loose due to the flaunching having cracked away. In both cases make a repair as described below for cracked flaunching.

Cracked flaunching
It is common for minor cracks to develop in the flaunching around the base of the pot, and although you will eventually have to replace it, you can make a long-lasting repair. But if the cracks are deep and the cementwork is loose in places, it must be removed and replaced with fresh cement mortar as described for replacing pots.

To repair cracks in flaunching, press in cement mortar filler or thick black bitumen mastic (caulking compound) with a filling knife. Alternatively you can inject a bead of non-setting mastic directly into the cracks by using a cartridge mastic gun.

Cracks in brickwork
Where the flaunching has cracked it is possible that the bricks in the top two or three courses have become loosened, with cracks developing in the mortar between them and the bricks themselves sometimes splitting. The chimney pots may even be built into the top two or three courses of the brickwork – if these pots become loose this can also crack the brickwork.

In this case you will have to re-lay the top courses of brickwork before replacing the pots and flaunching. Retain the projecting bricks, called corbelling, at the top of the stack as these help to throw rainwater clear of the stack, keeping the brickwork dry lower down.

If the chimney stack has any severe cracks that extend farther than the top few courses then there may be a serious fault in the chimney and you should seek the advice of a reputable builder or roofing specialist.

Decayed mortar joints
If the mortar between the bricks of the chimney stack is crumbling, this old mortar must be raked out and the bricks repointed as described in the chapter on Walls (see page 16).

This chimney stack, typical of much inner city property, has weathered quite well although the adjacent roof was in bad condition

Sealing a chimney stack

Capping a disused stack

A disused chimney stack can be sealed to prevent rainwater getting into the flue, although you must allow for an air supply within the chimney to prevent the stack becoming wet due to condensation and rain penetration through the brickwork. Before sealing a disused chimney stack it could be lowered if you feel this would improve the appearance of the house or if the old stack is dangerous or in need of repair. The technique for lowering is described below. You have basically three options for sealing a disused stack:

● If the chimney stack and pots are in good condition, the easiest way to seal the flues is to fit metal or clay capping pots directly into the tops of the chimney pots: simply clip the metal cap into place. To fit a clay cap, first insert the cap then press cement mortar into the gap between it and the pot.

● If the pots or flaunching are in bad condition it will be best to remove these completely. When the brickwork at the top of the flue is exposed, remove one or two bricks from each side of the flue by levering them out gently and replace them with air bricks, bedded on mortar. Seal the top of the flue by bedding a paving slab or slabs on mortar over the top of the stack. The edges of the slabs must overhang the sides of the chimney stack by about 25 mm (1 in) all round to throw rainwater clear of the brickwork.

● Alternatively, after making allowance for air bricks as described above, cover the exposed flues with roofing slates, then seal the top of the chimney by covering the entire surface with new flaunching, formed with sloping sides for drainage of rainwater.

Whenever a chimney stack has been sealed, or the brickwork has been repointed, paint the surface with a clear silicone water repellent, to keep the brickwork and the top of the stack dry. This will stop rain penetration without affecting the appearance of the stack and helps to prevent frost and water damage to the stack.

Lowering a dangerous chimney

For this job scaffolding or another firm working platform erected around or beside the chimney stack is essential.

1. Work steadily from the top of the chimney stack, removing bricks carefully by using a hammer and bolster chisel.

2. Take care not to let debris fall into the flue. Place the rubble in buckets and lower on a rope to a helper at ground level.

3. At the top of the lowered chimney build in two or three courses of overhanging bricks to form corbelling that will throw rainwater clear of the stack and improve its appearance.

4. Seal the top of the lowered chimney as described above, remembering to fit air bricks to ventilate the flue.

Chimney flashings

To weatherproof the join where the roof meets the chimney stack, flashings are fitted. These are usually made from lead, but they may also be made from zinc, aluminium alloy, copper, bituminous felt or a pre-formed rigid bitumen-asbestos material. Self-adhesive metal-backed flashing strips are the easiest to fit and form a good weatherproof seal.

Some flashings are formed by a triangular-shaped mortar fillet set against the stack and this type invariably gives trouble and should be replaced with self-adhesive flashing strips.

The design of chimney flashing varies according to the type of roof covering. With a single-lapped tiled roof and some slate roofs, the flashing at the side of the chimney stack will normally be a stepped flashing, inserted into the mortar joints, which is 'dressed' (beaten down) over the adjoining tiles or slates.

On a plain tiled roof, and some slate roofs, the flashing at the side of the chimney stack usually consists of separate pieces of metal called soakers, which are interleaved with the tiles. The soakers are turned up against the side of the chimney stack and then a stepped flashing covers the upturned edges of the soakers.

It is common for the top edge of the flashing to pull away from the stack where it is tucked into the brickwork and this will allow water to seep behind. Torn flashings can be repaired in the same manner that valley linings are repaired – see page 70. Chimney back gutters are replaced in the same way as valley linings (see

Cap a disused chimney stack by removing the old pot and flaunching, and bedding paving slabs on top (A); do not forget to insert airbricks in the stack to keep the flue ventilated. Alternatively, bed roofing slates in the top of the stack (B).

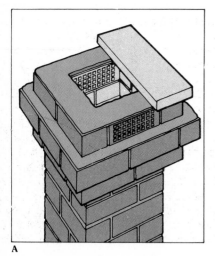
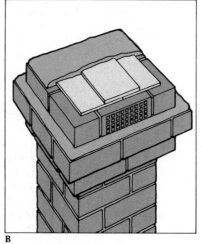

A   B

page 70), which involves removing adjacent tiles or slates, and this will also be necessary in order to replace soakers. Bear in mind these points when renewing flashings:

● To replace a flashing that has worked loose, rake out the old mortar and tuck the top of the flashing back into place, holding it in position with rolled up pieces of lead strip to form wedges. Dampen the mortar joint with water and trowel in fresh mortar.

● If a flashing is badly corroded it is best to replace it with new lead. Retain the old pieces and use them as patterns for cutting the new lead sheet accurately.

● Seal the gap behind a cement fillet flashing with a bead of non-setting mastic (caulking compound) if the gap is not too wide, or chip away the mortar and replace it with bands of self-adhesive flashing strip applied as described for strip flashings (see page 70).

Some chimney stacks are positioned against the outside house wall. Maintain the lower areas as for house walls

9. Gutters and downpipes

Guide to types

Gutters collect the rainwater that runs off the roof and feed it into a vertical downpipe, from where it is discharged into a rainwater gully; this either leads into the house drainage system or to a soakaway in the garden (see page 92), according to the requirements of the local authority. Sometimes, when rainwater is needed for watering the garden, the downpipe from a greenhouse or other outbuilding may discharge into a water butt (rain barrel) and can be drawn off from an integral tap when required.

On older houses cast-iron guttering is commonly found and, although it is still available from builders' suppliers for repair work, a demolition contractor may be a better bet if you are looking for a local source of supply. Be warned, though: it is expensive to buy and very heavy to transport.

Two other guttering materials that may be found are galvanized steel, which is not particularly strong and can be more prone to rusting than cast iron, and asbestos cement, which is easily damaged – by a ladder resting against it, for instance.

Plastic is nowadays the most commonly used material for gutters, because it is virtually maintenance free, light and easy to fit. Also quite widely used are gutters made from seamless aluminium sheet, which is formed on site by folding a roll of sheet aluminium into a gutter section in lengths to suit the building to which the gutter is being fixed.

The traditional shape for guttering is half-round, which is fixed by metal clips to the fascia board or protruding ends of the rafters. Many cast-iron, galvanized steel and aluminium gutters are formed into a decorative 'ogee' shape with a straight back, which allows them to be fastened directly to the fascia board. There are also square and rectangular gutters, which have a better flow rate size-for-size than ordinary half-round gutters.

Gutter sizes vary according to the area of roof they drain. When buying new gutters consult the manufacturer's literature regarding the recommended flow rates and maximum roof area. Obviously a gutter that has outlets at each end can carry more water than a gutter with a single outlet. In a typical system it is usual to use 100 mm (4 in) half-round guttering and 68 mm (2¾ in) downpipes.

Another type of gutter found on some (usually older) houses is the box gutter, which collects water between two adjacent sloping roofs. Such gutters are usually formed from timber boards waterproofed with sheets of zinc, lead, or roofing felt. Repairs are as for roof valleys and flashings (see page 70).

Common problems

Gutters have a vital role to play in keeping your house dry and sound. By neglecting gutter maintenance all sorts of problems with moisture penetration and decay will be created due to water running down the outside of the house: if left uncorrected, this will eventually allow the water to penetrate inside, ruining decorations and even rotting structural timbers.

If you take over an old or neglected house there may be quite a lot of remedial work to do to the gutters and downpipes, but generally an annual check is all that is required to keep the system in good repair.

Autumn is the best time to make an inspection because at that time of year faults are generally easy to see and there is time to take the necessary remedial action before the winter rains set in.

Do remember safety both when examining and repairing gutters. Working at a height is always dangerous, so follow the safety tips on page 86.

Fault Finder

An overflowing gutter is perhaps the easiest fault to spot but not always easy to remedy because the overflow may be due to one of three causes:

● The gutter may be blocked with leaves or other debris from the roof.
● The downpipe may be blocked somewhere along its length.
● The gully into which the downpipe discharges may be blocked.

Occasionally overflows are due to the gutters and downpipes not being sufficiently large for the area of roof they drain. This problem is shown by a tendency to overflow during heavy rain, even though the system is clear of blockages. In this case a new large-capacity guttering system should be fitted.

Leaking gutter joints, highlighted by a steady drip from affected joints during and shortly after rain, are a common problem with metal gutters but can also occur with badly fitted plastic systems.

Metal gutters sometimes develop leaks away from joints due to corrosion. Repairs are possible, although these should be treated only as a temporary measure: this fault is a warning that the old guttering is beyond its useful life and may even be dangerous. A new plastic guttering system will shortly be required.

Rusted metal gutters can be repaired if the damage is not too great – only close examination will reveal how far the rust has spread.

Types of gutter

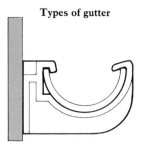

Half-round, *fixed in brackets screwed to the fascia board, rafters or brickwork, come in cast-iron, steel, asbestos or plastic*

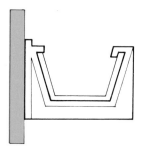

Square, *fixed in brackets as for half-round types, usually come in plastic, although other materials may be available*

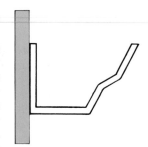

Ogee, *a decorative design in cast-iron or steel, must be screwed direct to the fascia board*

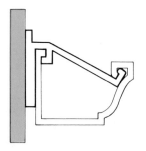

Moulded, *usually in aluminium or plastic, and often in ogee profile, can be screwed direct to the fascia board or mounted on brackets*

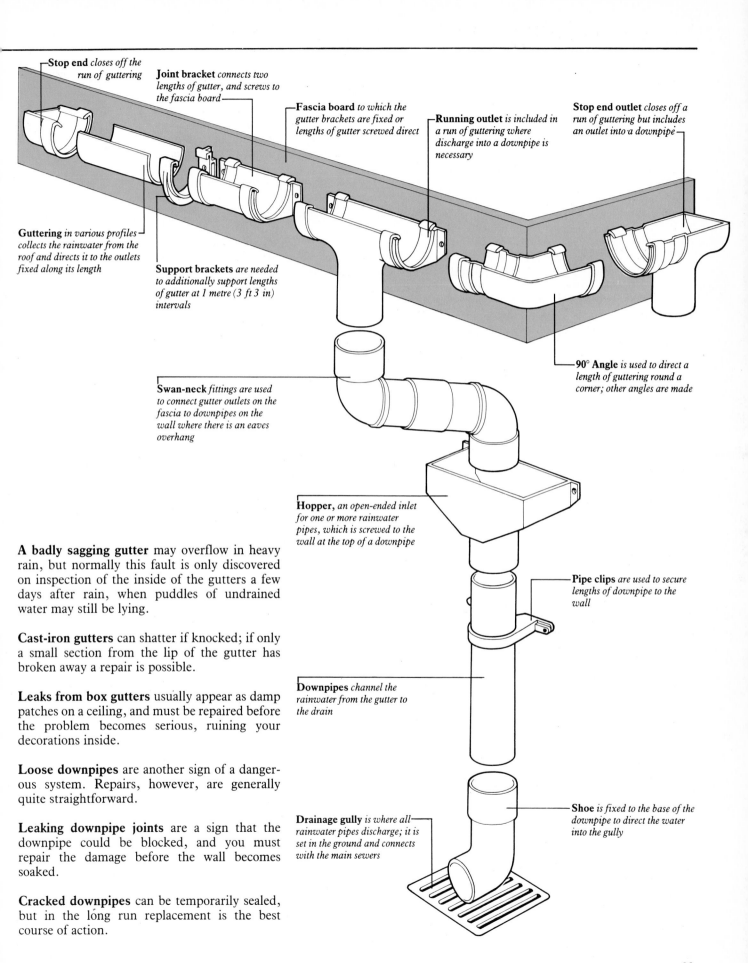

Stop end *closes off the run of guttering*

Joint bracket *connects two lengths of gutter, and screws to the fascia board*

Fascia board *to which the gutter brackets are fixed or lengths of gutter screwed direct*

Running outlet *is included in a run of guttering where discharge into a downpipe is necessary*

Stop end outlet *closes off a run of guttering but includes an outlet into a downpipe*

Guttering *in various profiles collects the rainwater from the roof and directs it to the outlets fixed along its length*

Support brackets *are needed to additionally support lengths of gutter at 1 metre (3 ft 3 in) intervals*

90° Angle *is used to direct a length of guttering round a corner; other angles are made*

Swan-neck *fittings are used to connect gutter outlets on the fascia to downpipes on the wall where there is an eaves overhang*

Hopper, *an open-ended inlet for one or more rainwater pipes, which is screwed to the wall at the top of a downpipe*

Pipe clips *are used to secure lengths of downpipe to the wall*

Downpipes *channel the rainwater from the gutter to the drain*

Drainage gully *is where all rainwater pipes discharge; it is set in the ground and connects with the main sewers*

Shoe *is fixed to the base of the downpipe to direct the water into the gully*

A badly sagging gutter may overflow in heavy rain, but normally this fault is only discovered on inspection of the inside of the gutters a few days after rain, when puddles of undrained water may still be lying.

Cast-iron gutters can shatter if knocked; if only a small section from the lip of the gutter has broken away a repair is possible.

Leaks from box gutters usually appear as damp patches on a ceiling, and must be repaired before the problem becomes serious, ruining your decorations inside.

Loose downpipes are another sign of a dangerous system. Repairs, however, are generally quite straightforward.

Leaking downpipe joints are a sign that the downpipe could be blocked, and you must repair the damage before the wall becomes soaked.

Cracked downpipes can be temporarily sealed, but in the long run replacement is the best course of action.

Cures for leaking gutters

Overflowing gutters

If examination shows that the gutter is blocked by leaves and dirt, these must be cleaned out. First put up a ladder fitted with a ladder stay at the top so that it is easy to get at the gutters without over-reaching. Clean a manageable section then move the ladder along so you do not have to lean too far sideways.

Scrape the debris into small heaps, using a piece of hardboard or plastic sheet cut to the shape of the gutter (below). Make sure that the debris does not drop into the downpipe. If the downpipe is fitted with a rainwater shoe (to divert the water into the gully) it is a good idea to

place a metal tray under the downpipe to prevent any dirt that drops into the pipe from falling into the drains. Use a garden trowel to collect the heaps of rubbish and place them in a bucket. If you scrape the rubbish straight over the edge of the gutters it will make a mess on the walls of the house.

Pour a bucket of water into the gutter at the top of the system and check that the water flows steadily into the downpipe and drains away quickly.

After cleaning cast-iron or galvanized steel gutters it is a good idea to wire-brush the inside of the gutter, which you should treat with water-proofing paint when the metal is dry.

Blocked downpipes

Place a tray under the blocked downpipe to catch debris. A straight downpipe can be cleared from the top using a long bamboo cane to which a bundle of rags has been tied at one end. If a swan-neck section (to connect the downpipe to a gutter on an overhanging eaves) is fitted, use a flexible drain clearing brush to clear the obstruction. If one of these is not available, then remove the swan-neck by lifting it out of the downpipe and clear the downpipe using a bamboo cane or a straightened-out metal coat hanger. If this still proves impossible due to the overhang of the roof, unclip the downpipe from the wall so that each section can be cleared individually. Use a hose to wash out the downpipe before reassembling it and reconnecting the swan-neck.

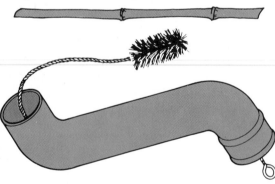

Leaking gutter joints

It may be possible to seal the joint in a leaking metal gutter without dismantling the gutter. Scrape dirt from the joint inside the gutter, brush this away and allow the gutter to dry. Inject a bead of non-setting mastic (caulking compound) into the joint, using a gun. General-purpose mastics can be used, although specialist mastics are available for this type of repair.

If sealing the joint with mastic does not cure the leak, the joint must be remade. The affected section of metal gutter must be removed as described on page 86. Carefully chip away the old red lead putty from the overlap and wipe the joint clean. Apply metal primer to the joint where the new putty is to go and apply a layer of metal-casement window putty or strips of thick mastic. Press the gutter sections together and tighten the joint with a new nut and bolt.

Problems with plastic gutters

Leaking plastic gutters are easier to repair than metal ones. Release the affected section by squeezing the side to remove it from its securing clip. Either wipe the old sealing gasket to remove any dirt that may be affecting the seal, or replace it with a new one; refix the gutter.

Corroded metal gutters

Cleaning and wire-brushing metal gutters may show that a leak is due to corrosion of the metal. Clean and dry the inside of the gutter after removing as much rust as possible. Use a car bodywork glass-fibre repair kit to repair the defect; reinforce the inside of the gutter with glass-fibre bandage. Use glass-fibre paste to smooth holes on the outside of the gutter. Sand smooth and repaint the gutter to hide the repair (see page 46).

Sagging gutters

If a metal ogee gutter has sagged because the fixing screws have corroded, the first step is to temporarily lift the section back into line by driving large nails into the fascia board just below the run, so that it can be lifted on timber packing pieces. Stretch a stringline along the gutter to help get it straight and check there is a shallow fall by using a spirit level. Drill new fixing holes in the back of the gutter and fix the gutter to the fascia using new galvanized gutter screws.

With half-round gutters, sagging may be caused by corrosion of the brackets or the bracket fixing screws. Correct the sag as described above then refix the gutter with new brackets and zinc-plated screws. Move the brackets slightly so they fix to a new part of the fascia. If the bracket screw holes are not accessible with the gutter in place the section must be removed and replaced as described overleaf for fixing new gutters.

Broken cast-iron gutters

It is best to replace broken sections of cast-iron guttering, but where perhaps only a small section at the edge has broken away a satisfactory repair can be made using glass-fibre matting and resin as used for car body repairs. Clean the inside of the gutter of rust and follow the procedure detailed in the instructions given by the manufacturers of the repair kit.

Rusted metal gutters

Use a wire brush and scraper to remove loose rust from inside the gutter. Allow the gutter to dry then apply a proprietary rust-killing and neutralizing liquid. When this is dry apply two coats of black bitumen paint.

Loose downpipes

With cast-iron downpipes, pull out the securing nails so that the loose section of pipe can be removed. The wooden plugs into which the nails were fixed will probably have come loose, so remove them and enlarge the holes slightly (A) so that new tapering softwood plugs can be inserted. Replace the downpipe and drive chisel-point downpipe nails into the plugs (B). If the joints are loose, fill with mastic (caulking compound).

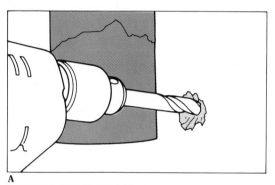

A

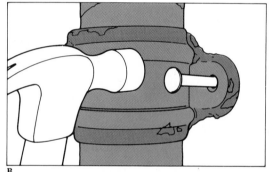

B

If plastic downpipes become loose, release the bolts holding the clips to the bracket blocks so that the downpipe can be lifted away. Move the bracket up or down on the wall slightly and refix the brackets using larger screws and plugs.

Leaking downpipe joints

Check that the downpipe is not blocked below the leaking joint, which should then be sealed by injecting non-setting mastic into the joint.

Cracked downpipes

Downpipe sockets may split if they are left open: this allows water to collect, which may freeze and burst the socket. Downpipes themselves may crack if they are accidentally hit or if they become blocked and water is allowed to freeze within them. In both cases it is best to replace the broken downpipes. Temporary repairs can be made by wrapping the pipes with pieces of metal-backed self-adhesive flashing strip or mastic tape. Alternatively the pipes can be repaired with glass-fibre bandage and repair paste.

Replacing a gutter system

Removing the existing guttering

Take care when removing the old guttering. It will not only be heavy but also the screws and bolts holding it together will probably be rusted and immovable.

1. Metal gutters are held together with nuts and bolts and the first stage in removal is to cut through these with a hacksaw. A mini-hacksaw will be ideal for the job: it is more convenient to use and less likely to damage the surface of the fascia board than a full-size hacksaw. Even when the nut and lower part of the bolt have been sawn off it is likely that the head of the bolt will be rusted in place, so drive this upwards with a nail punch and then tap the gutter joint with a hammer to break the seal of the mastic or putty at the joint.

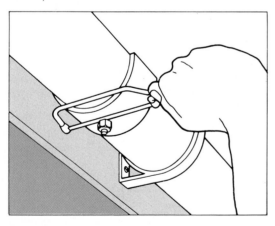

2. With half-round gutters, lift the sections from the brackets and take them down to the ground. Always lower sections on a rope or carry them down: never throw them – they are very heavy and could accidentally hit the ladder on the way down or, worse still, someone below.

3. Next, the brackets must be removed. Try undoing the fixing screws, but if this proves difficult, the answer may be to heat the heads of the screws with a narrow blowtorch flame (be careful not to set fire to the fascia) or the tip of a soldering iron. If this fails to loosen the screws, lever off the brackets from the fascia.

4. With ogee guttering, securing screws hold the lengths of guttering direct to the fascia and these screws must be removed before the guttering is released. Use the same loosening techniques as for bracket screws above.

5. Old downpipes are usually cast iron and are fixed to the wall by large nails, which pass through moulded-in lugs at the top of each section. Once the gutters are out of the way, move the swan-necks from side to side to break the seal and allow these to be lifted out. The downpipe can then be removed a section at a time by levering out the nails with the head of a claw hammer resting on a block of wood to protect the wall surface, or by levering the downpipe lugs away from the wall using a lever, such as a crowbar.

Fixing new plastic gutters

Although basically the same, the various plastic guttering systems vary slightly in the methods they use to fit the sections and brackets together and different makes may not be compatible. Choose a guttering and downpipe system from one manufacturer and stick to this throughout.

1. The first step in fixing new guttering is to ascertain the position of the gutter outlet. In the UK this is usually directly above the rainwater gully or hopper head, in the US, above the storm drain inlet. The position can be marked on the fascia board by dropping a plumb-line down to the gully.

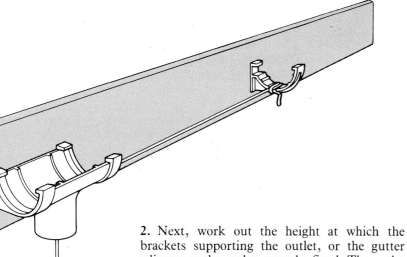

Fixing plastic downpipes

To fix downpipes, use offset connectors and a short length of downpipe to make up a swan-neck, to discharge the rainwater from the gutter into the downpipe (A). Use a chalked plumbline to mark the position of the downpipe on the wall. The brackets are usually in two parts – a wall block and a clip which should support the downpipe at each connector and at 2 m (6 ft) centres. Screw the wall blocks to the wall using screws and plastic wallplugs and attach the clips to the blocks with small galvanized nuts and bolts. When fitting the end of the downpipe into the spigot of the section below, allow a gap of 10 mm (3/8 in) for expansion of the pipes (B).

2. Next, work out the height at which the brackets supporting the outlet, or the gutter adjacent to the outlet, must be fixed. The outlet needs to be at the lowest point in a run of guttering and the end stop at the highest point, with the fall between them of 1 in 600 and 1 in 100 (between 5 mm and 25 mm in 3 m – 1/4 in and 1 in in 10 ft). Fix first the bracket farthest from the outlet so that the gutter will be close under the overhang of the roof at this point. Tie a length of string to this bracket, then run the string along to the bracket that will support the outlet. Hold the bracket in place against the fascia and use a spirit level to get the stringline level. Lightly mark the bracket position at this point, then – according to the distance between the two brackets – lower the outlet bracket on the fascia to give the required fall.

3. Screw the bracket in place using zinc-plated screws and, with the stringline tightly stretched between the brackets, fix the intermediate brackets in place on the fascia at the spacings recommended by the manufacturer.

4. The lengths of guttering usually simply clip into the brackets, which may be plain, or which may be union brackets for joining two lengths of guttering. It all depends on each manufacturer's system. Sometimes all the brackets are plain and lengths of gutter are joined independently of the brackets, using strapped unions.

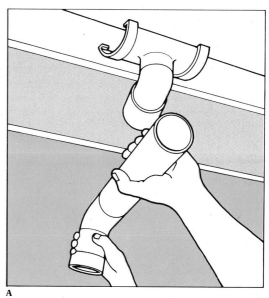

A

B

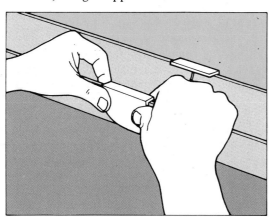

10. Drainage systems

For many householders, what happens when they pull out the bath plug or flush the w.c. remains a mystery. The disposal of soil and waste water has exercised sanitary engineers for centuries, and it is a tribute to their endeavours that many people never need to find out what happens 'down the drain' because nothing goes wrong. The trouble is that when something does malfunction, the results can be at best unpleasant and at worst catastrophic. So it helps to know what is involved.

The principle of water disposal is really quite simple. Waste water from baths and washing up, soil water from w.c.s, and rainwater from the house's gutters all flow under gravity to underground drains that lead from each property into the main sewers. Over the years the precise way in which appliances within the house have been linked to the drains has undergone some changes and what you find in your own house depends on its age (or on whether the system has been modernized since the house was built).

In a modern house you'll find what is called single-stack plumbing. A single large-diameter pipe, usually 100 mm (4 in) across, runs up through the house from the ground floor to the roof, where it is open to the air and capped by a cowl. At various points waste pipes from baths, basins, sinks, showers, and w.c.s are connected into it via specially designed branch fittings. The whole pipe may be within the house – usually boxed in behind plasterboard cladding, occasionally run in a specially constructed void in the building – or fixed to the outside wall. At ground level a slow (gradual) bend links this pipe (which is nowadays made of a plastic called upvc – unplasticized polyvinyl chloride) to the underground drain itself.

The waste pipe running to each appliance is fitted with a deep 75 mm (3 in) trap, which seals off the house from drain smells. The deep traps are designed to prevent the water seal being sucked out by siphonage when another appliance is emptied.

On older houses the so-called two-pipe system was used (the single-stack system only became common in the fifties). With this system the soil water from w.c.s was taken via a large-diameter soil stack direct to the underground drain. Other waste went down another stack to a trapped gully at ground level. Waste from upstairs appliances was fed out through the wall of the house to discharge into a hopper – an open 'bucket' at the top of the waste stack. Pipes from ground-floor appliances were taken to discharge over the gully, from where it entered the

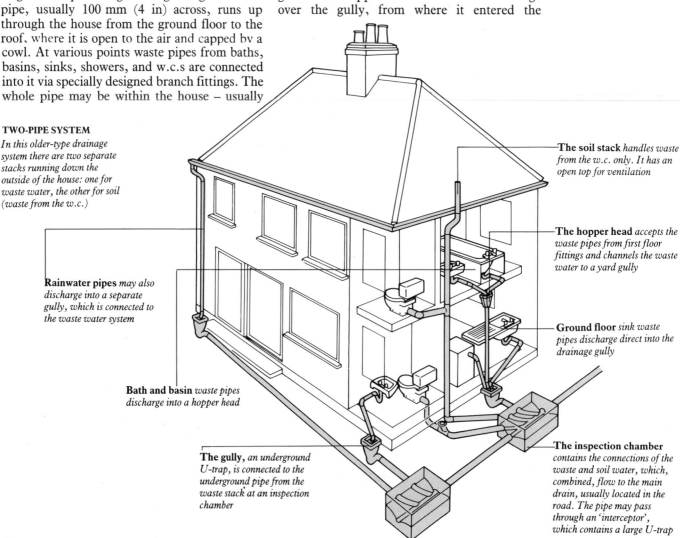

TWO-PIPE SYSTEM
In this older-type drainage system there are two separate stacks running down the outside of the house: one for waste water, the other for soil (waste from the w.c.)

Rainwater pipes *may also discharge into a separate gully, which is connected to the waste water system*

Bath and basin *waste pipes discharge into a hopper head*

The gully, *an underground U-trap, is connected to the underground pipe from the waste stack at an inspection chamber*

The soil stack *handles waste from the w.c. only. It has an open top for ventilation*

The hopper head *accepts the waste pipes from first floor fittings and channels the waste water to a yard gully*

Ground floor *sink waste pipes discharge direct into the drainage gully*

The inspection chamber *contains the connections of the waste and soil water, which, combined, flow to the main drain, usually located in the road. The pipe may pass through an 'interceptor', which contains a large U-trap*

underground drains via a separate drain run. Such two-pipe systems had to be fixed to the outside walls of the house, and the ugly sprawl of cast-iron pipework that resulted is familiar to everyone.

There is a variation on the two-pipe system found in some older multi-storey buildings. This is called the one-pipe system and was introduced because of the large amounts of pipework needed for the two-pipe system in such buildings. With this system all wastes flowed into a single large-diameter stack, which had an open-ended outlet at eaves level. Each waste pipe was connected into it and also into a small-diameter vent pipe, the object of which was to prevent siphonage emptying the traps of other appliances when one was emptied. The system is very rarely found in homes other than multi-storey ones, and is now obsolete.

Below ground, what happens depends to a certain extent on how your local authority handles its waste water disposal. In some areas all water from the house – including rainwater – goes into one sewer, while in other areas separate sewers and storm drains are provided, and in these areas you are not allowed to drain rainwater into a foul-water sewer. An alternative to storm water drains in some areas is to pipe rainwater into soakaways – rubble-lined pits that allow the water to soak into the subsoil.

Between the house and the sewer you will find one or more inspection chambers – rectangular pits through which the waste water runs in half-round channels. These chambers are always fitted where a drain run changes direction, and allow access to the underground section of the drains for clearing any blockages that may occur. They also act as junctions where two underground drain sections meet. Each chamber – often called a manhole – is fitted with a cast-iron or galvanized steel cover.

Underground drains are usually of glazed stoneware, although in many modern installations durable plastic drains and manholes are now being laid.

You may be one of the small minority of people whose homes are not connected to mains drainage. In this case the house's waste and soil water flow into either a cesspool or a septic tank. The former is just a holding tank, and has to be emptied quite regularly – an expensive process. The latter is in effect a miniature sewage treatment plant, processing the waste matter into harmless effluent, which is then discharged into the subsoil. A septic tank simply has to be emptied of sludge once or twice a year.

SINGLE-STACK SYSTEM
This is the drainage system now in common use: it consists of a single stack into which all waste pipes – soil and water – connect, and are channelled to an inspection chamber and on to the main drain

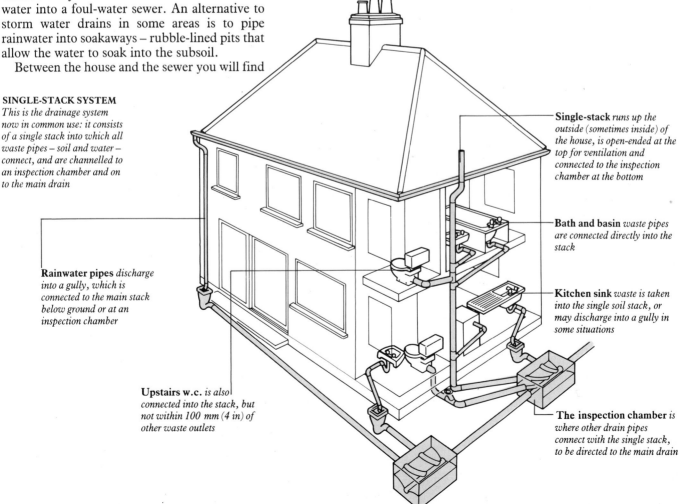

Single-stack *runs up the outside (sometimes inside) of the house, is open-ended at the top for ventilation and connected to the inspection chamber at the bottom*

Bath and basin *waste pipes are connected directly into the stack*

Kitchen sink *waste is taken into the single soil stack, or may discharge into a gully in some situations*

Rainwater pipes *discharge into a gully, which is connected to the main stack below ground or at an inspection chamber*

Upstairs w.c. *is also connected into the stack, but not within 100 mm (4 in) of other waste outlets*

The inspection chamber *is where other drain pipes connect with the single stack, to be directed to the main drain*

Clearing blocked drains

Blockages occur in waste pipes, soil pipes and underground drains for two main reasons – misuse and lack of care and maintenance. Knowing what to do when a blockage occurs can save a great deal of mess and inconvenience – even expense (24-hour plumbers charge a lot of money).

Blockages in waste pipes

The commonest problem with waste pipes is a blockage in the trap immediately below the appliance. Such a blockage is usually caused by foreign matter – solidified fat in the trap below a sink, or a mixture of scum and hair under a washbasin.

The blockage will usually build up over a period of time until the last straw breaks the camel's back and the blockage is complete (regular cleaning with, for example, hot water and caustic soda can prevent these blockages accumulating, but not everyone bothers with such good housekeeping).

Fortunately, blockages at this point were anticipated by the designers of even lead plumbing systems, and all traps can either be opened up or dismantled to allow the blockage to be cleared.

With lead traps on old plumbing systems, you will find a small plug in the lowest part of the trap. Undo this with a spanner (wrench) – but, before you do, you must brace the trap in place with a piece of wood to stop it bending as you undo the plug.

Insert a length of wire in through the eye and poke out the blockage. Have a bucket under the trap before you undo the eye, and fit the plug in the basin or sink, too. Then replace the eye and flush the trap through with hot caustic soda solution or drain cleaner.

With modern plastic plumbing systems, opening the trap is considerably easier. You will find either a U-shaped trap or a cylindrical bottle trap below the waste outlet. The former can be dismantled to allow the blockage to be cleared, and the sections removed can be flushed through and scrubbed out before being replaced. The fittings may only be hand-tight, but you may need a plumber's wrench to loosen stubborn ones. With a bottle trap you should be able to simply unscrew the base of the trap by hand, clean it out and replace it.

When you have dismantled a plastic trap, check that any seals or O-rings fitted are in good condition; replace them if they are not, since otherwise you will not get a watertight seal when you reassemble the trap.

Blocked w.c.s can be more difficult to clear, as there is no means of access to the trap. Try using a force cup or plunger, or feeding a

flexible wire round the trap bend to dislodge the blockage. If this fails, try a proprietary flexible 'snake' (you can buy or hire them) to clear blockages of this sort.

If all else fails, you will have to contact a plumber or your local authority emergency plumbing service for help.

Blocked gullies

Gullies taking waste water from upstairs hoppers, downstairs appliances or rainwater pipes can overflow for two reasons. Either the trap itself is blocked up with silt, debris and the like, or the gully grid is blocked with leaves, wind-blown paper and the like so that pipes discharging over it splash water over the surrounding area instead.

If the trap is blocked, the cure is to lift the grid and scoop out the debris from the trap with a gloved hand or an improvized implement such as an empty canned food tin or a bent garden trowel. Scour the sides of the gully thoroughly and wash it through with plenty of water from a hose before replacing the grid.

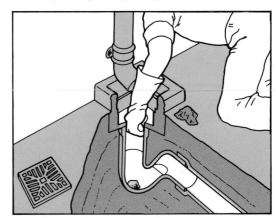

If the grid is blocked, lift off the grid, remove the debris then replace the grid. You can help stop the problem recurring by fitting a plywood or proprietary plastic cover over the gully, having first extended any pipes discharging over the gully so that they discharge below the cover.

Blocked drains

Often the first sign of a blockage in the underground drains is an offensive overflow from an inspection chamber or gully. The first thing to do is to find out exactly where the blockage is, and it is at this time that a knowledge of the layout of your drains is particularly useful.

If the overflow is from a gully and the trap is not blocked, work your way along the drain run from it to the nearest manhole and lift its cover. If the manhole is empty, the blockage is between

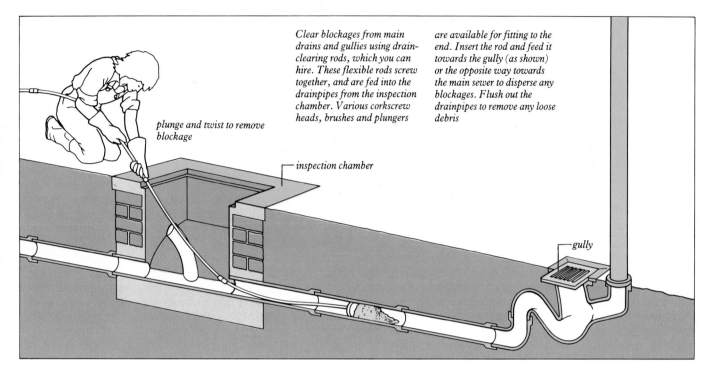

plunge and twist to remove blockage

Clear blockages from main drains and gullies using drain-clearing rods, which you can hire. These flexible rods screw together, and are fed into the drainpipes from the inspection chamber. Various corkscrew heads, brushes and plungers

are available for fitting to the end. Insert the rod and feed it towards the gully (as shown) or the opposite way towards the main sewer to disperse any blockages. Flush out the drainpipes to remove any loose debris

inspection chamber

gully

the manhole and the gully. If this first manhole is full (and overflowing), move to the next manhole along the run towards the sewer, and lift its cover. If this manhole is empty, the blockage is between it and the full manhole. If it too is full, the blockage is between the second manhole and the sewer, or at least in the outlet from this manhole (a common problem with old-fashioned intercepting traps – see **3.** below).

1. Having located the site of the blockage, the next task is to obtain a set of drain-clearing rods (you can hire them from plant hire shops; if they're closed, a garden hose turned full on may make an acceptable substitute). Attach a plunger to the first rod, then screw on one or more lengths of rod and feed the plunger into the manhole. Some people swear that you should work from the empty manhole below the blockage and push the rods up towards it, while others recommend working from the manhole above the blockage, feeding the rods into the outlet from this manhole and forcing the blockage on down the drain run. Either is acceptable (although if the blockage is between gully and manhole you will have to feed the rods up the drain run anyway).

2. Screw on extra rods as you push them up the drain. Always rotate the rods clockwise as you do this; if you turn them the other way you may unscrew one section, which you will then be unable to retrieve. Push the plunger up and down when you meet an obstruction; if this fails,

withdraw the rod and try a corkscrew attachment instead. When the blockage shifts attach the brush head and scrub through the drain run while running water from a hose through it.

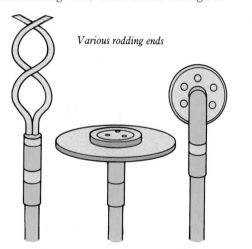

Various rodding ends

3. If you have an intercepting trap between your house and the road, a special type of blockage may occur. These traps, used some years ago to help vent the sewer, have a rodding eye in the outlet designed to allow you to rod the section between manhole and sewer (the trap was intended to keep sewer gas out of the house drain run). The rodding eye is fitted with an earthenware plug, and this can become dislodged, blocking the outlet from the manhole. If this occurs, you will have to retrieve the plug as best you can. Do not bother to refit it – it will only cause the problem to recur.

Laying land drains

Efficient garden drainage is essential for good plant growth – few plants can withstand constantly wet soil around their roots without rotting, and a lawn will tend to be mossy and unhealthy. A well-drained site is also necessary where you plan to build garden walls or lay paths. Although you can often overcome minor drainage problems by improving the texture and fertility of the soil – peat, compost and lime dug into a dry soil will aerate it, for instance – more serious defects must be corrected by laying land drains (weeping tiles). The job is quite straightforward, although digging trenches for the pipe runs can be laborious.

If you are not sure whether it is worth laying land drains (weeping tiles), you can make a simple test. Dig holes about 300 mm (1 ft) deep at several points around the garden shortly after heavy rain. If there is a pool of water in the bottom of the hole a few hours later – and assuming it has not been raining heavily since – the garden will probably benefit from improved drainage.

Your first consideration should be to work out how the drains are to be arranged and how the water is to be disposed of. If your garden slopes down to another garden below, for example, do not simply direct your surplus water into that: you will only succeed in making your neighbour's drainage suffer.

It is illegal to run your garden drains into a sewer, but if a soakaway (gravel-filled pit) for a roof is available, you may be able to run the surplus water into this.

Usually, however, a special garden soakaway is the best solution. Find a convenient low point in the garden to which you can direct the drain pipes (they must be laid with a slight fall), but make sure it is not near the house.

Making a soakaway

To cope with heavy rain, even a small garden will need a soakaway of adequate dimensions. It is simply a gravel-filled pit which allows surplus water to filter away to earth. The hole should be at least 1.2 m (4 ft) deep – not an easy depth to dig to on a heavy clay soil – and, simply to make it possible to excavate comfortably to that depth, the area covered should be at least 1.2 m (4 ft) across.

You will probably need a pick-axe to break up the soil at the lowest depth, and you may find it helpful to tackle the job in a series of short sessions spread between other jobs if you are not used to this sort of heavy work.

Fill the bottom 900 mm (3 ft) of the hole – or to within the top 300 mm (1 ft) if the hole is deeper or shallower than 1.2 m (4 ft) – with coarse rubble. Old bricks, large stones or

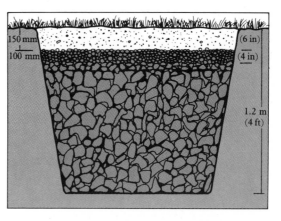

A **soakaway** may be necessary to ensure correct drainage of rainwater from the garden. To make the soakaway, dig a hole 1.2 m (4 ft) deep and fill the pit with coarse rubble such as old bricks, large stones or hardcore. Fill the hole to within 300 mm (1 ft) of the top, gradually using smaller stones. Compact the material a little. Add about 100 mm (4 in) of gravel then finish off with 150 mm (6 in) of soil. You can sow grass seeds or lay turf on top if the soakaway is in a lawn

hardcore, can all be used. Gradually use smaller rubble towards the top and compact it a little to ensure that it is fairly firm.

Cover the coarse material with about 100 mm (4 in) of gravel. The gravel is to stop the top dressing of soil washing down and clogging the drainage area. If you want to cover the soakaway with grass, or even shallow-rooting plants (do not choose a tree or shrub), cover the top 150 mm (6 in) with soil. Before you sow grass seed or lay turf, give the area plenty of time to settle, otherwise you may end up with a depression that is difficult to remove by top-dressing.

Where to lay the drains

Your test holes will have told you which parts of the garden need draining. Often only part of the garden becomes waterlogged; if so, confine the drains to this area to save draining parts of the garden unnecessarily.

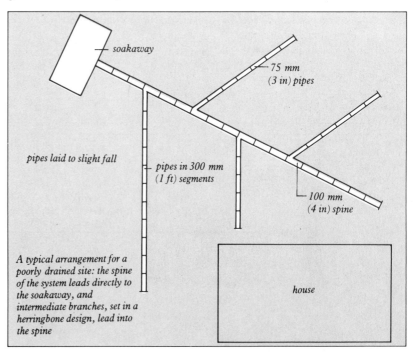

A typical arrangement for a poorly drained site: the spine of the system leads directly to the soakaway, and intermediate branches, set in a herringbone design, lead into the spine

Arrange the drains in a herringbone fashion (see illustration), each with a slight fall so that the water continues to drain to the lowest point. The 'spine' of the system should lead directly to the soakaway. You will need to sketch out the network on graph paper to make it easier to work to a scale – important so that you order the right quantities of materials.

The branches of the herringbone should not be more than about 2.4 m (8 ft) apart, but it will be needless expense and effort to have them closer than 1.8 m (6 ft).

If you have an established lawn in an area affected by the drains you want to lay, consider whether you would rather not bother with drains in this area, or whether you want to make a fresh start with the lawn. You *can* try to have the best of both worlds by lifting the grass where the drains are to go, digging a trench and relaying the turf, but this result is seldom satisfactory: the ground will probably sink later and the improved drainage may also mar grass growth at that point.

The drainage pipes must be set a minimum of 450 mm (18 in) below ground level to allow an adequate depth for cultivation, so bear this in mind when you dig your trenches.

Buying the drains

Traditional land drains (weeping tiles) are made of clay and resemble conventional pipes. They are about 300 mm (1 ft) long and 150 mm (6 in), 100 mm (4 in), or 75 mm (3 in) in diameter. Use the larger diameter for the main drain, the smaller one for side, branch drains. The pipes are simply butted together and most of the water enters at these joints, to be diverted along the pipe runs (although some water percolates through the walls of unglazed clay types). You can also buy plastic land drains, which have lots of holes for water to seep through. Plastic pipes are also quite flexible and can be curved to avoid roots, for instance.

To prevent the drains becoming clogged by soil entering at the joints, it is wise to cover the joints with old roof tiles or slates on clay drains or a piece of heavy-gauge polythene (polyethylene) on plastic drains.

Laying garden drains

1. Dig a trench at least 450 mm (18 in) deep from the affected area to the new drainage point. Remember to allow sufficient depth for cultivation of the ground above the pipes.

2. Lay the pipes with a fall of about 1:100. It is important that the fall is consistent, and a long straight-edged plank with a spirit level on top is the best way to ensure this. Use a small offcut of wood at the lower end of the straight-edge, under the spirit level, to represent the fall that you require.

3. Unless you can cut the trench accurately enough for the pipe to fit snugly into the bottom, with the right fall, you may have to pack more earth or gravel into the base to get a good fit.

4. Butt the lengths of pipe together, starting with the main run to the soakaway. Then lay the side branches. Cover the joints with tiles, slates, or squares of heavy-gauge polythene (polyethylene), then cover with about 150 mm (6 in) of course rubble topped with finer gravel to protect the pipes from subsequent movement of the ground, which could fracture or displace the pipes. Finally, replace the topsoil.

Left: Land drain pipes made of clay are easy to cut to length using a club hammer and bolster chisel; score the pipe first where you want to make the cut

Right: Set the pipes in the base of the trench and cover the joins between with a sheet of polythene (polyethylene) to prevent silt seeping inside and causing a blockage

11.Garden walls

There are several reasons why you may want to build a garden wall. It may be to restrain animals and people; to retain earth; or simply to act as a decorative feature. To a large extent the materials you use will be governed by the purpose of the wall.

A front garden wall, for instance, should be planned to complement the style of the house for a unified scheme. A regular-shaped, plain brick wall would look out of place in front of a pretty stone country cottage, where a dry stone wall would be more in keeping; a screen block wall might appear too prominent fronting an older terrace house, when a low brick or block wall would enhance the look of the building. Even details such as matching the colour of brick used in the house should be considered when choosing building materials for a wall.

Often, however, it may not be the shape, size or colour of the material but purely its newness which is wrong. Second-hand bricks or stones, which usually have a mellow, weathered appearance, are a good choice where you want the wall

to blend in immediately. They are available from demolition sites or some builders' suppliers, and have the added advantage of being cheaper than new materials.

Brick is most commonly used for garden walls; and there is a far wider choice of colours and textures than you might imagine. A local brick supplier will keep a selection of several different kinds and should be able to show you samples or a catalogue of other bricks, which can be specially ordered. The range of walls that you can build using bricks is vast; they can be formal, straight runs, or may incorporate curves and a highly decorative bonding pattern.

Concrete screen blocks are pierced with a variety of ornate patterns and avoid the hemmed-in feeling of solid walls; yet, combined with trailing plants, a screen block wall can still give a good degree of privacy, while allowing air to filter through. They are usually laid in a simple 'stack' bond – one directly above the other – and consequently the screen wall will not be as sturdy as a properly bonded wall. Their large

Screen blocks built on a low ornamental wall

size, however, does enable you to build a substantial wall fairly quickly.

'Reconstructed' stone blocks are manufactured from cement and natural stone aggregates cast in original stone moulds. The various colours and face textures available are specially chosen to match types of local stone found in different parts of the country. The blocks are laid like bricks and come in a range of sizes, some similar to brick and intended for a traditional brickwork bonding (and to be used in conjunction with bricks); others are larger 'modules' for use in a more random effect with the smaller blocks.

Natural stone is also available for garden walling, but this is much more expensive and more difficult to obtain than man-made types. Walls are usually built without mortar for a mellow, natural effect, and make a good base for planting between stones. Demolition sites are the best sources of natural stone; the variety of size and colour of stones is not a problem where an informal appearance is usually required.

The wall retaining this small bed has been constructed of random stone pieces bound together by mortar

This drystone wall has been constructed from carefully selected pieces and is used to retain a raised flower bed in this terraced garden

Designing a wall

Many factors govern the design of a wall and it is sensible to think seriously about them all before building. It is also advisable to draw a rough sketch of the proposed wall in location – colouring it in where appropriate – to get a useful visual impression of the size, shape and overall look of the project. When you are happy with the design, use string (or a line of blocks or bricks) to mark out the outline of the wall in the garden. Setting out the wall in this way will enable you to judge more accurately whether it is too long, too short, the wrong shape and so on.

As well as the practicalities, the aesthetics should also be considered when designing a wall. Take into account how the wall will fit into its surroundings – it should harmonize well both with the garden and the house, especially when building a front garden boundary wall. You must think about how it fits into the neighbourhood. An ornate, dominating wall might look good in isolation but could be an eyesore seen in the context of a whole road or a group of houses.

Choose a design which blends well in appearance and materials with its setting. Perhaps you will be able to join forces with a neighbour to build a complete wall across both properties, or at least decide on two sympathetic approaches.

The design of a low wall will be less problematic since its purpose will probably be to denote a boundary or enclose an area such as a vegetable patch. With a higher wall, built for privacy – perhaps to hide the whole house from passers-by or maybe just to give an element of seclusion to a patio – you have to be careful not to create a drab, solid, prison-like structure. It is often better to build a screen-block or open-bond brick wall, combined with conifers or climbers.

Do remember with higher walls that there are regulations governing heights and constructions – especially boundary walls – so consult your local authority before proceeding.

A long wall will require additional support from 'piers' – columns built in at intervals – and you can often make features of these.

Even a short wallspan can look boring if built in one shape and colour of brick or stone. You can introduce pattern and texture with a mixture of types of bricks, or perhaps even just a few in a second colour placed at random. The bonding arrangement of bricks also gives pattern and visual appeal. Multi-coloured shaped stones or screen blocks are sufficiently interesting in themselves and are better used alone in the simplest of bonds.

Trailing plants and flowers spilling over a wall soften the appearance of the building materials. You can create a cavity for soil in the top of the wall, or you could form a box-shaped planter from two leaves of walling. Dry stone walling is ideal for planting, as soil can be packed between the stones.

Mixing materials gives you the chance to bring individuality to a wall. For example, a dwarf brick or stone wall with high supporting piers fitted in between with screen blocks works well. But be careful not to mix materials or styles which are incompatible, such as a genuine dry stone wall combined with formal brickwork.

On the practical side, you must consider the cost and necessary building skills required to build a wall. Find out the cost of different materials beforehand so that you can work to a budget. If you are not confident about building a complicated design, you would be wise to settle for something less ambitious.

An **open-bond wall** (A) in brick can be made by leaving small gaps between bricks in alternate courses

Half-round roof ridge tiles (B) stacked on top of each other between supporting piers make a highly decorative screen wall

Natural stone or **reconstituted blocks** (C) make a traditional type of garden wall ideal for planting out with rock plants

Another **screen block wall** (D), using pre-made concrete pierced blocks, which come in a range of patterns, complete with piers and capping pieces

A

B

C

D

Foundations for garden walls

Any type of garden wall must have adequate foundations to spread its weight onto firm ground; this is usually a trench filled with a layer of compacted hardcore (broken bricks or concrete) topped with concrete.

The depth of the foundation – and of the individual layers – varies according to the thickness and height of the wall, and on the type of soil. Clay, in particular, causes movement at different times of the year, so on this type of soil it is worth excavating to a depth of about 1 m (3 ft 3 in) and using a thicker layer of hardcore and concrete. If in doubt, err on the cautious side and dig deeper. In general, the trench should be at least twice the width of the wall.

On sloping ground it will be necessary to make 'stepped' foundations so that the walling can itself be stepped down at intervals along its length yet still coursed.

1. Mark out the trench with taut stringlines attached to profile boards – two pegs with a cross piece nailed across their tops – which are driven into the ground beyond the area that will be occupied by the wall. Tie a pair of strings to nails driven into the cross piece to indicate the sides of the foundation trench, then dig out the earth to the required depth.

2. Level the bottom of the trench and drive pegs – marked from the top in increments of concrete and hardcore thicknesses – along its length at 1 metre (3 ft 3 in) intervals, then add the hardcore. Compact this thoroughly using a sledge hammer or stout post.

3. Mix the concrete on a hard, clean and dry surface, using the mix proportions described for each type of wall. Mix up only small batches at a time: tip out the sand, add the cement and mix up until it becomes an overall grey colour. Add water gradually and keep mixing until a uniform colour is achieved and the mortar has a 'plastic' consistency.

4. Shovel the concrete into the trench and work it around with your shovel to dispel air, then compact it to the top level of the pegs with a stout plank used edge-on in a chopping motion, followed by a sawing motion. Leave the foundation for one week for the concrete to harden before starting to build your wall.

Foundations for garden walls are set within a trench dug in the ground to a depth dependent on the soil type. Use a pair of stringlines attached to profile boards fixed at each end of the trench as a guide to digging. Level the bottom of the trench by using datum pegs (marked with the necessary increments of hardcore and concrete) driven into the base. Add hardcore to the base of the trench and compact it thoroughly with a sledge hammer or stout fence post. Fill any large voids in the hardcore with sand, then add the concrete. The concrete strip should be set fractionally below ground level. After about one week you can start to build your wall direct on the concrete base

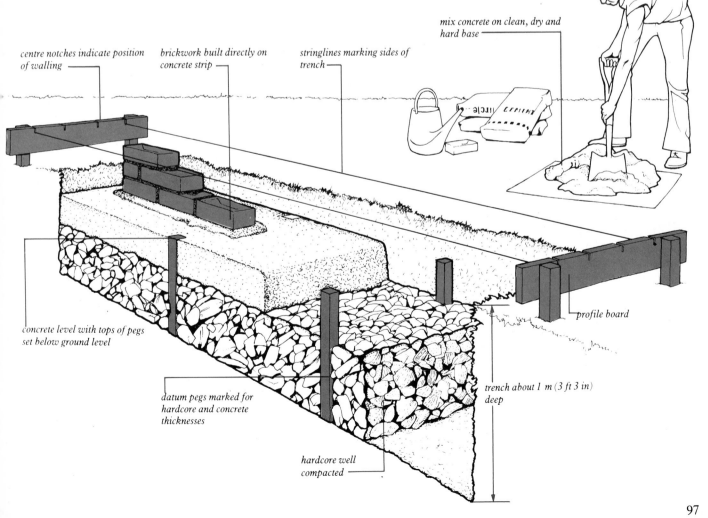

mix concrete on clean, dry and hard base

centre notches indicate position of walling

brickwork built directly on concrete strip

stringlines marking sides of trench

profile board

concrete level with tops of pegs set below ground level

datum pegs marked for hardcore and concrete thicknesses

trench about 1 m (3 ft 3 in) deep

hardcore well compacted

Building a brick wall

The following guidelines can be used for any wall up to 1 metre (3 ft 3 in) high. For a double-skin (single-brick thick) wall, dig a trench 500 mm (20 in) wide and at least 500 mm (20 in) deep. A layer of concrete 225 mm (9 in) thick on well-rammed hardcore is needed in the trench.

A single-skin (half-brick thick) wall needs a trench 300 mm (1 ft) wide and at least 350 mm (14 in) deep. Lay 150 mm (6 in) of concrete on well-rammed hardcore in the trench.

When you have laid the foundation strip reposition the strings on the profile boards to indicate the thickness of the wall centrally on the concrete.

Choosing a mortar mix
The strength of the mortar you use to lay the bricks depends on whether the wall is to withstand normal weather conditions or if it will be exposed to strong winds and heavy rain. Make a standard mix from 1 part cement; 1 part hydrated lime and 6 parts clean sand. A stronger mix comprises 1 part cement and 3 parts sand. Add a little liquid plasticizer or washing-up liquid (dishwashing detergent) to the mix to make it more workable, but avoid making it too sloppy or it will not support the weight of a brick. Aim for a stiff but workable consistency.

If you are working on a small project, it is worth buying a bag or two of dry mortar mix. Simply add water to the dry ingredients; one 50 kg (1 cwt) bag will make sufficient mortar to lay about 50 to 60 bricks. Never mix up more mortar than you can use in an hour, or it will start to set – faster on a hot day.

Bonding brickwork
Bricks can be laid in a number of bonding patterns, some plain, others ornate. The plain bonds are the best for a beginner since they involve far less cutting of bricks, which is also wasteful. Examples of three popular bonds are stretcher bond (single-skin wall), English and Flemish bonds (double-skin wall).

Whichever bonding pattern you choose,

Corners in brickwork
When you are building a brick wall it is best to build up the corners or ends first to about six courses. Step back the brickwork as you build, then fill in when you are satisfied that the corners are rising accurately. Make frequent checks with your spirit level held against the wall that it is not bowing outwards. Check also that each course is laid horizontally, using your string guidelines and the spirit level. Make up a gauge rod – marked in increments of a brick plus 10 mm (3/8 in) mortar joint – to check that the courses are uniform in thickness

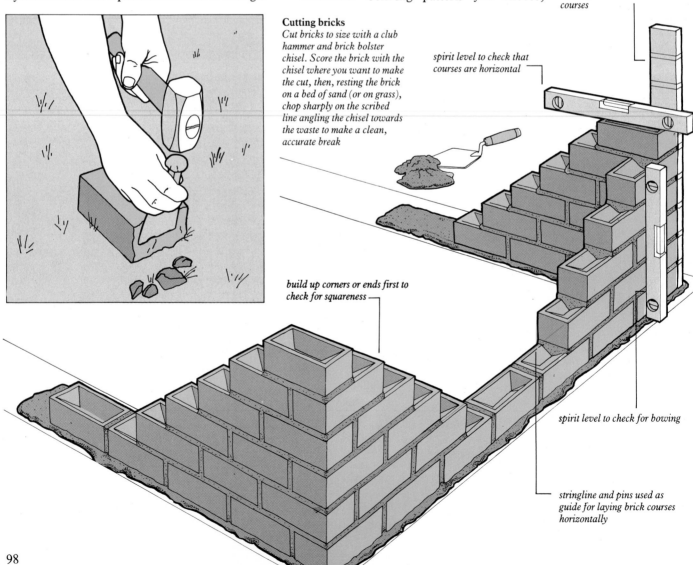

gauge rod to ensure consistent mortar joints between brick courses

Cutting bricks
Cut bricks to size with a club hammer and brick bolster chisel. Score the brick with the chisel where you want to make the cut, then, resting the brick on a bed of sand (or on grass), chop sharply on the scribed line angling the chisel towards the waste to make a clean, accurate break

spirit level to check that courses are horizontal

build up corners or ends first to check for squareness

spirit level to check for bowing

stringline and pins used as guide for laying brick courses horizontally

remember that the vertical joints of a wall must not coincide between two adjoining courses – they are always staggered for greatest strength.

When you are deciding on a bond it is a good idea to 'dry lay' (without mortar) the first three or four courses to check the fit. Note down the positions of any cut bricks.

Laying the bricks

1. Starting at one end of the foundation trench, trowel a 15 mm (⅝ in) thick band of mortar inside the string guidelines set up for the brickwork. Hold a spirit level vertically against the outer string and, with the point of the trowel, scribe a line in the mortar the length of the proposed wall.

2. Lay the first brick against the scored line and check that it is horizontal using a spirit level. Use the handle of your trowel to tap it level. If you lay too much mortar it will be difficult to level the brick; remove the brick, scoop off a little mortar and re-lay the brick. If the mortar has lost its 'stickiness' scrape it all off and start again. If you lay too little mortar remove the brick and add some more. When you have laid the brick scoop off the excess mortar squeezed from below.

3. Lay a second brick at the other end of the trench (or about six brick lengths away if the wall is long) and place a long straight-edged piece of timber across the two bricks. Rest a spirit level on top to check the level and tap down the second brick with the handle of your trowel until the two are horizontal.

4. To complete the first course, lay the intermediate bricks between the end bricks and 'butter' the end of the subsequent bricks with mortar where they butt up to the previous laid brick. Scoop some mortar onto your trowel and scrape it onto the end of the brick. Form a

wedge of mortar on the brick; this helps to bed it evenly with sufficient suction.

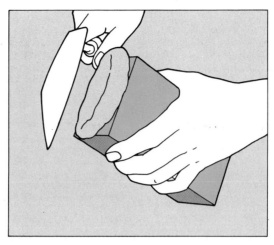

5. Build up the ends of the wall about six courses to form a 'stepped' structure at each end. As a guide to laying the intermediate bricks of each course horizontally, stretch a stringline between two pins slotted into a mortar joint on the two ends of the wall. A piece of wood marked off in brick-course (plus mortar joints) increments (see opposite) makes a handy check that the vertical courses are uniformly thick.

6. As you complete each course, check that the wall is not 'bowing' outwards or leaning by holding a spirit level diagonally across the face of the bricks. Shaping the mortar joints between bricks for neatness and weather resistance should be done as each course is completed, or when the mortar has stiffened slightly. The simplest joint is formed simply by drawing a piece of dowel or metal rod across the mortar.

7. Finish off the top of your wall neatly with a course of special shaped bricks – half-rounded and bevel-edged types are popular – or set a row of standard bricks on end or edge.

Building ornamental stone walls

Decorative walling blocks are available in a range of colours – notably reds, yellows, greens and buff tones – and with either exposed aggregate or split-faced finishes. They are laid in the same way as bricks in formal courses yet, because of their moulded faces, suggest a softer, more informal effect.

Decorative stone walling blocks need foundations, unless the wall is to be built on soundly laid paving slabs.

Set out the site using stringlines and profile boards as described for making foundations (see page 97). For a dwarf wall less than 750 mm (30 in) high, lay 50 mm (2 in) of well-compacted hardcore with 75 mm (3 in) of concrete on top. On particularly soft ground, or if the wall is to be higher than about 600 mm (2 ft), then dig a trench three times as wide as the thickness of the wall and deep enough to allow for 65 mm to 100 mm (2½ in to 4 in) of well-compacted

hardcore below 100 mm to 150 mm (4 in to 6 in) of concrete.

The mortar needed for building the wall should comprise 1 part cement to 5 parts soft sand. Mix up only small batches at a time on a hard, clean surface.

If you are following a fairly complicated design using different shaped stones or several colours, then keep a plan of the wall at hand to serve as a reference while building.

A wall that retains soil needs an allowance for drainage. The easiest way to allow for this is to leave open vertical joints at about 1.5 m (4 ft 6 in) intervals about 75 to 150 mm (3 to 6 in) above ground level. Where there is a likelihood of excessive water draining through the wall – if the wall is at the foot of a bank, for instance – avoid the blocks becoming stained by painting the back of the wall with bituminous paint before filling in with soil.

Reconstituted walling blocks *can be laid with mortar just like bricks to give a decorative finish that resembles a dry stone wall. The front faces of the moulded blocks are rough to resemble original split stone. Coping slabs are also made for finishing off a wall*

1. Lay a 12 mm (½ in) thick bed of mortar at one end of the foundation strip. Place the first end or corner block in position and tap it down level to leave the mortar about 10 mm (⅜ in) thick. Be careful not to smear any mortar on the face of a block; it will cause a stain that is difficult to remove.

2. Lay a second block at the other end of the wall (or about six block lengths away). Place a straight-edge and spirit level across the two blocks and tap down the second block until it is level.

3. You can now fill in the course with more blocks. When placing a block to butt up to a previous one, butter either the end of the block to be laid, or the end of the previous one with mortar. The latter method is usually preferable, as the mortar tends to slide off the new block as it is lowered into position.

4. Build up the wall as for brickwork, checking each block against the previous one with a spirit level. Ensure that the wall is not bowing outwards by holding the level across its face.

5. When the mortar has partially set rub the joints with a piece of dowel or metal rod to give a half-round profile, or rake them back with a pointing trowel to a depth of about 6 mm (¼ in).

6. Normally, coping stones are used to finish the top of the wall both for decorative appearance and to protect the wall surface from rainwater. Bed the coping stones in mortar in the same way as the blocks.

Making a screen block wall

Screen wall blocks are laid in stack bond between supporting piers made from special pilaster blocks. You must always plan out your screen block wall so that it will use full-size blocks and pilasters; because of their pierced pattern you cannot cut the blocks to size. Commonly available screen blocks measure 305 mm (1 ft square) and 102.5 mm (4 in) thick (these dimensions include an allowance of 10 mm/⅜ in for mortar joints); pilaster blocks are 200 mm (8 in) square. Pilasters for use in straight runs of walling have grooves to take the screen blocks in opposite sides; those for corners have grooves in adjoining sides; end pilasters have only one groove.

If working on a sloping site, you will have to build a low stepped wall out of bricks or ornamental stones first. These should be above the ground level so that no part of a screen block is below ground.

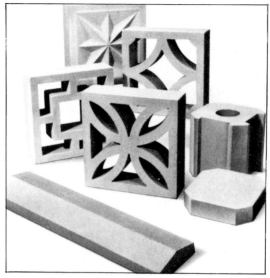

Screen walling blocks are moulded from concrete with a variety of pierced designs. They are laid in stack bond between piers made up from pilaster blocks. Coping stones finish the wall at the top and deflect rainwater; pilaster capping stones protect the tops of the piers

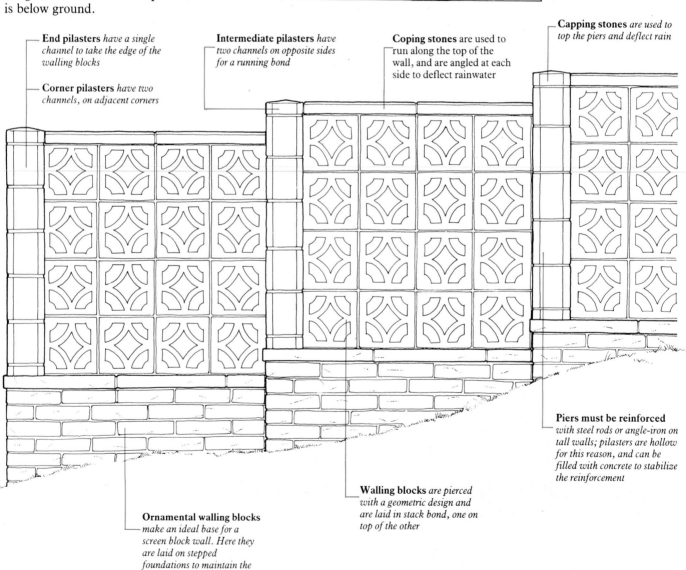

End pilasters *have a single channel to take the edge of the walling blocks*

Corner pilasters *have two channels, on adjacent corners*

Intermediate pilasters *have two channels on opposite sides for a running bond*

Coping stones *are used to run along the top of the wall, and are angled at each side to deflect rainwater*

Capping stones *are used to top the piers and deflect rain*

Piers must be reinforced *with steel rods or angle-iron on tall walls; pilasters are hollow for this reason, and can be filled with concrete to stabilize the reinforcement*

Walling blocks *are pierced with a geometric design and are laid in stack bond, one on top of the other*

Ornamental walling blocks *make an ideal base for a screen block wall. Here they are laid on stepped foundations to maintain the level coursing of the wall*

Start building the screen wall by erecting the end or corner piers, then fill in with pierced blocks. In addition to the end piers, intermediate piers will be required at intervals no greater than 3 m (9 ft 9 in) to give the wall the rigidity it lacks in its bond.

With walls over three courses high you must reinforce each pier with an iron rod or length of angle iron set into the foundation concrete. The hollow pilaster blocks are lowered over the rods and filled with concrete. Obviously, the reinforcing rods should be set at their precise points when you cast the foundation concrete and must be held vertically.

For the foundation, use 100 mm (4 in) of hardcore and a 100 mm (4 in) layer of concrete, comprising 1 part cement; 5 parts ballast (mixed aggregate). Make the mortar mix for the wall with 1 part cement; 5 parts builder's sand; it should be fairly pliable. White joints can be made using white cement and a light-coloured sand; for grey joints use grey cement. The pilaster blocks are filled with a fluid mortar mix comprised of 1 part cement; 3 parts sand, which stabilizes the piers.

1. Set out the first course of pilasters and screen blocks dry on site and mark the area it will cover; note particularly the positions of the supporting piers.

2. Make the foundations for the screen wall as for brickwork (see page 97), setting reinforcing rods at the pier positions. Set up stringlines to indicate the width of the pilaster blocks – 200 mm (8 in) apart.

3. Lay one end pilaster block on a bed of mortar, aligning it with the string guidelines. Check it for level both horizontally and vertically, using a spirit level. Next lay the other end pilaster block and any intermediate pilasters. Build up each pier to three pilasters high, check them for alignment then pour in the strengthening mortar (if needed).

4. Once the piers are in place, you can lay the screen blocks. Spread mortar on to the foundation concrete between two piers and trowel some into the groove of the pilaster. Then lay the first screen block, locating it in the pilaster groove and tapping it level. Trowel mortar on to the edge of the next block and butt it up to one already laid, leaving a 10 mm (⅜ in) vertical joint between the two.

5. Check each block for level as you lay it. If necessary, tap it down gently with the shaft of a club hammer, but place a length of wood on top of the block to protect it from cracking. Continue laying blocks between piers, stacking them one on top of the other, until you need to add more pilasters. As you build up the wall check it for horizontal and vertical alignment. Clean up the joints by scraping off excess with a trowel when the mortar has stiffened. Try not to drop any mortar on the face of the screen blocks: because they are light in colour, they will mark easily.

6. Finally bed a row of coping slabs in mortar along the top course of blocks and a pilaster cap on each pier. Point the mortar joints using a piece of dowel or metal rod to give a neat, half-round profile.

Dry stone walls

A genuine dry stone wall appears at first glance to have been almost thrown together at random – with stones of assorted shapes and sizes placed without regard for any bonding pattern. Yet this traditional craft requires considerable skill in order to make a strong, sturdy structure. The wall actually tapers from a broad base to a slightly narrower top and should consist of courses of large, regular-shaped stones alternated with rows of irregular ones; the gaps are filled with chippings or soil for planting. For greater stability, set each stone at an angle of 15 to 20 degrees.

Materials are hard to come by, and the laying technique fairly difficult so you would be wise to attempt only walls up to about 1 metre (3 ft 3 in) high. Dry stone walls of this size do not require concrete foundations. Instead you should lay the stones in a rubble-filled trench.

1. Dig a trench, about twice as wide as the intended width of the top of the wall, to a depth of about 600 mm (2 ft).

2. Fill the trench with small pieces of rubble and gravel to form a smooth bed. This foundation will allow for good drainage.

3. Select your stones carefully. Alternate courses should be made of large, regular stones, which span the full width of the wall and form uniform horizontal joint lines, similar to a standard brick wall. Make up the intermediate courses from irregular-shaped, random-sized stones, with chippings used to fill gaps.

4. Examine each piece of stone and lay it so that its grain runs horizontally – if the grain is vertical there is a risk of splitting under the pressure exerted from above.

Dry stone walling blocks

There are a number of manufactured dry stone walling blocks available, which are much easier to use than natural stone, and which can produce excellent results.

The blocks are commonly about 600 mm (2 ft) wide and about 75 mm (3 in) thick. On the back of each block there are usually one or more grooves, which are intended as splitting points: a single block can be divided into two or more smaller units, as required, revealing a natural aggregate texture at the edge. To split a block, place it, groove uppermost, on two pieces of stout wood so that there is a gap below the groove (a multi-grooved block should be laid on soft sand or soil). Place a bolster chisel in the groove and give a couple of sharp taps with a club hammer; this will result in a clean break.

Low walls of less than 600 mm (2 ft) do not require special foundations – a compacted gravel

Genuine dry stone walls (above) must be set on firm foundations for stability. Use large, regular-shaped stones alternated with courses of smaller, infill stones of irregular shape. Rig up a wooden frame to act as a guide to laying the wall to the correct wedge shape

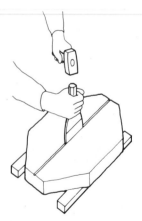

Cutting a stone walling block along its pre-formed groove

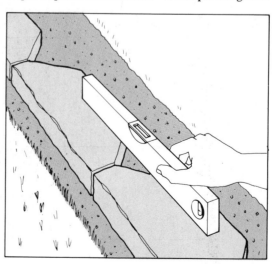

Use a spirit level to make sure the wall is flat

in horizontal courses. A little soil added between occasional courses is useful for planting, and likewise a small vertical gap should be left between the stones, both for planting and for drainage. Vertical joints should be staggered in successive courses.

In an earth-retaining wall, use a single course of wide stones protruding from the back about halfway up the wall. This will penetrate well into the soil to give the stones above a more stable base, preventing slippage.

Modular dry stone walling

There is another type of dry stone walling block which, in fact, is laid with mortar. During manufacturing a pattern is moulded on to each block, giving it the appearance of being eight smaller blocks. Half-size blocks are also made for the ends of the wall so that it is possible to stagger vertical joints between blocks. To avoid any uniformity or repetition a variety of different faces is produced.

These blocks have 'frogs' (indentations in the top edge as with some bricks to give a better mortar bond) and these must be laid uppermost. Concrete foundations are needed, using a mortar mix of 1 part masonry cement; 4 parts sand. Keep the vertical and horizontal joints to about 6 mm (¼ in) thickness, and finish off the top of the wall with special coping slabs.

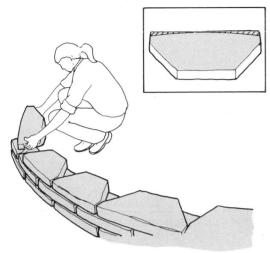

If laying dry stone walling blocks to a curve, you will have to trim the modules to shape using a club hammer and bolster chisel

or hardcore layer is sufficient. Any wall above this height must have a concrete foundation as described for an ornamental stone wall.

Recommended building techniques vary according to the type of block, but, in general, the basic rules are the same: they are simply stacked, leaving staggered vertical joints. Because the blocks are laid without mortar, you can build a large wall fairly quickly.

Begin at a corner or end and build the blocks

Modular dry stone walling blocks, showing the face decoration imitating individual stone pieces

Identifying dangerous walls

There are a number of reasons why garden walls deteriorate: they may be built on inadequate or poorly laid foundations; there may be a lack of piers in a long wall; no facility for drainage in an earth-retaining wall; weak mortar used in building; or poor bonding. Badly shaped pointing or poor quality bricks or blocks can contribute to a wall's failure; using a single skin where two would have been more appropriate is another reason. The wall may simply have been badly built.

A seemingly sound wall may suddenly collapse, but usually there will be some early warning signs. Although some faults can actually seem worse than they are it is safest to screen off a dangerous-looking wall until it has been inspected and any necessary repairs carried out.

Some danger signs are obvious: a wall leaning off true vertical, for instance, or bricks or blocks which have become dislodged. All walls move a little and the resulting stress can leave a crack; normally it is the mortar joints which are affected, and, in fact, they are deliberately made weaker than the bricks so that any cracks will follow this least resistant line. Cracks are more difficult to analyse: a crack which runs through a couple of mortar courses in a zig-zag might only be a superficial fault needing cosmetic repointing. Where a crack splits a brick vertically there is more pressure on the wall, and the problem is even more serious when several bricks are affected.

It is a good idea to inspect and test walls regularly. Prod the mortar joints with a sharp blade to see how firm they are. Pay attention to the base of an earth-retaining wall – constant exposure to damp soil can have a weakening effect on both bricks and mortar. If necessary dig away the earth to make a thorough inspection of a suspect wall.

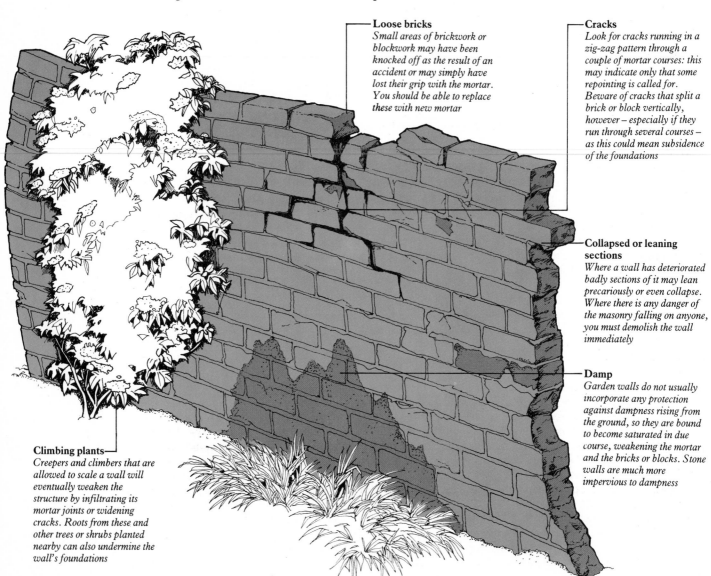

Loose bricks
Small areas of brickwork or blockwork may have been knocked off as the result of an accident or may simply have lost their grip with the mortar. You should be able to replace these with new mortar

Cracks
Look for cracks running in a zig-zag pattern through a couple of mortar courses: this may indicate only that some repointing is called for. Beware of cracks that split a brick or block vertically, however – especially if they run through several courses – as this could mean subsidence of the foundations

Collapsed or leaning sections
Where a wall has deteriorated badly sections of it may lean precariously or even collapse. Where there is any danger of the masonry falling on anyone, you must demolish the wall immediately

Damp
Garden walls do not usually incorporate any protection against dampness rising from the ground, so they are bound to become saturated in due course, weakening the mortar and the bricks or blocks. Stone walls are much more impervious to dampness

Climbing plants
Creepers and climbers that are allowed to scale a wall will eventually weaken the structure by infiltrating its mortar joints or widening cracks. Roots from these and other trees or shrubs planted nearby can also undermine the wall's foundations

12.Fencing

Fences serve a variety of purposes – as a boundary marker, to restrain animals and pets, or for privacy. They can be simple designs, from a simple chain suspended between posts as a border to a lawn or where the front garden meets a pavement, or more substantial timber panels, which give maximum privacy and security to your property.

Choosing a fence
One factor you must consider when choosing a fence is its likely lifespan and the extent of maintenance costs. Any timber fence, for example, is subject to eventual rotting, though this can be delayed for many years provided that some sensible precautions are taken.

The longest-lasting fences of all are those made of plastic, although they are mostly used as low barriers to denote a boundary.

The only way timber can be protected from the elements is with a good wood preservative brushed or sprayed on every other year at least. Apart from the posts, no part of a timber fence should be allowed to touch the ground; either a gap can be left below it or the gap can be filled with gravel boards – horizontal timbers fixed between the posts. These boards will, of course, decay but it is far easier to replace one than to have to be faced with repairing an integral part of a fence.

At the outset, however, you should buy a fence that has been pre-treated with timber preservative. After that it is up to you to keep it well treated.

Problems with wood rot
Concrete posts and gravel boards solve a lot of the rot problems but not everyone is keen to see concrete in the garden – they prefer the aesthetic appeal of timber. If you want timber posts, then make sure they are oak or chestnut. It is well worthwhile asking for posts which have been 'tanalized'. This is a vacuum/pressure impregnation treatment, which drives preservatives right into the wood, giving it extra protection against decay. If you cannot get hold of such posts then make sure that the bottom part of each post, which will be buried in the ground, is well soaked in preservative for 24 hours before fixing. Stand them in a bucket and brush the preservative on to them frequently – there will not be any waste since excess preservative will just drip in to the bucket.

Rainwater settling on the top of a post can cause it to rot from the top downwards. At the very least it is worthwhile sawing the top of the post to a single or double bevel (creating an inverted V-shape) so that rainwater will slide off. Far better, though, is to make or buy some caps;

ready-made wood caps are simply nailed to the top of the post.

If you prefer, pieces of scrap wood can be cut to shape and soaked in preservative before being nailed on. Alternative capping materials are small sheets of lead, zinc or roofing felt, turned down the sides of the post and nailed in position. The top of a panelled fence or a close-boarded fence can also be capped with a strip of wood to keep away rainwater.

All the nails used to make a fence should be rust-resistant – choose either galvanized or aluminium alloy types.

Fixing fence posts
There is always debate on whether a post should be fixed with concrete or be sunk into well-firmed earth. The problem is which is less likely to encourage rotting. Generally speaking, the decision will be reached by the height of the fence and the stability of the ground. Certainly, without concrete the ground will have to be really firm to keep posts stable, but even then it may not be able to support high fence posts. So, for a low fence on stable ground, you have the choice; for all high fences, or where the ground is weak, use concrete. Provided that the stump of the post in the hole is placed on hardcore and is also supported by hardcore around it, there should be adequate facility for rainwater to drain away before any harm can be done.

Arranging fence panels
Often the job of erecting a fence starts with having to clear away an old fence. The most time-consuming part of the job is digging out the old posts, which can entail a lot of excavating in order to remove old concrete and hardcore. Normally you would have to do this since, as fence posts have always been set about 2 m (6 ft 6 in) apart, the old concrete would probably lie just where the new posts have to be inserted. If, therefore, a lot of posts have to be removed, it would be quicker and easier to include a short panel at the beginning of the run so that the positions for the new posts would be staggered between the positions of the old posts.

Another problem is where there is a patio and a post has to be positioned along it. With paving slabs laid on sand the relevant slab can be removed quickly and a hole dug. This would, of course, mean having to cut the slab to re-lay it around the post, so, if preferred, the slab could be left out and the space used as a small flower patch or you could fill it with gravel or cobblestones. Where paving slabs or crazy paving bedded on mortar gets in the way then this would have to be first broken up to clear the way for a post.

Types of fence

Panel fences
A selection of designs is available: vertical or horizontal close-boarded, interwoven larch, waney-edge larch and double-slatted. Panels are normally 1.8 m (6 ft) wide. Heights are 600 mm, 900 mm, 1.2 m, 1.5 m and 1.8 m (2 ft, 3 ft, 4 ft, 5 ft and 6 ft). Odd widths can be supplied to special orders if needed to finish off a run. Timber or concrete posts can be used.

Close-boarded
Vertical boards are fixed to horizontal arris rails which, in turn, are fixed to posts of timber or concrete. The boards can be square sawn or have one edge thinner than the other (called feather-edged). Horizontally fixed versions are also made. Shiplap cladding is often used instead of boards.

Picket
Sometimes called a paling or palisade fence. The palings can be plain (square ended) or ornately shaped. Palings are fixed to arris rails supported by posts. A gap of about 75 mm (3 in) is usually left between the palings. This type of fence is normally built no higher than about 1.2 m (4 ft). A kit-type paling fence is available, which comprises ready-made sections for fixing to posts with metal brackets.

Ranch-style
Horizontal sawn wood planks fixed to posts. For fences up to 900 mm (3 ft), the planks are generally about 75 mm (3 in) wide; above this height the planks can be 125 mm or 150 mm (5 in or 6 in) wide. Normal thickness of planks is about 19 mm (¾ in). Main posts 125 mm × 75 mm or 100 mm (5 in × 3 in or 4 in) are fixed at 2 m (6 ft 6 in) intervals with 90 mm (3½ in) square posts midway between. Planks are located in slots in the posts, or fixed to the posts with galvanized nails. These fences are either treated with preservative or painted white.

Double ranch-style
Exactly the same as a single ranch-style, except that the planks are nailed to both sides of the posts. The planks on the reverse side are positioned to coincide with the gaps left between the planks on the other side, so creating a semi-solid fence.

Split-chestnut paling (Stockade fencing)
Cleft chestnut stakes are linked at the top and the bottom with galvanized wire. Normally you buy a roll of fencing of this kind, which is about 9 m (30 ft) long and from 900 mm (3 ft) to 1.8 m (6 ft) high. Softwood posts or chestnut poles are used as fixing points for the fencing.

Trellis panel
Normally used to add height to a solid fence without creating a hemmed-in feeling. This type would be 300 mm (1 ft) high. However, as a screening, possibly for growing climbing plants against, 900 mm (3 ft) or 1.8 m (6 ft) fences are available.

Post and wire
Galvanized steel wire fixed to posts of concrete, timber or steel. Thinner posts are used between the main posts to add extra support. Height is optional but, since this fence normally just denotes a boundary, they are normally about 900 mm (3 ft) or 1.2 m (4 ft) high maximum.

Wire netting
Open-mesh fencing available in rolls of 10 m,

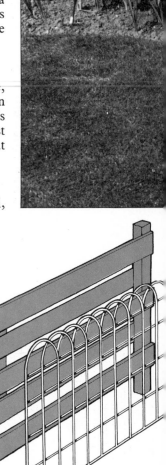

25 m, and 50 m (33 ft, 82 ft and 164 ft) and in heights from 300 mm (1 ft) to 1.8 m (6 ft). Mesh sizes vary from 10 mm to 100 mm (³⁄₈ in to 4 in). For extra strength the netting can be fixed to horizontal wires stretched between posts of timber, angle iron, or special wire stakes.

Welded mesh (Chain link)

A stronger version of wire netting. The steel wire is welded at each joint. Rolls are normally 6 m or 30 m (20 ft or 100 ft) long and heights are from 450 mm (1 ft 6 in) to 1.8 m (6 ft). The mesh can be anything from 12 mm × 12 mm to 50 mm × 50 mm (½ in × ½ in to 2 in × 2 in). Galvanized or plastic-coated versions are available. Posts can be timber, metal or concrete.

Decorative wire

Plastic-covered steel wire with a hooped arrangement at the top. Rolls are 10 m or 25 m (33 ft or 82 ft) long and heights can be 100 mm, 400 mm, 600 mm, 750 mm or 900 mm (4 in, 1 ft 4 in, 2 ft, 2 ft 6 in, 3 ft). Lower types can be self-supporting simply by driving the ends of the wire into the ground. Higher versions must be supported by timber or angle-iron posts.

Spiked chain

Steel links and diamond-shaped spikes form a chain. The material can be galvanized or have a plastic or black-japanned finish. The chain is fixed to timber or concrete posts.

Wattle

Although it is not built to last longer than about four years, wattle fencing is good for providing cover for young or tender plants. It is made from long, thin flexible branches woven around thin upright posts, which are driven into the ground.

A selection of fencing types
Below, from left: Horizontal close-boarded fence with feather-edged boards (often shiplap cladding) between two posts; wavey-edged boards come in panels; vertical close-boarded types have arris rails let into the posts to support the boards; ranch fencing is normally used quite low for boundaries; double ranch style has horizontal boards fixed at each side of the posts; decorative wire fencing is available in rolls, and typically plastic-coated; picket fencing is a medium-height type good for boundaries; wattle fencing is a temporary barrier for protecting your plants; wire netting comes in rolls which you stretch between posts; welded metal mesh is a tougher version; interwoven fencing panels are one of the most popular, and economical types; a chain link fence

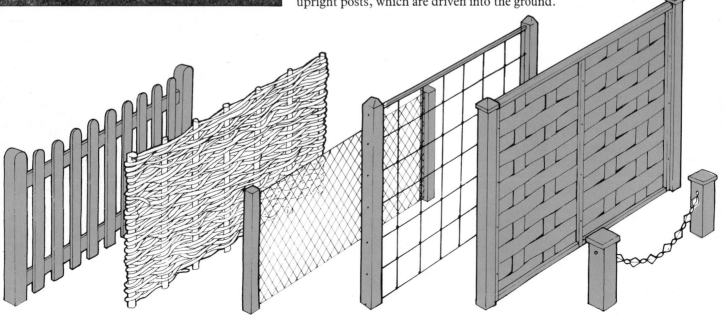

Erecting a panel fence

1. The first job with erecting any fence is to stretch a taut stringline from the beginning to the end of the proposed fence run as a guide to positioning the posts. Fix the stringline to pegs driven into the ground.

2. The first post is usually fixed to the house wall. A tall post needs to be fixed with three bolts (top, middle and bottom) and a low post needs just two bolts. The bolts need to be about 6 mm (¼ in) diameter. First drill holes through the post using an electric drill, then select a larger bit to make a slightly countersunk hole for each bolt head. The bolt heads must lie below surface so that the edge of the panel can be fixed tight against the post.

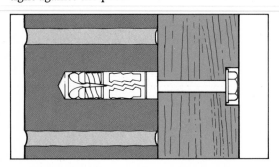

3. Place the post against the house wall, align it with the string and check it for vertical with a spirit level. Use a sharp implement to mark off the positions of the holes on the wall.

4. Remove the post, drill holes in the wall, then replace the post and insert the bolts.

5. Each post hole can be dug with a narrow spade (the smaller the hole the better) or a post hole borer. The latter resembles a large corkscrew; it is twisted back and forth into the ground, occasionally withdrawing it to deposit earth gathered on the blades. The depth of a hole is governed by the post height. For high fences allow for 600 mm (2 ft) of post to be buried; for lower fences (up to 1.2 m/4 ft) only

450 mm (1 ft 6 in) of post needs to be buried. In both cases dig holes about 150 m (6 in) deeper so that the bottom can be lined with hardcore for drainage of rainwater.

6. Dig the next hole and insert the post. Check that its top is level with the top of the preceding post by laying a long straight-edged piece of wood across the two posts and placing a spirit level on top.

7. Check that the post is aligned with the string guideline. Offer it up to the edge of the panel,

check it is vertical with a spirit level, then nail the edge of the panel to it as before. At this point you should again check the post for alignment, if necessary adjusting it by packing hardcore around its stump in the hole.

8. Use a drill to make holes for the fixing nails in the edges of the panel. You will need to use three 75 mm (3 in) long galvanized nails on each side of the panel. That means six nails at each end of each panel. Pre-drill the nail holes to prevent the panel edge splitting when the nails are banged in. With the panel supported in place against the post, the nails can be driven in.

9. Check with a spirit level that the top edge of the panel is horizontal. Then drive a nail into the post and force a length of timber up under the nail to hold the post in place temporarily. From then on the procedure for erecting the complete fence, panel by panel, is the same.

10. When the fence is complete, mix up a dryish concrete mix of one part cement; four parts ballast (mixed aggregate) and tip this into the hole around the post. Firm it well down with a stick. Add some small pieces of hardcore to fill out the hole. Finish by shaping a sloping layer of concrete around the post so that rainwater will

drain away. Leave the wedges supporting the posts in place for about four days until the concrete has hardened.

11. Cap the fence posts with a shaped wooden square, or cut a sloping profile (below).

Fence post capping *pieces are intended to protect the post from rot by shedding rainwater quickly. They can be either plain squares nailed on (A); angled post tops (B); rounded tops (C); bevelled wood squares (D); or pointed tops (E)*

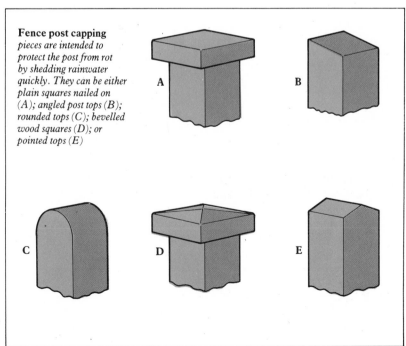

Fitting a close-boarded fence

The posts are normally set at 3 m (10 ft) spacings. They may have two or three slots in them to receive the arris rails (smaller fences only require two rails).

The basic technique for stretching a string guideline and fixing posts is the same as for a panel fence. The important aspect is that the slots in the posts for the arris rails are exactly in line. There are two methods that can be used to ensure this. The first and last posts in the run can be inserted and a taut string line stretched between the tops. The string can be checked for horizontal using a spirit level or, if you have one, a line and spirit level (a small spirit level which can be suspended from a stringline). Alternatively set in the posts one by one as the fence is erected and check their levels as described for panel fencing.

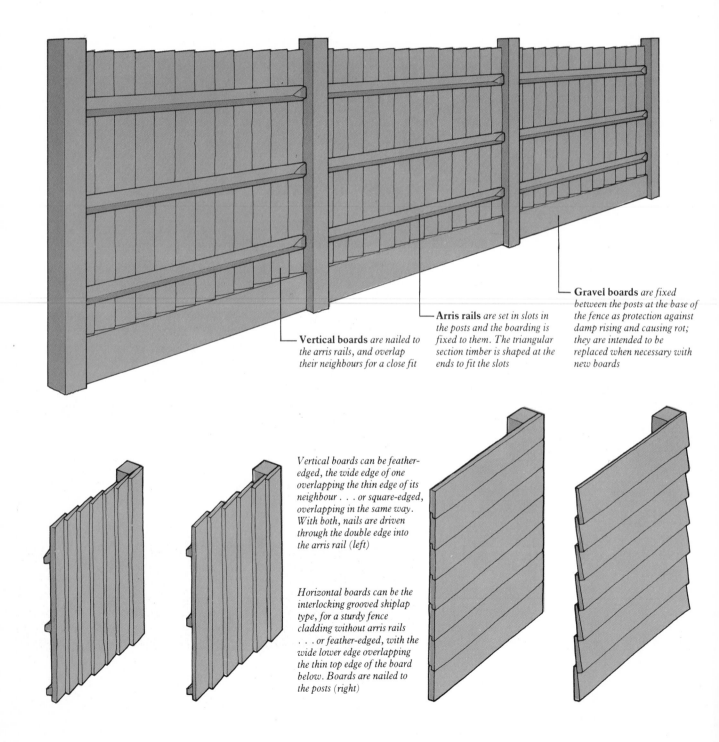

Gravel boards *are fixed between the posts at the base of the fence as protection against damp rising and causing rot; they are intended to be replaced when necessary with new boards*

Arris rails *are set in slots in the posts and the boarding is fixed to them. The triangular section timber is shaped at the ends to fit the slots*

Vertical boards *are nailed to the arris rails, and overlap their neighbours for a close fit*

Vertical boards can be feather-edged, the wide edge of one overlapping the thin edge of its neighbour . . . or square-edged, overlapping in the same way. With both, nails are driven through the double edge into the arris rail (left)

Horizontal boards can be the interlocking grooved shiplap type, for a sturdy fence cladding without arris rails . . . or feather-edged, with the wide lower edge overlapping the thin top edge of the board below. Boards are nailed to the posts (right)

1. The arris rails supplied may not have the ends shaped to fit into the post slots. This can be done using first a saw to create roughly the right shape then a plane to finish off and make the rail the correct shape to fit snugly in the post slot. Brush preservative on the rail ends.

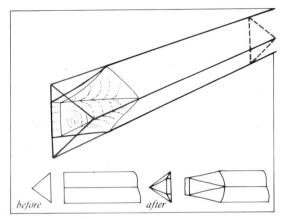

before   *after*

2. Insert the rails to about half the depth of the post and secure with alloy dowels, tapped into place with a hammer. Use two dowels about 38 mm to 45 mm (1½ in to 1¾ in) long for each rail end.

3. When the first rails have been fixed into the first post, the next post can be roughly positioned and the other ends of the rails located in the relevant slots. Check that this post is level with the top of the first post and is aligned with the string guideline at the base.

4. Raise the post upright, check it with a spirit level, then wedge it in place as described for panel fencing. Continue fixing posts and rails until the basic framework is complete. Fix the posts with concrete and hardcore and leave for a few days for the concrete to harden.

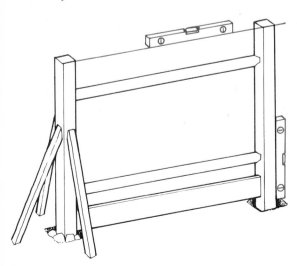

5. Gravel boards are used on close-boarded fences and if these are intended to slot into the posts (ready-made slots will be available in the posts) then they will have to be inserted, along with the arris rails, as the fence is erected. The alternative is to fix them later to battens driven into the ground (see page 117).

6. When the vertical boards are fixed, they will either be overlapped (feather-edged boards) or butted up (square sawn). Usually feather-edged boards are used. Fix the first board against the first post with its thickest edge near the post. Fix subsequent boards by overlapping the thin edge of the previous board with the thick edge of the next board by about 12 mm (½ in), then insert a nail through the two boards into the arris rail behind. Insert each nail at an angle to stop it pulling out. Check each fourth or fifth board for vertical. The overlap margin might have to be increased or decreased slightly with the last few boards to give a snug fit against the post. Alternatively, continue with 12 mm (½ in) overlaps and trim the last board down its length to fit the space.

A solid fence offers security and helps to prevent you from being overlooked

Erecting a wire fence

Wire mesh fences
Wire netting is fixed to posts set between 2 m and 2.4 m (about 6 ft and 7 ft) apart. Galvanized line wire is stretched between the posts and the netting is supported by this.

1. Welded wire mesh is fixed to 3.15 mm (⅛ in) galvanized line wire stretched between the posts. Set the posts at 2 m (6 ft 6 in) intervals and strain the wires taut between them. Use two lines for fences under 1.2 m (4 ft) high and add a third line midway between the top and bottom wires for higher fences. Brace each end post by fixing a supporting post to it. Set all posts in a coarse concrete mix.

Post and wire
Set the posts 3 m (10 ft) apart. Brace the end posts with struts and fix intermediate posts for strength. Stretch 4 mm (⅛ in) galvanized steel wire between the posts and secure with staples or tie wires.

Decorative wire
Low fences are self-supporting by pushing the ends into the ground but they are really only used for marking out areas of lawn or planting beds. Higher fences are fixed to timber or angle-iron posts set at regular intervals – about 2 m (6 ft 6 in) apart is usual.

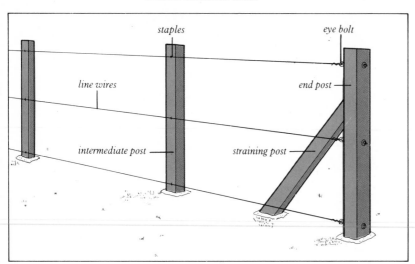

staples · eye bolt
line wires · end post
intermediate post · straining post

2. Fix the edge of the wire fence to the first post using 15 mm × 1.60 mm (⁹⁄₁₆ in × ¹⁄₁₆ in) staples or with tying wire. Then unroll the fence; pull taut, and attach to the line wires with tie wire and to the remaining posts with staples or tie wire.

Split chestnut paling (Stockade fencing)
End posts of 100 mm × 100 mm (4 in × 4 in) are braced with 75 mm × 75 mm (3 in × 3 in) struts. Fix thinner intermediate posts, 75 mm × 75 mm (3 in × 3 in), at regular intervals. Unroll the fence, pull taut, and fix to the posts at the top and bottom using staples. It is important to retain the tension of the fence while it is stapled to prevent it sagging later.

eye bolt
staples

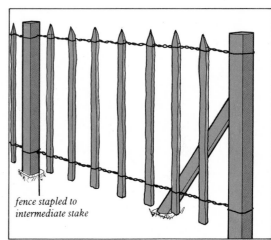

fence stapled to intermediate stake

Constructing other fences

Rustic fencing

This type of fencing is made up from lengths of unsawn timber, which has its bark left on for a natural look. Poles are available in various lengths and diameters for you to construct your own designs. Although you have free rein in the designs you choose, there are a number of methods of joining the various lengths of wood to ensure a sturdy construction (see below).

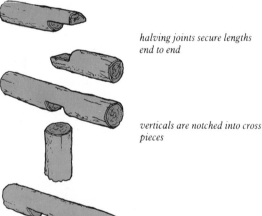

halving joints secure lengths end to end

verticals are notched into cross pieces

diagonals share a notch with verticals

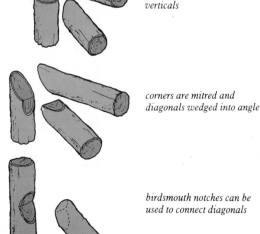

corners are mitred and diagonals wedged into angle

birdsmouth notches can be used to connect diagonals

Picket fencing

This popular see-through type of close-boarded fencing is useful where you want a decorative boundary.

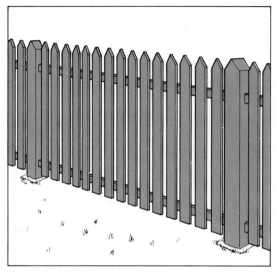

Plastic ranch-style fence

Construction varies according to type. Mostly the horizontal planks are slotted into pre-formed mortises in the posts. Fences up to 1 m (3 ft 3 in) high usually have two horizontal planks; higher fences have three or more planks. Normally posts are fixed at 1.5 m (4 ft 6 in) centres; accurate positioning is important for the posts to accept the planks. Set about one-third of the total height of a post below ground level and secure with hardcore and concrete.

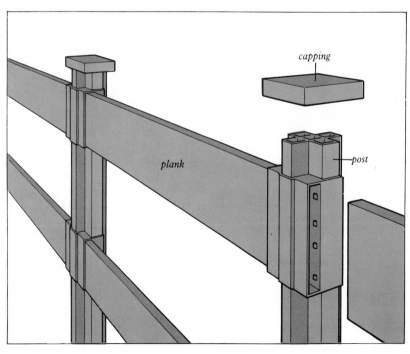

capping

plank

post

Fence repair and maintenance

Protection against rot

Rot is the main enemy of timber fences. The most susceptible parts are the posts, which decay at soil level, though any other parts of the fence in contact with soil are equally vulnerable. Always leave an air gap of around 50 mm (2 in) between the bottom of the fence and the ground, or insert a gravel board (see page 112).

It is sensible to treat the complete fence every other year at least by brushing or spraying on a good wood preservative. Do this in the autumn on a day when the timber is dry, and rain is not expected for a day or so. Rainfall immediately after applying preservative can lessen its effectiveness.

Dig a hole around each post so that the preservative can be brushed on to the part below ground level. Plants can be harmed by preservative so cover them with well-weighted-down polythene (polyethylene) sheets.

Fixing rotten posts

When a post has rotted at the base, the decaying stump will have to be sawn off back to sound wood and the remainder refixed to a concrete spur. The post is bolted to the spur.

1. Dig down to about 600 mm (2 ft) and place the spur in the hole so that it rests against the fence post.

2. Push a bolt into each hole and tap the head with a hammer to leave indentations on the post to indicate the drilling positions needed for each bolt.

3. Drill holes right through the post using a brace and auger bit. Make sure you keep the bit horizontal, or it will not align with the bolt.

4. Coat the post with preservative, especially the sawn edge.

5. Insert and tighten the bolts, keeping the nuts on the spur side.

6. ·Pull the post vertical (check with a spirit level on both faces) and support it with temporary struts tacked at the top of the post.

7. Pack hardcore around the base of the spur to support it, then pour in dryish concrete (1 part cement; 5 parts ballast). Compact it well; leave for 48 hours to set before removing the struts.

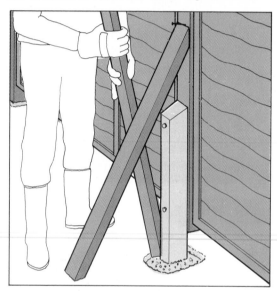

The alternative to using a spur is to insert a new post. This means temporarily supporting the fence on each side of the post before removing the old post. A panel fence is removed by withdrawing the nails securing it to the post. With a close-boarded fence, the arris rails on one side will have to be sawn through close to the post. When the new post is in place, these can be resecured by fixing a 'box' of 50 mm × 50 mm (2 in × 2 in) battens around the mortise slot, then fixing the arris rail to the box with rust-proof screws or nails. Or you can buy a special steel bracket to rejoin the rail to the post, which is fixed with 50 mm (2 in) galvanized nails.

One way to increase the life of posts or – if the decay at the base is slight – to refix old posts, is to use a proprietary metal spike, which is driven into the ground. The spike has a square recess at the top into which the post is bolted.

If an arris rail is badly decaying, it will have to be replaced completely, which means partially dismantling the affected part of the fence. If there is just a single crack it is far simpler to support it with a special bracket (A). Should the end

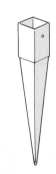

A concrete spur is set alongside the old post and is bolted to it. The base is packed with concrete

A metal fence post spike *is the best way to increase the life of a slightly rotten post. Simply drive the spike into the ground and insert the post end in its square recess, and secure with a bolt*

of a rail be damaged, then support it with a bracket as for post repairs (B).

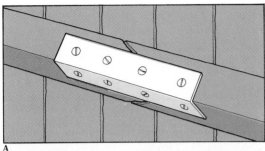

A

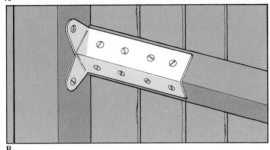

B

If a rail has simply become loose in the post and rattles in the wind, first drill a hole through the post into the rail. Cut a shallow groove in a length of dowel (the dowel should be the same diameter as the hole), along its length. Coat it with waterproof adhesive. Tap the dowel into the hole to secure the rail to the post. The groove in the dowel allows excess adhesive to escape.

A new arris rail

If a new arris rail is being fitted, buy one that is 85 mm (3½ in) longer than the space between the posts. This allows for about 40 mm (1½ in) at each end to be cut to a tenon shape and to enter the slot in the post. For refixing techniques see page 113.

Post tops

Posts can rot from the top downwards, too. If this happens:
1. Saw off the affected timber.
2. Apply preservative.
3. Fit a protective cap (see page 111).

Gravel boards

These eventually rot, but it is far easier to remove and replace them than to have to dismantle a fence and renew feather-edged boards. To replace gravel boards:
1. Drive 50 mm × 50 mm (2 in × 2 in) battens into the ground alongside the posts (remember to coat them first with preservative).
2. Nail gravel boards to the battens leaving a 12 mm (½ in) gap between the top of the gravel boards and the base of the fence.

Feather-edged boards

Old unprotected boards will become brittle and rotten. Remove the nails holding a board to the arris rail; if the nails will not budge then use a nail punch to bang them through into the arris rail, releasing the board.
1. Coat the replacement board generously with preservative.

2. Reposition it by sliding its thin edge under the thick edge of the neighbouring board.

3. Refix it by nailing through its thick edge and by nailing through the thick edge of the next board, using rust-proof nails.

Fitting a new wooden post

If, despite your preventative measures, a fence post becomes irreparably rotten, you will have to replace it. It is possible to remove the defective post and insert a new one without having to dismantle the entire fence.

1. Prop up the fence panels at each side of the faulty post with long wooden battens pinned to the arris rail (close-boarded fence) or top of the panel (panel fence). Prise away a feather-edged board from each side of the post (or lever out the fixing nails on a panel fence). On a close-boarded fence you will have to saw through the rails where they enter the slots in the post (A).

2. Tie strong rope around the post near the base, using stout nails to secure it. Tie a sturdy length of timber – the new fence post is ideal – end-on to the old post and wedge it up on a stack of bricks. Lean on the end of the post to lever the rotten one from the ground (B).

A

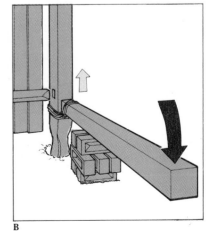

B

3. Prepare the hole for the new post and bed it in place. Pour in concrete to retain it then secure the arris rails to the sides with a steel bracket (see above). Renail a panel fence to the post.

13. Garden gates

Garden gates are available in a number of materials and are normally chosen either to match the style of fencing or the style of the house; what may be ideal in the country may look entirely out of place in a town, and vice versa. So choose a style with care.

Timber gates

Various timbers are used for gates, and although all need some routine maintenance, timber is still a good choice because it has the ideal appearance for most situations. Also, close-boarded timber gates over 1.5 m (4 ft 6 in) high offer good security. Timber gates are available, or can be made, to match all styles of timber fencing and in addition will blend in with hedging and other types of fencing.

Front entrance gates for boundary marking and to restrict the movements of children and pets need to be 900 mm (3 ft) or 1.2 m (4 ft) high. These gates are widely available in the standard ranges of most joinery and fencing manufacturers. The standard widths are 900 mm, 1050 mm, 1.2 m and 1.5 m (3 ft, 42 in, 4 ft and 5 ft) and therefore by buying a pair of gates drive widths of up to 3 m (9 ft 9 in) can be closed.

The standard pattern gate of this type is redwood with exterior-grade plywood infill panels. Another popular style is a feather-edge gate, which is ideal for use with a close-boarded fence as well as with hedges and brick walls. Also commonly available are several ledged-and-braced gates with shaped palings to match various styles of paling fences in a similar style. Before buying check that a front garden gate is made from sturdy timber, which ideally should be pressure-impregnated with wood preservative. If it has not been treated in this way then apply a coat of clear wood preservative, which should be allowed to dry before the gate is given any decorative finish.

For wider than normal entrances, a single farm-style gate could be the answer. There are various styles of five-bar gates, which may be made from pressure-impregnated softwood or from hardwood. The latter are harder to paint than the softwood types, but they look attractive if given a water-repellent wood-stain finish. Gates of this type are available in widths ranging from 1.2 m to 3.6 m (4 ft to 12 ft). In most cases the diagonal cross brace is fixed from low on the hinge side although there is a 'universal' five-bar gate available with twin diagonal cross braces that allow it to be hung on either side. The Yeoman style of gate, which has a distinctive curved hanging style to which a slanting brace is attached, is also a good choice for a driveway gate. For use in residential areas there are styles

of five-bar gates which have closely spaced vertical palings, which are useful for containing small pets as well as young children.

The traditional type of timber gate for side entrances is the ledged-and-braced gate. This type of gate has three horizontal rails braced with diagonal rails and may be close-boarded, open-boarded or clad with feather-edge boards to match feather-edge fencing. The standard width for this type of gate is 900 mm (3 ft) and standard heights are 900 mm, 1.2 m, 1.5 m, and 1.8 m (3 ft, 4 ft, 5 ft and 6 ft). For additional strength this type of gate may also be ledged, braced and framed.

Framed interwoven and many overlap gates are available to match interwoven and overlap fencing panels and these gates blend well with the panels to give a rustic appearance. As they are made out of similar timber to the fencing panels, these gates tend not to be of very strong construction.

Plastic gates

Plastic front entrance gates are available to match some styles of plastic fencing, but as most plastic fencing systems tend to be ranch style it is common to make up gates as required using standard plastic fencing planks. An open-boarded ledged-and-braced gate is quite easy to make using plastic planks, which can be joined with galvanized bolts.

Just some of the vast selection of garden gates available:
1. *Standard front gate with redwood frame and exterior-grade plywood infill panels*
2. *Ledged-and-braced with close-boarded verticals*
3. *Ledged-and-braced gate with feather-edged vertical boards*
4. *Diamond style gate*
5. *Interwoven gate, which matches fencing panels for unified look*
6. *Small five-barred gate in the traditional farm style*
7. *Palisade-style gate with slim pointed palings*
8. *Wrought-iron gate with decorative scrolls, ideal for the suburban garden*
9. *Full-height wrought-iron gate with decorative patterns suits a setting in an archway*
10. *Plastic gate and posts for ranch-style fencing*

Metal gates

There are two types here, so be careful when buying and comparing prices. The cheaper types are made from mild steel, but the heavier gates are made from wrought iron, which is stronger and more resistant to corrosion. Both types are available in traditional ornamental scroll-type styles as well as plainer modern designs. They can be used singly or in pairs both as front garden gates or as side entrance gates. For the latter, curved tops are popular, particularly for combining with a brick arch. These gates are available in a range of standard widths and may be supplied with metal posts on which hinge pins and latch fastenings are already fitted. They may be made to measure to fit between existing pillars or posts, in which case the side for hinge fittings must be stipulated.

Types of gate posts

Timber

Oak is the best timber for gates posts, although it may warp and the surface tends to split. If the posts are to be painted it is better to use pressure-impregnated softwood posts. The minimum size for gate posts is 100 mm (4 in) square, although this should be increased to 125 mm (5 in) square if the gate is more than 1.8 m (6 ft) high or more than 1 m (3 ft 3 in)

wide. The posts should be long enough to allow 450 mm (18 in) to be set underground if the gate is up to 1 m (3 ft 3 in) high by 1 m (3 ft 3 in) wide, and 600 m (2 ft) underground if the gate is higher or wider than 1 m (3 ft 3 in).

For farm-style gates 150 mm (6 in) or 175 mm (7 in) square posts will be required. These should be long enough to allow 900 mm (3 ft) or 1.2 m (4 ft) to be set in the ground respectively.

Metal posts

These may be circular, square or rectangular in cross-section. The manufacturers will supply a post suitable for the gate it is to support. Make sure the new posts are painted with rust-resisting primer before installation, and treat the below-ground parts with black bitumen paint.

Concrete posts

Standard concrete fencing posts are used, to which 100 mm × 38 mm (4 in × 1½ in) preservative-treated timber is bolted to allow the gate hinges to be fitted.

Brick, stone and concrete block piers

These must be set on substantial foundations built at least 500 mm (20 in) into the ground. The minimum size for a brick pier is a brick-and-a-half square (about 340 mm/13½ in).

Hanging a gate

1. Unless the manufacturer specifies the distance at which the gate posts are to be set apart, the first stage in fitting is to lay out gate and posts on the ground where they are to be fitted. You will also need to lay out the hinges and the gate catch so that sufficient clearance can be left between the edge of the gate and the posts to allow them to be fitted. Do the same if you are fitting double gates, but place a 6 mm (¼ in) thick batten between the gates where they close together to ensure adequate clearance. Measure the distance between the posts and cut a batten to this length – use this as a gauging rod to help in setting the posts the correct distance apart.

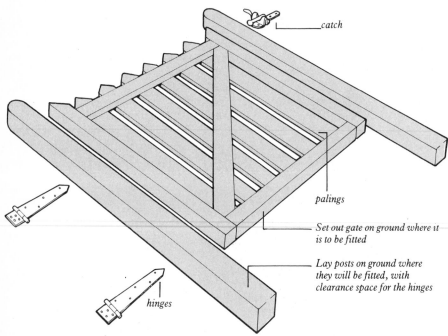

catch

palings

Set out gate on ground where it is to be fitted

Lay posts on ground where they will be fitted, with clearance space for the hinges

hinges

2. Excavate for the post holes so that after fitting there will be a clearance space of about 50 mm (2 in) under the gate. Set the bottom of each post on bricks or on a piece of concrete

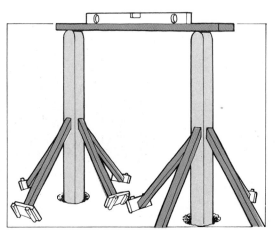

paving slab so that the post will not sink further into the ground. Make sure that the post is vertical on all faces and use temporary struts to hold it in position. Set the second post in the ground, using the gauging rod to ensure it is at the correct distance from the first post. Place a straight-edge across the post tops so that a spirit level can be used to ensure that the posts are both at the same height.

3. Pack rubble around the base of both posts and add a 75 mm (3 in) thick collar of concrete around each at ground level. Concrete and metal posts are both best fixed by surrounding them solely with concrete. On soft ground there will be a tendency for the tops of the posts to be pulled inwards, so dig out a 150 mm (6 in) deep by 300 mm (1 ft) wide trench between the posts and fill this with concrete, which will form a 'bridge' at soil level between the posts.

4. Position the gate in the opening so that the diagonal brace between the top and bottom rails runs between the bottom rail on the hinge side and the top rail on the side where the catch will be fitted. Stand the gate on bricks or offcuts of timber so that there is a gap of about 50 mm (2 in) beneath it. Check with your spirit level that the rails are horizontal and ensure that there is a gap of about 6 mm (¼ in) between each edge of the gate and the posts. Use small timber wedges to hold the gate in this position. It will be easier to position double gates if they are clamped together with G-clamps, using a 6 mm (¼ in) batten between the meeting edges to hold them the correct distance apart. On sloping ground make sure that the gates either swing away from the slope, or that the gates are high enough to clear the ground when opened.

5. If the gates are being hung with tee-hinges, these are simply held against the gate and post so that the screw holes can be marked and drilled. If you are going to use the more substantial cranked steel strap and plate hinges, fit the strap part of each hinge to the top and bottom rail of the gate before the gate is positioned. The cranked part of each strap should protrude an equal distance from the side of the gate. After the gate is positioned push the pin plate flaps into place in the straps and screw them to the rear face of the post. Check that the gate swings satisfactorily, then drill through the hinge strap so that the coach bolt can be fitted to hold the strap firmly to the rail. Fit the gate latch next, carefully aligning the parts so that the latch operates smoothly.

6. Concrete posts may be pre-drilled to allow the fittings to be mounted direct, but it is more common to use the holes to bolt 100mm × 38 mm (4 in × 1½ in) preservative-treated timber mounting pieces to the posts. When hanging a gate between existing posts, mount the timbers on the inside or rear faces of the posts, according to the width of the gate.

7. Make or order gates to suit the positions of hinge pins already built-in to existing brick, stone or concrete block piers. If this is not possible, saw off the pins and discard them; then mount the gate on timber mounting blocks bolted to the faces of the piers using sturdy expanding bolts.

8. If the gate is to be hung on new piers, hold the gate in position using timber struts, then build up the piers on each side, setting the hinge and catch fittings into the mortar joints as the

piers are built. Do not hang the gate on a new pier until the mortar has set.

9. Tall timber and metal side gates restrict access around the side of the house; they are usually hung so that the gate closes against the house wall. If possible hang the gate so that it swings on a sturdy post and closes against a catch post, which can be fixed to the house wall using large expanding bolts. Hanging the gate the other way round so it swings from the post mounted on the house wall can exert considerable pressure on the expanding bolts, which will need to be fixed even more securely.

Below: *Two examples of the diverse range of garden gates that are possible. When choosing, try to pick a gate that matches existing fencing, or at least provides an interesting contrast*

Repairs for timber gates

Garden or boundary gates are used virtually every day, so it is not surprising that they eventually show signs of wear.

Correcting sagging gates

Of the various types of gates, those made of timber give the most trouble. Sagging is the most common problem; usually the gate drops on the side of the latch, resulting in the latch stile scraping on the ground. This makes the gate difficult to close and the latch hard to operate – and it can even wear out the timber if the defect is left untended. The problem may be caused by a loose joint, or loose or worn hinges, so the first step is to partially open the gate, grasp the latch stile and try to lift the gate. This should highlight the fault.

If the gate seems fairly firm, the sagging is probably due to the gate being made from insufficiently thick timber, being made without a diagonal brace, or because the gate has been hung incorrectly so that the brace is on the wrong side. In each case the solution is to fit a new diagonal brace.

To fit a new diagonal brace between the bottom rail on the hinge side and the top rail on the latch side, first close the gate and insert a wedge under the latch stile to lift the gate into its correct position. Measure up for the brace and cut it from 100 mm × 38 mm (4 in × 1½ in) timber, treat it with wood preservative, then fix it in place with waterproof glue and zinc-plated screws or nails. Make sure it is firmly wedged between top and bottom rails.

Sometimes large close-boarded gates sag because the brace is insubstantial. In this case lift the gate into the required position using wedges and then fit a wire brace between the top hinge on the post side and the opposite corner. Use straining wire fitted to metal plates at each corner and tension the wire using a fencing turnbuckle (barrel strainer).

Worn or broken hinges

Lifting the edge of the gate will highlight worn or broken hinges, which should be replaced. If the problem is simply that the hinge securing screws have worked loose, these should be removed and replaced with longer zinc-plated screws. If it is impossible to fit longer screws either plug the enlarged screw holes with hardwood dowels, or remove the hinges and replace them in a slightly different position so that the screws can go into new wood. When worn or broken hinges are replaced, use larger hinges.

Tightening loose joints

When lifting the latch stile of a gate reveals loose joints this could be a sign that the gate is affected by rot, which may be in its early stages. Probe the wood with a penknife blade to make sure it is sound; if you find rot, repair as described below.

The joints may have just worked loose because the gate has been misused by slamming. If only one or two joints are loose it may be possible to repair these individually, otherwise the gate must be dismantled so that all the joints can be remade. Isolated joint repairs can be made by drilling at right angles through the tongue of the joint and inserting a hardwood dowel smeared with adhesive into the joint. Where the loose joint is a through mortise and tenon type the repair can be made by making a chisel cut into the end grain of the tenon and then driving a small hardwood wedge coated with adhesive into the slot to swell the tenon and tighten the joint.

When a gate has to be dismantled to repair all the joints, it should be reassembled using a waterproof resin adhesive. Each mortise and tenon joint should be drilled and a hardwood dowel glued in place to reinforce it. The gate should be kept square and tightly clamped up on a flat surface while the adhesive is setting.

If the gate cannot be dismantled, an easier, although less attractive, repair of loose joints can be made by screwing metal corner plates over the affected joints.

Treating rotting timber

Probe the surface of the timber with a penknife blade to reveal the extent of the rot. If the gate is badly decayed the only solution is to replace it, but if only one or two rails are affected it may be possible to dismantle the gate and replace just these rails. Treat the new timber with clear wood preservative before finishing.

If the rot is not too severe, prise out the worst of the rotted timber and leave the remaining area to dry out. (Drying can be accelerated by playing a hot-air paint stripper over the affected area.) Treat the remaining wood with a wood hardener liquid, which will give a firm base when dry for a high-performance glass fibre-type wood filler to be used. These two-part fillers harden rapidly and after about 15 minutes can be sanded to leave a smooth surface. To protect the surrounding areas from further rot, insert wood preservative sticks into holes drilled about 50 mm (2 in) apart around the vulnerable areas such as joints. Conceal the repair by repainting.

Rusted latches and hinges

If the metal is badly eaten away by the rust, replace the affected fittings. Otherwise wire-brush the fitting to remove loose rust, or use a flap-wheel sander in an electric drill. Treat the

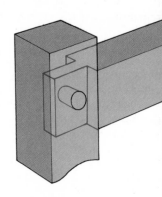

Reinforce loose joints in gates with glued dowels fixed through the tenons

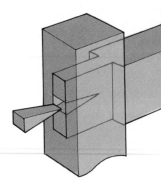

Wedge loose tenons apart by driving in triangular offcuts of timber

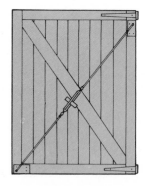

A badly sagging close-boarded gate can be restored to shape using a straining wire and turnbuckle arrangement attached to two metal plates fixed at diagonal corners of the gate

fitting with a rust-neutralizing primer before repainting. Finally, lightly oil moving parts.

Refixing loose posts

If a freestanding gate post has worked loose, dig out a collar of soil about 150 mm (6 in) deep and 200 mm (8 in) wide around it. Hold the post vertically and ram large stones or bricks into the ground around it before levelling off the surface with concrete.

On soft clay ground this may not be sufficient treatment. Here, you will have to dig a 150 mm (6 in) deep and 300 mm (1 ft) wide trench between the hinge post and the catch post and fill this trench with concrete, which will form a rigid bridge to firmly link the two posts together.

Correcting a leaning post

It is difficult to correct a leaning post without resetting it in the ground. However, if the lean is not too bad it may be possible to prevent it becoming worse by fixing a straining wire and turnbuckle (barrel strainer) between the top of the leaning post and the base of a firmly fixed adjacent fence post. Finally the gate can be made vertical by packing out the edge of the leaning post with timber offcuts to form a vertical edge to which the hinges can be fixed.

Repairing a broken post

It may be possible to make a repair to a broken post with a concrete spur (see page 116). If you decide to replace the post you may be faced with a section that has broken off at ground level. In this case hire a 600 mm to 900 mm (2 ft to 3 ft) long timber auger of about 25 mm (1 in) diameter and use this to bore down into the end grain of the broken post. Drill out as much as possible, then use a cold chisel or crowbar to split up the posts so that the timber can be removed in manageable pieces.

If the post has broken off above ground level you may be able to lift the post straight out of the ground using two car jacks. Drill the post so that sections of angle-iron can be bolted to each side, under which the jacks can be placed.

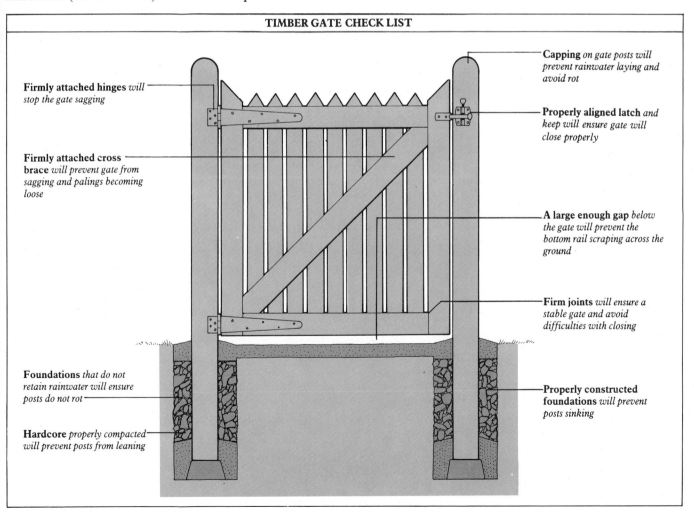

TIMBER GATE CHECK LIST

Firmly attached hinges *will stop the gate sagging*

Firmly attached cross brace *will prevent gate from sagging and palings becoming loose*

Foundations *that do not retain rainwater will ensure posts do not rot*

Hardcore *properly compacted will prevent posts from leaning*

Capping *on gate posts will prevent rainwater laying and avoid rot*

Properly aligned latch *and keep will ensure gate will close properly*

A large enough gap *below the gate will prevent the bottom rail scraping across the ground*

Firm joints *will ensure a stable gate and avoid difficulties with closing*

Properly constructed foundations *will prevent posts sinking*

14. Paths and drives

The drive or path leading to your front door is the first and last thing visitors see and so their impressions of your house will, to a large extent, be governed by its appearance. Therefore it should be both attractive and hard-wearing to complement a well kept house. There is a host of materials which are suitable, so you can design any pattern you choose.

Always think about a drive as an extension of the house. Ideally, the two should blend together in character and appearance. A green-walled house, for example, might look far from happy with a red brick drive leading up to it; whereas a white house could look drab with a grey area of concrete surrounding it. A period house or cottage is not likely to be enhanced by a whole area of square paving slabs, and a modern bungalow would not be suited to a large area of gravel around it.

Cost, of course, is going to dictate your choice and, possibly, the speed or skill associated with laying the material. The two, largely, go hand in hand. The easiest materials to handle are gravel and asphalt, which require no more than spreading and rolling. Stone chippings, logs and stepping stones also fall into this category.

Concrete has to be considered carefully. It is a strenuous material to work and it should not be used in large areas without at least giving it an interesting surface texture.

Bricks and concrete blocks work well in any setting. They offer an enormous choice of bonding arrangements and blend well with almost any style of house.

Perhaps the most popular material of all is paving slabs, for crazy paving (flagstone pattern). Colours, shapes and textures abound.

Materials	Foundations
asphalt	**drive:** any firm surface such as gravel, ash or concrete **path:** as above
cast concrete	**drive:** 100 mm (4 in) layer of hardcore, well compacted, with layer of ballast to fill large voids **path:** well-compacted ground is sufficient. Fill soft patches with stones or hardcore
cobblestones	**drive:** unsuitable **path:** use only in small areas. Bed in mortar on firm concrete base
concrete pavers	**drive:** 100 mm (4 in) layer of hardcore, well-compacted, topped with 60 mm (2½ in) bedding sand, plus edge restraints **path:** well-compacted ground, with layer of bedding sand and edge restraints
gravel	**drive:** well-compacted hardcore base 100 mm (4 in) thick, with kerbstones to prevent stones spreading **path:** well-compacted hardcore base 100 mm (4 in) thick

Materials	Foundations
logs	**drive:** unsuitable **path:** well-compacted earth
quarry tiles	**drive:** unsuitable **path:** set in mortar on a concrete base
Paving slabs/stepping stones	**drive:** 125 mm (5 in) layer of well-compacted concrete with sand-blinding layer **path:** on well-compacted ground or 100 mm (4 in) hardcore base
stone chippings	**drive:** 100 mm to 150 mm (4 in to 6 in) well-compacted hardcore **path:** 75 mm to 100 mm (3 in to 4 in) hardcore **surface dressing:** any firm surface is adequate

Choose materials for drives and paths with care for the longest-lasting surface. It is important to have substantial enough foundations for the weight of traffic a path or drive is likely to receive; see this table for requirements.

A gravel drive suits an older-style property. Here, the entrance to this imposing house is kept subtle in tone and texture so as not to detract from the lines of the building

Right: *Burnt brick pavers used to form a meandering narrow path across a lawn incorporate a planting area to break up the run*

Left: *Concrete block pavers laid in a herringbone design make a grand, sweeping entrance to a house. The top edge of each block is bevelled to accentuate its shape and the pattern*

Laying concrete block paving

Concrete block 'flexible' paving is laid dry – that is, no mortar is used in the laying: the blocks are bedded down on sand. Both rectangular and shaped blocks are available. Rectangular blocks for drives measure 200 mm × 100 mm (8 in × 4 in) and are 60 mm to 65 mm (2¼ in to 2½ in) thick. Some have bevelled top edges which, apart from adding to their overall 'established' effect, are less likely to be chipped than square-edged types. Shaped blocks – zig-zag and curved types, for example – cover the same approximate area; the edges are shaped so that neighbouring blocks interlock. Grey, red and multi-coloured blocks, which resemble old, weathered bricks are available.

Although the blocks can be laid and compacted with a club hammer on a stout length of timber, it is better, especially for larger areas, to use a mechanical plate vibrator. Enquire at a local plant hire shop for a machine with a rubber sole plate. If you have to make do with a metal-soled vibrator, use it over an old carpet or rubber mat to prevent scratching the surface of the blocks. If you have a lot of blocks to cut – you will have to cut some for filling in edges – hire a hydraulic stone splitter. Otherwise you will have to cut individual blocks using a bolster chisel and club hammer.

Site preparation

A drive laid with concrete block paving requires a sub-base of well-compacted hardcore (aggregate). First, remove all vegetable matter and topsoil. When digging out the site check the height of the house d.p.c. plus any gate or door which may not open if the surface is raised.

Any inspection covers or drain gratings should be boxed out with timber battens. The battens can be removed when the driveway is complete and the spaces filled with concrete. Blocks can be laid right up to a pre-cast inspection cover.

Edge restraints are needed to prevent the blocks moving. Permanent walls – those of the house or garage – provide adequate support but elsewhere 125 mm × 50 mm (5 in × 2 in) pre-cast concrete kerb edging should be bedded in concrete. Straight and curved kerbs are

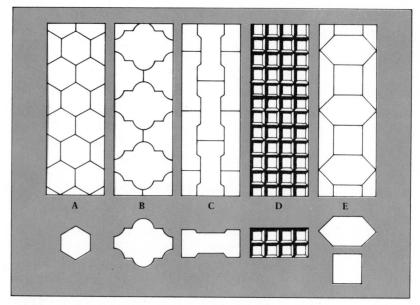

Various patterns you can make using block pavers:
A Hexagonal
B Multi-curved
C Interlocking
D Squared modules
E Hexagonal and squared

available. Allow 24 hours for the kerbs to set firmly. Alternatively you can fix planks to stout pegs driven into the ground outside the perimeter of the area you are going to pave.

The sub-base must be smoothed and completed using a roller, or if you have hired one, a plate vibrator. For drainage a fall of about 50 mm in 2 m (2 in in 6 ft) will be sufficient.

Laying bedding sand

Spread sand between the edge restraints using a rake. Then use a straight-edged board to level it off to about 60 mm (2½ in); this will be reduced to about 50 mm (2 in) after the blocks have been vibrated. Work in areas of about one metre wide. After levelling the sand, make sure it is not disturbed.

Laying the blocks

1. Lay the first blocks against an edge restraint. Make sure the pattern is being formed correctly; use a board to kneel on to prevent disturbing the levelled sand or blocks already laid. Butt the blocks up together closely.

2. Work with full size blocks as far as possible, since stopping to cut blocks causes hold-ups. To cut a block with a hydraulic stone splitter, first score the cut line on the face of the block, then place it in the jaws of the machine; operate the lever to make the cut. When cutting by hand, place the block on a firm, level surface. Score the cut line all round with a bolster chisel and club hammer, then make a final firm blow to cut the block cleanly.

3. Complete each levelled area before going on to level the sand over the next metre or so.

COVERAGE AND PATTERNS

Fifty blocks will cover an area of 1 sq metre (3 sq ft). About 1016 kg (1 ton) of sand is sufficient for laying about 10 sq m (30 sq ft) of blocks. Order sharp (concreting) sand.

The blocks can be laid in various patterns. Almost all are suitable for foot traffic, but for a driveway a 45° or 90° herringbone pattern is needed. This pattern will prevent the blocks moving under the pressure of braking or turning cars.

4. When a fairly large area of about 4 or 5 square metres (12 or 15 sq ft) has been laid, compact the blocks with the plate vibrator. Make about three passes over the blocks. Do not take the vibrator within 1 m (3 ft) of an unsupported edge of blocks.

5. When the whole drive has been laid, spread a sprinkling of sand into the joints. This will finally lock the blocks firmly together. A helper will be needed to keep brushing sand in front of the vibrator to ensure it is forced down into the joints. The drive is then ready for use.

Future maintenance
It is possible that weeds will start to grow in the joints after a year or so. Although these can be pulled up as they appear, the possibility of them growing can be eliminated altogether by treating the drive with a chemical weed killer each spring. Dilute the chemical with water and sprinkle it over the drive with a watering can.

Laying by hand
Provided the drive is not to be used by vehicles, the blocks can be compacted by hand as previously described. Use a slightly thinner layer of sand, then moisten it with a watering can fitted with a fine spray head. The sand should be just moist enough to remain in a ball after being squeezed in the hand. Follow the normal techniques for laying and screeding then, to complete the job, direct sand into the joints using a watering can.

When laying blocks use a board to stand on to prevent disturbing sand or blocks already laid

Using concrete

Concrete can be used for a wide variety of jobs around the house and garden – paths, drives, steps, foundations for walls, bases for garages, sheds or summerhouses, plus a host of other small building projects, such as flower planters or coal bunkers.

Normally concrete is made using a mix of cement, sand and either gravel or stones. There are several types of cement available, but the one that is used for most jobs around the house and garden is called Portland cement, which is light grey in colour and is normally supplied in 50 kg (1 cwt) bags. Portland cement is not a brand, it is a type of cement. It can be bought in smaller-sized bags but, although easier to lift and store, the amount is only suitable for small jobs and repair work.

The sand and gravel or stones are called 'aggregates'. Although these can be bought separately, it is normal to buy them already mixed together. In this form the mix is called all-in ballast or, simply, ballast (mixed aggregate).

Concrete is made by mixing cement and ballast together with water. The proportion in which they are mixed is normally 1:4 or 1:5 by volume, dependent on the purpose for which the concrete is needed.

The table (opposite) shows you how to calculate the number of bags of cement you will need and the amount of ballast to order. All you have to do is to measure the area to be concreted and then multiply the result by the thickness to be laid. So, if you are planning a drive which is to be 2 m (6 ft) wide, 8 m (24 ft) long and 100 mm (4 in) thick, you would multiply 2 m × 8 m × 0.1 m (6 ft × 24 ft × 0.3 ft) to find out the number of cubic metres or feet of concrete needed.

Refer to the table under the column headed 'amount per cubic metre/foot' to calculate how much you need and then add about 10% for wastage to tell you how much to buy. Do not order the materials too far in advance since they will have to be stored somewhere. The bags of cement will start to harden after only a couple of weeks if moisture in the air penetrates through the paper bags. Store them off the ground and preferably under cover in a dry garage or shed. A platform of strong boards is an ideal base. If the bags have to be kept outside then cover them completely with strong plastic sheeting.

The ballast is likely to attract animals and wind-blown leaves or dirt so, again, keep it covered. The alternative to mixing your own concrete by hand or with a concrete-mixing machine is to buy ready-mixed concrete. This is by far the best method for most people because it takes a lot of hard work out of the job and the

project will be completed far more quickly. There are two ways of buying ready-mix. You can simply phone up and order the amount you want, which will then be delivered at a pre-arranged time by the supplier. If the supplier is able to get near the site then the concrete can be unloaded where required, leaving you only with the job of levelling and smoothing it. However, if the site is at the back of the house, you will have to wheelbarrow it there. This is tough work so you will need as many helpers and wheelbarrows as can be assembled. The supplier might simply dump the load in the road and leave you to move it. Since it will start to harden within a couple of hours (less in hot weather), you must move it quickly.

Do make sure you are aware of the arrangements that have to be made with the delivery firm, in case illness or bad weather lead to cancellation. A number of firms operate a system whereby they will deliver part-loads in accordance with your requirements and speed, which is ideal if you cannot enlist a lot of support. Remember that handling concrete can be very tiring for anyone not used to heavy work and be realistic in your calculations.

It is also possible to buy concrete in bags of dry materials all ready for mixing with water. The cement and aggregates are supplied in the correct proportions in the bag. This, however, is an expensive method of making concrete, though it is a handy method where small jobs and repairs are concerned. Store the bag as stated above for concrete.

Tools for the job

For preparing the site and setting up the strong support boards which act as a mould and retain the wet concrete while it is setting (called 'formwork'), you will need a spade, fork, garden roller, hammer, saw, spirit level, tape measure, stringlines, wooden pegs and a builder's square. A builder's square is handy for marking out right-angled corners when making formwork for a rectangular slab of concrete. Make one using

A selection of the tools and equipment you will need when laying concrete: spade, fork and garden roller for preparing the foundations; hammer, saw, spirit level, tape measure, stringlines, wooden pegs and a builder's square (see below) for setting out the formwork; a powered mixer and two large shovels for mixing the concrete, plus two buckets for adding water to the mix and measuring out proportions of cement and ballast. Additionally you will require a rake, a tamping beam and a steel float, wood float or coarse broom for finishing off the new surface

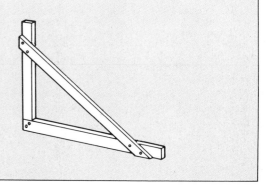

Make up a builder's square *from three lengths of softwood screwed together to form a right-angled triangle. Make the lengths 450 mm, 600 mm and 750 mm (1 ft 6 in, 2 ft and 2 ft 6 in) and use a lap joint at the corner between the shortest pieces, setting the longer brace on top. The angle between the short pieces must be 90°*

Use	Mix-your-own Proportions (volume)		Amount per cubic metre (36 cu ft)	Yield per bag of cement	Ready-mix specification (UK only)
General purpose (Most uses except foundations and exposed pavings	Cement	1	6.4 bags	0.15 m² (5 cu ft)	C20P to BS 5328, medium to high workability. 20 mm maximum aggregate
	Sand	2	680 kg (13 cwt)		
	20 mm aggregate	3	1175 kg (23 cwt)		
	Combined aggregates	*4*	*1855 kg (36.5 cwt)*		
Foundation (Footings, foundations and bases for precast paving)	Cement	1	5.6 bags	0.18 m³ (6 cu ft)	C7.5P to BS 5328, high workability. 20 mm (¾ in) maximum aggregate
	Sand	2½	720 kg (14 cwt)		
	20 mm (¾ in) aggregate	3½	1165 kg (23 cwt)		
	Combined aggregates	*5*	*1885 kg (37 cwt)*		

Table supplied by the Cement and Concrete Association

three pieces of wood – 750 mm × 600 mm × 450 mm (2 ft 6 in × 2 ft × 1 ft 6 in). Join the pieces. Provided the proportions are accurate, the angle between the shortest sides will be 90°.

Mixing equipment

A concrete mixer is certainly needed for larger jobs. For hand mixing use two shovels and two buckets of the same size. Keep one shovel and bucket for measuring out the cement and the other for measuring out the ballast and water and for mixing. You will also need a rake for roughly levelling the concrete.

A tamping beam is needed to level off the concrete. A simple piece of 100 mm × 50 mm (4 in × 2 in) timber will suffice for a narrow path; for wider sections use 150 mm × 50 mm (6 in × 2 in) timber, fitted with strong, makeshift handles. The timber, in both cases, must be about 300 mm (1 ft) wider than the formwork.

A steel float, wood float or soft or coarse broom can be used to provide a finish to the concrete.

If a hard surface is not available for hand mixing concrete, make a platform of about 2 m × 1 m (6 ft × 3 ft), using timber boards or 18 mm or 25 mm (¾ in or 1 in) thick plywood.

Preparing the site

Apart from a rectangular base for a shed or garage, which is built to a pre-determined size and in a set position, all other projects should first be planned on paper and then marked out in the garden using stringlines stretched between timber pegs.

• First completely clear the site of all weeds and roots. How much soil you have to remove from the site will be determined by where you want the concrete surface to finish, bearing in mind the house d.p.c., the pavement outside the front gate, the level of the lawn and so on. Hardcore foundations are not vital below concrete: it can always be laid directly onto firm, well-compacted ground. Just use stones or broken bricks to reinforce any soft patches then roll thoroughly to compact it.

• Where the soil is weak or the soil is clay or peaty, or where the concrete is to serve as a driveway, lay a 100 mm (4 in) thick layer of broken bricks or stones then compact it well with a sledge hammer or garden roller. Fill any voids with sharp sand.

• Concrete has to be laid inside strong support boards, which act as a mould to retain the wet concrete until it has hardened. The boards, which are called the formwork, can be any reasonably straight-edged lengths of wood about 12 mm to 18 mm (½ in to ¾ in) thick. Old floorboards are ideal.

• Define the site of a path with taut stringlines tied to pegs driven into the ground; a curved path can be indicated by rope, hosepipe or bricks. The formwork boards are then positioned following the guidelines. They can be supported on the outside by strong stakes set about 1.2 m to 1.8 m (4 ft to 6 ft) apart. Ideally, the boards must be the same depth as the intended thickness of the concrete. However, if you do not have sufficient boards that are deep enough you can rest them on bricks or old tiles to raise them to the correct height.

• If a path was made absolutely flat rainwater would lie on it, so a slight crossfall must be allowed for. A sufficient fall would be 12 mm in 1 metre (½ in in 3 ft) from one side of the path to the other. Such a slope would not be noticeable to the eye. Set the correct fall by placing a thin wedge of wood (known as a 'shim'), 12 mm (½ in) thick, on the formwork on one side of the path. Place a straight-edged length of timber resting on the shim and on the formwork at the other side of the path. Place a spirit level on the straight-edge and tap down the formwork with the shim on it until the spirit level gives a horizontal reading.

• A curved path adds a little complication since the formwork has to be bent. To bend formwork simply saw through the wood to half its depth at about 100 mm to 150 mm (4 in to 6 in) spacings. This will enable it to be bent comfortably to shape. You will probably need extra support pegs alongside this curved formwork to retain it in position, since there will be a tendency for it to spring back.

• When constructing a base for a shed or garage it is important to get it level. Setting out the area is a little more involved too. Stringlines tied to pegs fixed well outside the concrete area are needed. The corners can be checked with a builder's square to ensure they are at true right-angles. A check for exact squareness can be made by measuring across the diagonals. They should be exactly the same. Formwork can then be erected and the stringlines removed. It is important to ensure that the formwork is horizontal on all sides and that each side is level with each other. This can be done by placing a long straight-edged piece of timber spanning the formwork and placing a spirit level on top.

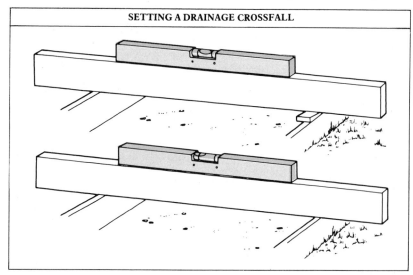

SETTING A DRAINAGE CROSSFALL

It is important that the path slopes gently to one side to enable rainwater to drain away quickly (see above)

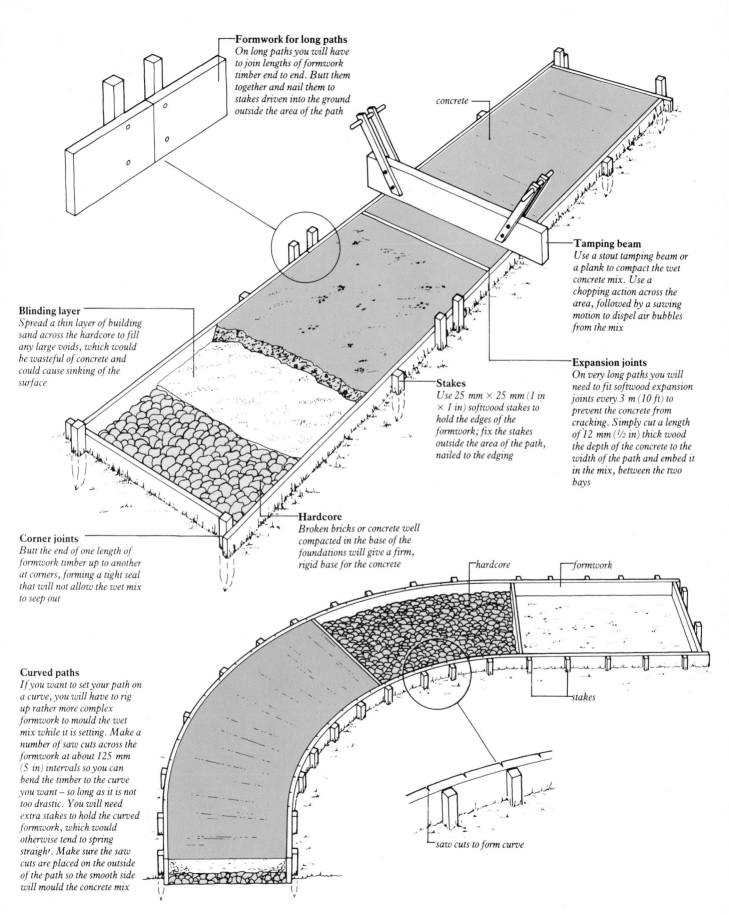

Formwork for long paths
On long paths you will have to join lengths of formwork timber end to end. Butt them together and nail them to stakes driven into the ground outside the area of the path

concrete

Tamping beam
Use a stout tamping beam or a plank to compact the wet concrete mix. Use a chopping action across the area, followed by a sawing motion to dispel air bubbles from the mix

Blinding layer
Spread a thin layer of building sand across the hardcore to fill any large voids, which would be wasteful of concrete and could cause sinking of the surface

Expansion joints
On very long paths you will need to fit softwood expansion joints every 3 m (10 ft) to prevent the concrete from cracking. Simply cut a length of 12 mm (1/2 in) thick wood the depth of the concrete to the width of the path and embed it in the mix, between the two bays

Stakes
Use 25 mm × 25 mm (1 in × 1 in) softwood stakes to hold the edges of the formwork; fix the stakes outside the area of the path, nailed to the edging

Corner joints
Butt the end of one length of formwork timber up to another at corners, forming a tight seal that will not allow the wet mix to seep out

Hardcore
Broken bricks or concrete well compacted in the base of the foundations will give a firm, rigid base for the concrete

hardcore

formwork

Curved paths
If you want to set your path on a curve, you will have to rig up rather more complex formwork to mould the wet mix while it is setting. Make a number of saw cuts across the formwork at about 125 mm (5 in) intervals so you can bend the timber to the curve you want – so long as it is not too drastic. You will need extra stakes to hold the curved formwork, which would otherwise tend to spring straight. Make sure the saw cuts are placed on the outside of the path so the smooth side will mould the concrete mix

stakes

saw cuts to form curve

131

Mixing and casting concrete

Hand mixing

When mixing concrete by hand or machine it is important to keep the proportions of the cement and ballast correct. Each batch of concrete should comprise, for example, one bucket of cement and four of ballast. If you want to mix a larger batch in one go, you would use, say, two buckets of cement and eight buckets of ballast.

1. Measure out the ballast into a heap, then make an indentation and add the cement.

2. Turn over the heap until the cement and ballast are thoroughly mixed. At this point the pile should be an overall grey colour.

3. Make a deeper hole in the pile and pour some water in. Then start turning over the mix until the water is absorbed. Make a further hole in the top of the pile, add more water and mix again.

4. Getting the right consistency is important – the mix must be neither too dry nor too sloppy. If the back of the shovel is used to flatten the concrete then the surface should remain solid but moist.

Machine mixing

A small mixing machine can be hired locally. Normally a smaller machine, called a 5/3½ or 'half-bag' size is suitable. It can be powered by petrol (gas) or electricity. Electrically operated types are more convenient if there is an electricity supply nearby. It is best to position the mixer close to the ballast and cement and alongside the formwork. If the mixer has to be positioned away from the site then you will need to tip the concrete into a wheelbarrow for transportation.

When you hire a mixer find out exactly how to operate it. Always stand it on level ground and put blocks under the wheels to prevent it moving. You must not leave a mixer idle for any length of time, such as a lunch break, without cleaning it out. The best method is to spray a jet of water into the drum with a hosepipe, and then to tip out the watery remnants of the mix. If you are leaving it idle for a short time, tip in half the ballast and water for the next batch of concrete to be mixed and leave the drum revolving.

1. To make a batch of concrete with a mixer, keep to the stipulated proportions for the ingredients. Tip half the ballast followed by half the water into the revolving drum. Allow this to mix for about half a minute then add all the cement and the remainder of the ballast.

2. Leave the mix to turn over for about another

minute and a half. The mix should drop cleanly off the blades inside the drum but must not be too watery. Test a mixed batch for correct consistency by using the shovel test described for hand mixing. You then can add more or less water if needed.

3. If you are using a bag of dry-mixed concrete, you must always pour the complete contents out of the bag and mix them up dry until a uniform grey colour is attained. If you do not need to use the complete bag then shovel some back in for storage. This mixing is necessary because the cement in the bag tends to settle at the bottom; if you just used the top half of the bag you would be using mainly ballast in your mix.

Laying and compacting the mix

1. Tip the concrete into the formwork. Use your shovel to force it well down beside the formwork so that no air-pockets remain. Air-pockets in the mix are a prime cause of edges crumbling later.

2. Use the back of a rake to spread the concrete roughly level and slightly above the top edge of the formwork. Allow an excess of about 10 mm (⅜ in) for every 100 mm (4 in) of intended finished thickness.

3. Place the tamping beam (a heavy batten used for levelling the concrete) across the formwork. By resting it on the top edge of the formwork and then working it backwards and forwards in a chopping followed by a sawing movement, the concrete will be levelled with the top edge of the formwork.

4. Continue mixing and adding concrete until the job is complete. If you want to leave the job half-finished overnight, place a length of timber across the formwork and concrete up to it. The next day you can remove the timber and continue concreting by making a butt joint, spreading out and compacting the mix as before.

A

B

C

D

Add the cement to the ballast then mix the ingredients thoroughly without water (A)

Make a crater in the heap and add a little water, then fold in the sides of the crater (B)

Mix the ingredients and water until you achieve an even texture free of dry pockets (C)

Add the remaining water slowly; continue to mix until you reach the right consistency (D)

Below: There are various ways to provide a finishing texture to concrete: slightly rippled, applied with a soft broom (A); fairly smooth, applied by wood float (B); shiny-smooth, applied with a steel float (C); swirling, with a shovel back (D)

Finishing the concrete

After levelling off the concrete with the tamping beam the surface will have a rippled appearance, which can be slight or exaggerated depending on how carefully the compacting was carried out. In either case you can leave the concrete to set just as it is for an acceptable surface finish.

You cannot stand on fresh concrete of course, so if the area is too wide for you to reach across with the brush, a platform spanning the concrete is needed. A strong plank resting on the formwork is the most suitable.

There are lots of other ways to finish the surface. Brushed finishes are easiest to achieve since it is the bristles and the time at which the brush is used on the setting concrete that determines the results rather than any skill. Try out the chosen finish on a small corner of the concrete to see if it is what you want.

Types of finish

For a rough, pronounced ripple, draw a nylon or stiff-bristled broom across the surface as soon as the concrete has been compacted. Do not put pressure on the brush or it will spoil the surface. Hold the brush at a shallow angle and just indent the surface with the bristles. It is normally better to have the ripples running across a path or drive rather than down its length. Always keep the

brush moving in the chosen direction only. A smoother ripple is achieved by using a soft broom, again immediately after compaction of the concrete.

For a very smooth finish use a steel float. Never use a float too vigorously or excessive amounts of water will be drawn up to the surface and this will leave the concrete weak and prone to dusting or surface damage. It is usually better to leave the concrete until it has started to stiffen before using the float. This will give a tight, smooth finish.

A wood float gives a fine glass-paper texture. A coarser texture is created simply by allowing the concrete which gathers on the face of the float to remain while the float is used. Use a float by skimming it over the surface. If pressure is exerted, marks will be left.

A textured aggregate finish can be applied, after compaction, using a soft broom on the surface, then allowing it to stiffen slightly. Subsequent gentle brushing and spraying with water will wash away fine aggregate leaving the coarse aggregate slightly proud of the surface. If you want to go a stage further, spread a thin, even layer of coarse aggregate on the surface of the fresh concrete and then firm it in with a wood float.

'Mock' crazy paving (flagstone pattern) can be achieved by first using a steel float to smooth the concrete, then allowing the surface to nearly harden. A pointed implement is then used to scribe the irregular shape of paving into the concrete.

Protecting the wet concrete

Concrete which dries out too quickly is prone to damage later. Hot sun or frost are particularly bad for setting concrete.

In hot weather allow the surface to harden, then cover it with a large polythene (polyethylene) sheet. Tape the joints between sheets and keep the edges weighted down with bricks. Alternatively, use hessian sacking (burlap) as protection and keep this damp by sprinkling it with water. Leave the covering material in place for about three days.

Ideally you should never concrete when there is a danger of frost as this will freeze the water in the concrete and weaken – or even possibly crack – the surface. If a snap frost catches you out, cover the surface of the concrete with polythene (polyethylene), then straw, then more polythene (polyethylene). Weight down the edges to stop the wind blowing underneath.

A   B
C   D

Using small-scale materials

Gravel

Gravel is available in a variety of colours, including white. It is easy to lay but can have disadvantages in use. The main problem is that it becomes disturbed by cars and foot traffic and so has to be rolled or raked regularly to maintain its appearance. Rain can wash the stones away and when they are wet they tend to be picked up on shoes and carried into the house. Unless contained with some type of kerb the gravel will also tend to spread onto adjacent lawns or flower beds. The other main problems with gravel are that it is not easy to ride a bike over it or push a pram or carriage across it, so you may have to incorporate a paved path through it.

Economy is the main advantage of a gravel drive, together with speed of laying over a large area. It looks best on wide, longer drives rather than in small areas. Break up a gravelled area with small areas of planting.

Laying a gravel path

1. Lay a base of 100 mm (4 in) of well-compacted hardcore (broken bricks and concrete). If planting areas are to be included, then box these off and do not lay hardcore on them. Lay a thin dressing of sand over the hardcore to fill any large voids. Finally, spread a 6 mm (¼ in) layer of gravel on top.

2. Rake the gravel level, then compact the whole area with a garden roller. Repeat the process with a second layer of gravel to bring the total thickness to about 12 mm (½ in).

3. It is important to lay the gravel to a reasonable fall of about 1 in 25, so that the drive will drain efficiently. If the gravel stays damp for long periods it will tend to sink in patches. Weeds protruding through the gravel can be a problem, but a once-yearly treatment with a suitable weedkiller will prevent heavy growth.

Stone Chippings

Chippings are available in 25 kg (½ cwt) bags and one bag will cover about 2.5 metres square (2.5 yards square). Colours available are grey, white, grey-green and dark pink. Any firm surface is suitable for surface dressing with stone chippings, but a new site needs a well-consolidated foundation of hardcore. For a driveway the soil must be excavated to a depth of 100 mm to 150 mm (4 in to 6 in), depending on the nature of the subsoil. Soft clay sub-soils require deeper foundations. A path is constructed similarly except that an excavation of 75 mm to 100 mm (3 in to 4 in) is adequate.

Laying stone chippings

1. Ram the base firm with a sledge hammer or stout fence post before adding hardcore and ramming this down also. Place coarse material in the base with finer rubble on top. Finally spread a binding layer of mixed aggregate over the surface and roll it flat.

2. Check that there are no depressions and that the surface slopes to ensure good rainwater drainage. It is worthwhile adding concrete kerbs to give a neat edge.

3. Stretch stringlines as a guide along the edges of the area, then set the kerbs in concrete over rubble. Tap them down until they are in line, then secure them in place with more concrete.

4. Spread bitumen emulsion (tar paint) over the area to serve as a binder and to hold the chippings in place. How much you spread depends on the nature of the surface. Open-textured loose surfaces such as rolled ballast will require about 4 kg per square metre (9 lb per square yard). Firm, dense surfaces will need half the amount. On concrete and other smooth surfaces use about 1.4 kg per square metre (3 lb per square yard). Bitumen emulsion is sold in 25 kg and 50 kg drums (or ½ cwt and 1 cwt drums). Treat the foundation with a weedkiller and ensure no weeds remain before the emulsion is spread.

Asphalt

Cold macadam is available in bags in a choice of red, black or green. It is a straightforward material to lay and can be used on any firm surface – such as gravel, ash, or concrete. The only preparation needed is the removal of weeds and vegetation (treat the area with a weedkiller a week or so before laying) and then brushing to remove loose dirt.

When you have removed weeds and loose dirt from the path or drive, pour on a layer of bitumen emulsion (tar paint) to bind the surface

Laying asphalt

1. If the surface is loose or of concrete, apply a layer of bitumen emulsion (tar paint) first to bind the surface.

2. When the emulsion has turned from brown to black, empty the macadam from its bags and rake it out to an even thickness of about 18 mm (¾ in) over the surface.

3. Compact the area with a dampened garden roller, then fill any depressions with more macadam and re-roll the surface.

4. Decorative stone chippings can be added to the surface to make it more attractive. Sprinkle these across the macadam from a shovel and bed in using the roller.

Cobblestones

Cobblestones must be set deeply in mortar if they are to be comfortable to walk on. They are most effective when used mainly to break up an area of paving or concrete.

Laying cobblestones

1. Lay a base of concrete (1 part cement; 5 parts ballast) and about an hour later, when the concrete has started to set, spread a 12 mm (1 in)

layer of mortar (1 part cement; 3 parts sand) on top. The time element between laying the concrete and mortar is important in order to ensure a good bond between the two.

2. Keep the cobbles in water so that they are laid wet. This will ensure that they will not draw water from the mortar, and so weaken it. Set the cobbles in the mortar so that they are bedded in to about half their depth. Press them down level all over by using a straight-edged board. If any mortar sticks to the top surface of the cobbles, remove it by lightly washing and brushing the surface about three hours after laying, when it will not smear.

Quarry tiles

Quarry tiles make an unusual and attractive path. They are either brown or red and come in many shapes and sizes. Thicknesses are from 12 mm to 30 mm (½ in to 1¼ in).

Laying quarry tiles

1. A concrete base (1 part cement; 5 parts ballast) must be laid first. Fix battens on each side of the path to serve as a guide to the surface level of the tiles.

2. Spread mortar (1 part cement; 3 parts sand) between the battens then level it off by drawing a T-shaped timber across it that will leave the mortar surface the same distance below the battens as the thickness of the quarry tile being used. Work in areas of about 600 mm (2 ft) square at a time.

3. Lay the tiles on the mortar, tapping them down with a block of wood and checking for level by laying a straight-edged timber across the guide battens.

4. Allow 24 hours for the mortar to harden before pointing the joints with mortar. Wipe away surplus mortar from the face of the tiles immediately using a wet cloth.

Slabs

Paving slabs forming a path are laid as described for patios on page 60. For a drive you must use hydraulically pressed paving slabs at least 50 mm (2 in) thick and no greater than 450 mm sq (18 in sq). A 100 mm (4 in) foundation of well-compacted hardcore is needed below a 75 mm (3 in) base of concrete (1 part cement; 5 parts ballast). Use a box-and-cross layer of mortar for each slab and tamp down the slabs well so that the mortar spreads out underneath to give good support.

Informal stepping stone paths

Stepping stones make an eye-catching path through a lawn. Ordinary square paving slabs or shaped types can be used. They often look more attractive if they meander from the gate to the front door in gentle curves. The only point to watch in the design is that the stones are set at a comfortable distance apart for walking. Also, for ease in mowing the lawn, the surface of the slabs should be set slightly below surface level.

Laying stepping stones
1. Experiment with designs for laying the slabs to determine the best arrangement. Just lay them on the lawn in different patterns until you are satisfied. If you are choosing a curved arrangement it is probably better to leave them for a week or so to ensure that the design is satisfactory.

2. The ground around the perimeter of each slab can be cut using a spade. Slice out the turfs to a depth of about 75 mm (3 in). Lay each slab on a bed of sharp sand or fine soil and tap down level using the shaft of a club hammer.

Irregularly shaped stones *placed in random fashion across a lawn make a stylish stepping stone path that blends in well with its surroundings*

A path with log rounds

A wood log path is the most natural way of blending a walkway into a garden. It is not, however, a long-lasting method, since wood is prone to rot by damp and insect attack. This can be averted to an extent by treating the logs with a thorough coat of preservative before laying them. It is also possible to give extra protection by laying a polythene (polyethylene) membrane below a bed of sand. Puncture the polythene (polyethylene) at regular intervals of about 150 mm (6 in) to ensure rainwater drains away.

Laying logs

1. The danger with wood paving is that it can be slippery when wet, so it is best to scatter gravel between the logs, some of which will naturally find its way on to the wood by wind and foot traffic. This will provide extra grip.

2. The best situation for a log path is in a sunny part of the garden. If in a shaded area, the wood will stay damp and moss will be encouraged. Use rough-textured wood and give an occasional wire-brushing to keep the wood less slippery.

3. Use sawn logs about 75 mm (3 in) thick and in diameters from 250 mm to 1 m (10 in to 3 ft). Lay the logs either as stepping stones or close together as a continuous path.

4. Arrange the logs in the required formation, then dig around them as for paved stepping stones. Set them down on loose soil or polythene (polyethylene) and sand as previously described. If available, old railway sleepers (ties) can be used in much the same way as logs for a tough, long-lasting surface.

Sawn log rounds *laid at intervals along a path give a natural effect in a wooded garden, where a more harsh, man-made material would be totally unsuitable*

Repairing paths and drives

Concrete

Concrete can crack, break at the edges or sink in patches. The problem can always be traced back either to inadequate foundations, or to an error made when laying the concrete. Odd patches can be repaired quite easily, but if the defects extend over a large area the only satisfactory solution is to break up the entire area and cast a completely new surface as described on pages 132-3.

Filling cracks
These are due mostly to settlement. It is not worthwhile repairing a crack until all movement has stopped.

1. Use a bolster chisel and club hammer to undercut the crack at the edges, making it wider below the surface so that an inverted V-shape is formed.

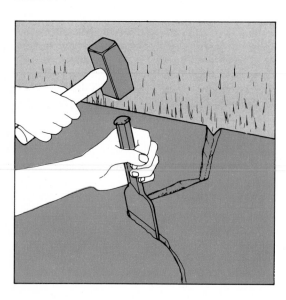

2. Brush out all dust and lightly dampen the crack with water.

3. Brush a coat of pva adhesive into the crack, ensuring that all surfaces are covered. The pva acts as a primer and ensures that the repair material will adhere well.

4. Mix up a mortar of one part cement; three parts sand and add some pva adhesive to the mix. Ready-mix mortar can be bought in small bags. Keep the mortar fairly dry.

5. Pack the mix well down into the crack using a trowel, ensuring it is well packed into all crevices and edges.

6. Level off the mortar with the surrounding surface using a float.

Repairing crumbling edges
Apart from poor foundations, edge defects can be caused by failure to tamp the concrete well down beside the formwork when the concrete was laid. Another possibility is that the formwork was removed too quickly, leaving the edge weak.

1. Break up the crumbling edge using a cold chisel and club hammer until you reach sound edges.

2. Brush away all dust and chippings and consolidate the exposed foundation hardcore with a heavy weight. Add extra hardcore if needed and consolidate it well.

3. Place a length of timber alongside the area and bring its top edge flush with the concrete surface. Drive stakes into the ground, or use bricks, to hold the formwork solidly.

4. Brush pva adhesive along the exposed edges of the concrete.

5. Mix up a batch of concrete using one part cement; five parts ballast (mixed aggregate) and add some pva adhesive to the mix to improve adhesion.

6. Press the mix well down into the side of the formwork, gradually building up to the surface level, finishing off with a float.

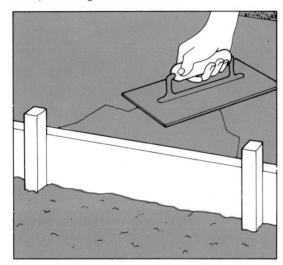

7. Allow a week before removing the formwork.

Depressions
Depressions are caused either by subsidence or by not levelling off the concrete when laying it. They are a nuisance because they allow puddles to form. A depression less than about 12 mm (½ in) deep cannot be filled successfully. The solution is to break up that part of the surface, consolidate the hardcore (adding more if needed) and refill the area with new concrete. Level this off with the surrounding surface using a timber straight-edge. Include pva adhesive in the repair as described above for cracks. A deep depression can be filled as follows.

1. Brush pva adhesive over the area.

2. Mix up one part cement; three parts sand (adding pva adhesive to the mix).

3. Spread the mix into the depression and level off with a float.

Paving slabs
Slabs can sink, start to rock or get cracked. Sometimes it is possible to lift a slab completely after chipping away the pointing around it. A cracked slab can be broken into smaller pieces

using a club hammer before removing it.

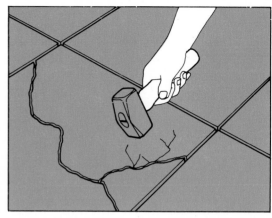

1. Mix up bedding mortar of one part cement; five parts sand.

2. Spread it in five dabs or in the band method described on page 60.

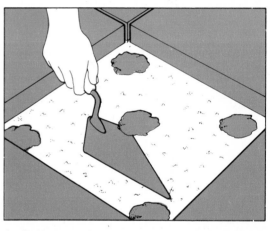

3. Re-lay the old slab (or a matching new one) and gradually tap it down with the shaft of a club hammer until it is level with surrounding slabs. Lay a spirit level across it to check it is level.

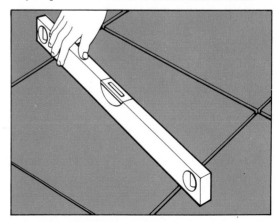

4. Repoint the joints to match the original.

Broken bricks

1. Remove the broken brick and chip out any old mortar.

2. Mix up a small amount of new mortar and spread this in the gap.

3. Lay the new brick. If it will not tap down far enough then remove it and skim off some mortar. If it sinks too far, add more mortar.

4. Tap down the brick again and check with a straight-edge that it is level with surrounding bricks. A concrete block is usually laid on sand, so it should be re-laid the same way.

Asphalt

The most common problem with asphalt is that depressions form in the surface, causing puddles to form in wet weather.

1. Cut out the depression using a bolster chisel and club hammer to leave a square patch.

2. If it lies alongside an edge, set up a piece of timber to act as formwork.

3. Fill the area with macadam slightly above the surrounding surface.

4. Compact with a roller. If the edge is being treated then remove the formwork after about 24 hours.

Repairing an asphalt drive

If an asphalt drive is being resurfaced, depressions can be filled with cold macadam. Sweep the area clean before starting.

1. The surface should be dry. If necessary cover it with polythene (polyethylene) for 12 hours beforehand and choose a day when rain is not likely. Roll the drum of tar paint for a few minutes to ensure thorough mixing, then pour some into a watering can for application.

2. On a hard surface the emulsion can be poured from the can and spread with a broom. On a loose surface, tie a dessert spoon beneath the spout of the can to act as a baffle.

3. Pour the emulsion to leave a film about 3 mm ($\frac{1}{16}$ in) thick. Avoid puddles forming or the film being too thin. Cover a section of about 5 metres square (5 yards square).

4. Use a shovel to sprinkle the chippings over the emulsion immediately a section is completed. The chippings should cover the surface in a single layer.

5. After completing two or three sections, use a garden roller to compact the chippings. When the area is finished give a final complete rolling.

15.Pergolas and trellises

A pergola or trellis can provide delicate shade over a patio, a leafy walkway through the garden, or an effective screen, especially when covered with climbing plants. You do not have to be a proficient carpenter to make even the most ornate structure, and you will find that there is a vast number of materials which you can use to create an array of designs.

You must be careful that your pergola or trellis does not look contrived or pretentious. A traditional rustic or sawn timber pergola that links one part of the garden to another, for example, or which leads to a focal point, such as a statue, or garden ornament, can help to unite various elements of the garden. If the garden is not large enough to make a long walkway, a rustic arch can be just as effective – perhaps at the side of the house where a narrow side garden or passage leads into a larger back garden. The height of the building will prevent the pergola from appearing as if it is sticking up incongruously into the air, and plants and creepers will soften its appearance.

Both trellises and rustic structures can also be used to screen off less attractive parts of the garden, such as the compost heap or dustbins, or to obscure a poor view.

The patio may be improved by the addition of a pergola, providing shade for eating under. Overhead beams of trelliswork supported on timber, or brick, or scaffold pillars can be used to enclose the patio, making more of an outside room. Be cautious about covering the top with glass or corrugated plastic roofing sheets – dirt and leaves are likely to collect on the top (which could be awkward to clean), and during heavy rain it can be very noisy.

As the picture on page 147 shows, a trellis is also useful in raising the height of a boundary fence without blocking out too much light or causing shadows.

Whether you want a rustic pergola or a sawn timber structure depends on how it will fit into your garden. In the formal setting of a patio, for example, sawn timber is usually more in keeping; in a rose garden, the natural look of timber is likely to be more suitable. Both are relatively easy to work with, as all the joints you can use are fairly basic, but you can get away with less precision if you use rustic poles.

An oriental-inspired *pergola attached to the side of a low house makes the ideal space for sitting out in comfort. The structure is formed with stout black-stained posts and bevelled cross timbers; bright yellow blinds can be drawn between the roof beams when shade is required. A profusion of plants make the pergola – although vivid in appearance – blend in perfectly with its surroundings*

Designing a pergola

A basic pergola

Here is a simple design to make, with no difficult carpentry. Screw the side beams to the uprights down through the halving joint (see below), then fix the cross-member with the other half of the joint. To reduce the amount of timber used, the uprights can be placed at every second cross-member without it looking too sparse or weakening the structure.

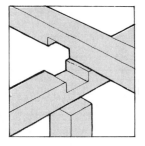

The side beams are screwed into the ends of the uprights, down through the halving joints that connect them to the cross pieces

Oriental pergola

In the right setting, a simple but strongly made pergola painted white can give the garden an oriental look, especially if the beams are bevelled at the ends. If you want a pergola that does not look as though it leads somewhere, make it bold, simple and upright.

The top, bevelled, beams are notched onto matching side beams, which in turn are notched onto the ends of stout uprights. This type of structure makes an ideal focal point in the garden.

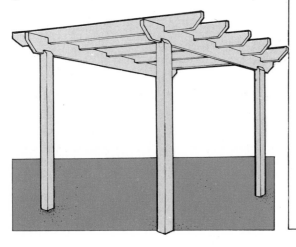

A pergola need not lead anywhere: this oriental-style structure serves as a shady bower for sitting out in the heat of the day, when trailed with climbers

Sinking a post

The upright posts, which support the pergola, must be firmly secured in the ground. Dig a hole – using a post hole borer, which you can hire – and fill the base with well-rammed hardcore to ensure a firm surface and proper drainage. Wedge bricks round the post to make sure it's held securely, then fill in around it with concrete. As with any outdoor timber, the posts must be thoroughly treated with preservative before they are used

timber post should be about 100 mm (4 in) square

concrete formed into bevel at top for drainage

well-rammed hardcore or broken brick pieces ensure good drainage

A stepped pergola
Pergolas do not have to lead in a straight line. If you have the space, a stepped pergola can be much more interesting.

Metal supports
Against a modern home, metal scaffold poles do not look amiss for the upright supports. Once covered with climbers they can be very effective. Paint the poles black or white to suit the design.

Brick supports
Brick pillars look impressive whether they are used for a freestanding pergola or for one against the wall of a house.

A pergola against a house wall
A wooden pergola against the house, such as the one featured on the previous page, can be used to link a patio with the home. The rafters have to be substantial to look in proportion with the building. The outer cross rails must be securely fixed to stout uprights and the whole pergola attached to a sturdy wall plate.

Rustic pergolas
Rustic pergolas are popular in rose gardens and gardens in a traditional setting. Because the joints are not as firm as on most sawn-timber structures, make sure the poles are substantial. A typical design is shown below.

A rustic pergola offers the opportunity for an adventurous design

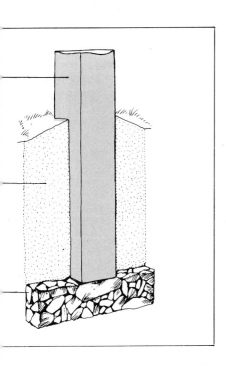

Constructing a pergola

A rustic pergola

Whether you make a pergola or just an arch, the construction principles are the same. In either case it pays to work out the design carefully beforehand, so you will know how much timber will be needed.

You can use some of the designs on the previous two pages as a starting point, and modify them to suit your own needs. Do not be tempted to make the structure too fussy; it may be better to use a few poles that are really stout than lots of thin, less substantial pieces. You can join the poles together by simply nailing through them but, for really tough fixings, cut notches in one or both pieces to be joined, slot them together and reinforce with nails.

A good garden centre or a fencing company are the most likely places to stock a good range of rustic poles.

It is always best to go along yourself to choose the wood that you want – even though you'll probably have to have it delivered because of the long length of some pieces.

The uprights will have to be set into concrete to give the structure rigidity. Allow about one 40 kg (88 lb) bag of dry-mixed coarse concrete for each upright.

You will need some poles at least 2.4 m (8 ft) long for uprights. Even this will only give about 1.8 m (6 ft) of clearance with the base driven into the ground: not really adequate if you plan to cover the structure with climbing plants because you would probably have to stoop to walk through. Try to allow at least another 600 mm (2 ft) for clearance.

Construction

1. Treat the ends of the uprights that will be set in the ground with a wood preservative such as creosote. Because the bark will prevent sufficient preservative being absorbed, strip it off the section that will be in the ground. Make sure the timber is dry before treating. Although you can just paint on the preservative you will achieve greater saturation if you stand the poles in containers of preservative for up to a week, brushing them with the liquid periodically.

2. Once treated, lay out all the pieces on the ground and examine them carefully in relation to your plan. If you cut them before you have chosen the best pieces for each part you may run into difficulties later.

3. Plan the actual assembly carefully. Even with a helping pair of hands, you will find it difficult to make the main joints once part of the pergola is erected. You can, however, assemble any small sections on the ground first, then fix these to the framework while someone supports it.

4. Make sure the uprights are well anchored. If you are only making an arch, you may be able to assemble the whole arch, then position it for concreting-in. You will find it easiest to use a post-hole borer (which can be hired) to make the holes, but if you only have one or two holes to make you will probably manage with a spade.

5. Rest the base of the supporting poles on a piece of broken brick, then wedge bricks or rubble around the base. Check with a spirit level to make sure that each post is upright. This may be difficult with a particularly uneven rustic pole, but you can simply judge by eye.

6. Cut the pieces for the sides and top to length allowing for any joints. Do not cut them all until you know how well the first ones fit. The main joints are shown here in the illustrations. Cut notches by sawing down to the required depth and remove the waste using a chisel. Sloping struts that have to be sawn at an angle might have to be cut by trial and error. Hold the piece into position first, mark the cut line, then saw it. Check that the angle is right and, if it is, mark and repeat for the other end.

7. Nail the joints, using galvanized nails and a claw hammer – useful for withdrawing nails that bend. Get someone to hold a club hammer at the other side of the joint so you have firm resistance as the nail is driven home.

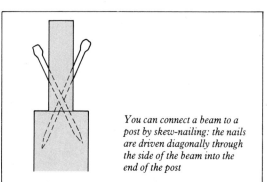

You can connect a beam to a post by skew-nailing: the nails are driven diagonally through the side of the beam into the end of the post

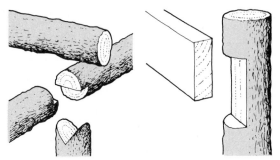

Fix cross rails to the ends of uprights by cutting out half the thickness of the rail with a saw and chisel, then slot it onto the end of the post. Nail or screw through into the end of the post

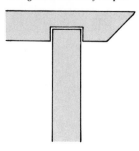

Connect two rails with cross-halving joints: cut matching notches in the timber half its thickness and piece them together to restore the original measurement. Fix with glue and screws

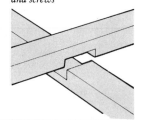

Butt up two rails over a post by cutting notches in their ends to hook over the post. Nail or screw through the rails into the post

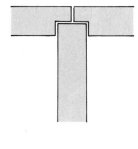

Far left: rustic joints can be made by notching the ends of two posts to connect them end to end; 'birdsmouth' a post and rest the rail on top. You could also fit a third rail between the two rails. Skew-nail all pieces to the post and to each other. Left: join sawn softwood rails to a rustic pole by cutting a notch in its side to take the square-section timber

A sawn-timber pergola

You can buy a sawn-timber pergola in kit form from some garden centres, but it is not difficult to make one yourself to your own design. The key to a sawn-timber pergola is to retain simplicity of outline.

Start by carefully measuring how much wood you will need. The supports could be brick, but this makes it a more ambitious project. A freestanding pergola usually looks effective with wood supports, although scaffold poles can also be used where the other end of the horizontal joists are fixed to the wall of a building. Timber posts should be at least 100 mm (4 in) square.

For a light structure overhead beams 150 mm × 50 mm (6 in × 2 in) should be adequate; for a stronger structure, perhaps adjoining the house, you would be wise to use 225 mm × 50 mm (9 in × 2 in) timber.

Buying timber

Any good timber yard should stock suitable wood, and some d-i-y shops have stocks of sawn timber, although probably not in very long lengths. Bear in mind that you are unlikely to be able to carry home very long lengths of timber in the car, so make sure that deliveries are made to your area.

Western red cedar is a good choice and could last for about 20 years without preservative treatment. Redwood (also called red or yellow deal) can also be used, if treated. Whitewood, also called white deal, is less satisfactory in the garden because it does not take up the preservative so well.

You may prefer to use metal scaffold poles for the uprights, and you should try a large builder's supplier; if they cannot supply them they will probably tell you where you can get them in your area.

Fixings and brackets

For fixing rafters to a house wall you will need metal joist hangers, which are used in house construction. These are normally stocked by builder's suppliers.

You would also be wise to buy a selection of metal T-braces, L-brackets and dowels for connecting and reinforcing joints; they should be stocked by a good d-i-y store. Use brass screws or galvanized nails where necessary to prevent rusting.

Because you are likely to plant climbers against the posts, use a solvent- or water-based preservative. Solvent-based preservatives may be harmful to plants when wet, but they are safe when dry. Always check the label before you buy to make sure it is suitable.

Constructing the pergola

1. Treat the timber with preservative (you do not need to treat Western red cedar). Do this beforehand so that all areas are thoroughly treated, especially the part that is to be set within the ground.

2. Insert the posts as described for rustic poles, and use a spirit level to ensure they are set upright. Use halving joints, as shown opposite and reinforce with galvanized nails.

3. Treat any sawn edges – including the inside faces of the joints – with preservative. Scaffold poles should be sunk at least 1 metre (3 ft 3 in) into the ground.

4. If you are fixing one side of the pergola to a building, the exact height will be influenced by the position of the joist hangers: these must be fixed into a mortar joint between courses of bricks. To fit a hanger, remove sufficient mortar with a cold chisel and club hammer, and mortar the hanger into place. Slot in the ends of the rafters.

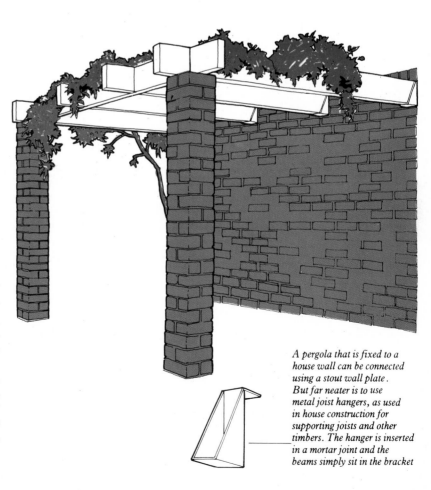

A pergola that is fixed to a house wall can be connected using a stout wall plate. But far neater is to use metal joist hangers, as used in house construction for supporting joists and other timbers. The hanger is inserted in a mortar joint and the beams simply sit in the bracket

Screening with trelliswork

Making a trellis

Whether you are making a trellis to add height to an existing fence, to provide a screen for a patio or some other, perhaps less attractive, part of the garden, or to fix to a wall so that climbers can take hold, the basic principles are the same.

Western red cedar is a sensible choice because it has a natural rot resistance, but in the UK 'deal' is more readily available and cheaper. Choose yellow deal (also called redwood) not white deal (also known as whitewood), as the former can be treated more effectively for outdoor use. Always use a suitable wood preservative that will not harm plants, unless the trellis is intended simply to extend the height of a fence and not as a support for plants.

The dimensions of the wood will be influenced by the size and scale of your trellis, but 50 mm × 50 mm (2 in × 2 in) timber is suitable in most cases. If you think that this looks too thick and 'chunky' for laths spaced quite closely together, reduce it to 50 mm × 25 mm (2 in × 1 in) or even 25 mm × 25 mm (1 in × 1 in).

Always sketch out the trellis on squared paper first and calculate how much wood you will need. The main design option you will be faced with is whether to opt for a square or diamond pattern. You will find the square pattern easier to assemble and if the strips are quite widely spaced (say 300 mm/1 ft) it will not look too overpowering.

If you are fixing the trellis above a fence, the most practical and firm way of fixing it is to run the support posts behind the fence posts. If these run the height of the old fence plus the new trellis you can bolt them to the old fence posts and nail the trellis to these. Timber 100 mm × 50 mm (4 in × 2 in) should be adequate for these supports.

You will also need timber of this size for the ends and top if you make a freestanding trellis.

For a wall trellis, fix 50 mm × 50 mm (2 in × 2 in) vertical supports to the wall about 1.5 m (5 ft) apart, and screw the assembled trellis to these with zinc-plated screws.

Buying materials

Any good d-i-y shop or timber merchant will be able to supply suitable timber; d-i-y and hardware shops will sell the coach bolts you will need to fix the supports to the old fence posts. Remember that you will need galvanized nails and zinc-plated woodscrews. If you are fixing into a wall, you will also need wallplugs.

Construction

When you come to make your trellis, it is best to assemble it on the ground and erect it where you want it in one piece.

1. Lay out the horizontal laths and position the vertical pieces on top; 300 mm (1 ft) intervals is about right for a fence extension, but 600 mm (2 ft) may be better for a wall trellis.

2. Where the pieces intersect fix with a single galvanized nail. Measure the diagonals periodically to check that they are equal (and the trellis therefore square).

3. Before fixing the trellis to its support, apply a wood preservative which is safe for plants (avoid creosote).

4. If you are fixing the trellis to a wall, drill holes to take the vertical supports at about 1.5 m (5 ft) intervals, using a masonry drill. Make sure the exact spacing matches the position of the vertical pieces on the trellis. Plug the wall and fix the supports with zinc-plated screws. Use a spirit level to ensure that the battens are vertical. Then fix the trellis using zinc-plated screws.

Trellises can transform *a corner of your garden into an area lush with foliage. Here a latticework arrangement fixed to a high garden wall provides a base for a climbing plant, while a matching trellis on the adjacent angle retains a thickly-grown section and screens the area from being overlooked*

To make a decorative fence extension

The fence extension illustrated combines a simple, nailed trellis of 25 mm × 25 mm (1 in × 1 in) timber with a decorative fretwork panel over the gate, linked by a plain timber beam.

1. Lay the horizontal trellis bars, cut to length, on a firm, flat surface, about 125 mm (5 in) apart, and parallel.

2. Cut the vertical pieces to length and lay on top, spaced about 125 mm (5 in) apart. Mark the position of the two verticals at each end.

3. Nail on the end pieces, using galvanized nails, and check that the section is square. Check that the remaining pieces are evenly spaced, then make a pencil mark where each is to go. Nail them into position.

4. Measure the distance between the gate posts, and make the frame to go over the gate. You will probably have to cut sections for the hinge and latch. Shape the ends of the cross-piece to make it look more attractive. Bolt this section to the gate posts.

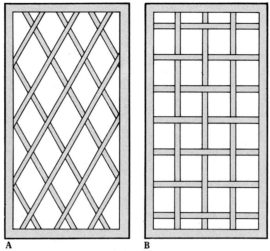
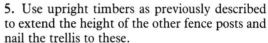
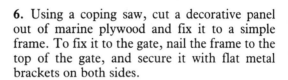
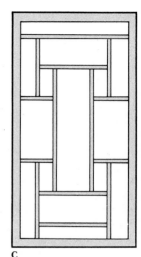

A B C

5. Use upright timbers as previously described to extend the height of the other fence posts and nail the trellis to these.

6. Using a coping saw, cut a decorative panel out of marine plywood and fix it to a simple frame. To fix it to the gate, nail the frame to the top of the gate, and secure it with flat metal brackets on both sides.

Three designs for a decorative trellis extension to a fence: diagonal (A); basketweave (B); and geometric (C). You can alter the size of the square, rectangle and diamond shapes simply by spacing out the bars, or closing them together. Each allows plants to entwine around them, creating a semi-solid screen

Use one of the trelliswork designs shown above to create a screen on top of an existing fence, for privacy, or simply as a means of training climbing plants for a delicate cover. Bolt the trelliswork frame onto the fence post for a really rigid fixing. Add a decorative touch by making a fretwork arch above the gateway, cut from marine plywood and fixed to a slim frame. You can cut any design you like

16.Sloping gardens

A sloping garden can be a handicap or an asset: much depends on how steep the site is and how good access between levels is.

Although it can be more difficult to work on, a sloping garden gives much more scope for landscaping than a flat site, where you might expend considerable effort simply to create even a small change of level to add interest.

With care you can transform even the steepest slope into a split-level scheme by digging out areas to create flat terraces, or by lessening its overall height. Plan your garden so that you have to move as little earth as possible. By removing just a little earth in one part and adding it to another, for instance, you may be able to achieve a sufficiently large level area for planting out,

then make small steps up to the next level (see pages 151 to 157). Provided the slope is not too steep, a lawn and borders built on an incline can be quite effective, so do not feel that you have to achieve exact levels. What is important is access with garden equipment such as the lawnmower and wheelbarrow.

If you have a really steep slope you may be able to cut out shallow terraces (effective if you have plants cascading over the edge of each terrace), or simply leave the shape of the ground as it is and plant a suitable ground cover.

On page 150 we tell you how you can level or terrace a slope, and on page 151 there is practical advice on constructing steps, with exciting ideas for making them look interesting.

Below: *The crest of this sloping garden has been planted out with lush and colourful plants, and the area outlined with small stone blocks – a theme that is carried through in other features in the plot*

Right: *A steeply sloping site has been styled to resemble a natural hillock, with plantings of trees and bushy shrubs and an irregularly shaped pond for visual interest*

Levelling a slope

If the slope is gradual you may be able to lay a small course of bricks or stones as a transition from one level to another. If you prefer something softer, try creating a small bank and cover it with plants.

The drawings on this page show you how to calculate the fall of your land, level it by cutting and filling, and terrace it when the fall is just too great to level.

If you make a terrace you will need steps to link the levels.

Calculating the fall of your slope

It is useful to calculate the fall of your slope before you decide on the area to be levelled. You will need a long, straight-edged length of wood and a spirit level. Place the spirit level on top of the straight-edge, then place one end of the straight-edge at the top of the slope (A). Drive a peg into the ground below the opposite end of the straight-edge (B) until the spirit level registers horizontal. Measure the distance from the bottom of the straight-edge to ground level (C) and make a note of it.

Move the other end of the straight-edge to the peg position, resting on the ground, then repeat the operation again (D). When you reach the bottom of the slope, add the figures together to give you the total fall of the land (E).

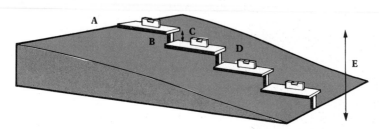

Cutting and filling

1. The 'cut-and-fill' method of levelling allows you to move the minimum amount of earth. First remove the topsoil from the whole area so thats it does not become buried. Place it nearby but not on the part to be levelled.

2. Sink a peg to ground level in the centre of the fall (which you will have worked out from your previous calculations: see above). Using a spirit level on a straight-edge, fix pegs to the lowest point of the area that you are levelling.

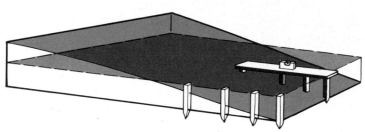

3. Gradually remove soil from the higher level and deposit it at the lower level. As you cut far enough into the slope, use the straight-edge and spirit level to check that you are removing the right amount.

4. Finally, firm the filled part to remove large voids, then return the topsoil. Rake this level.

Making a terrace

On a steep slope you will have to make a terrace. It will be more attractive to look at, and stronger if you make several smaller steps rather than one big one. It also provides more space for planting. You will need a retaining wall at each terrace to hold back the earth: this must be made firmly on proper foundations (see pages 94 to 106 for details of building walls).

It may be necessary to brace the bank while you make the foundations. Use a concrete mix of one part cement to four parts ballast (aggregate) and 'special quality' bricks, ordinary quality that you know are suitable for garden walls, or concrete walling blocks.

Insert a damp-proof course (vapor barrier) in the wall and leave 'weep holes', or insert drainage pipes near the base to allow excess water to drain freely away.

It is worth placing a layer of heavy-gauge polythene (polyethylene) behind the wall to reduce the risk of efflorescence forming. A layer of gravel at the bottom, behind the wall, will also help drainage. Fill the gap behind the soil.

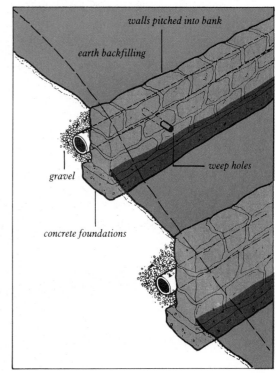

walls pitched into bank

earth backfilling

weep holes

gravel

concrete foundations

Designing garden steps

Steps are not only a means of access between levels in a sloping or terraced garden, they can also be an important part of the overall scheme, linking otherwise neglected areas or dividing two distinct parts, such as a raised lawn and a vegetable patch. There are basically two types of step construction: cut into a bank or slope, or freestanding, linking one flat area with another on a higher level.

Types of steps

Steps that are to receive regular use by everyone must be safe in all weather and strongly built. Bricks, paving slabs or cast concrete are good choices for solid, rigid steps. You could even use bricks for the risers (the height of the step) and paving slabs for the treads (the part you walk on), although there are many other combinations of materials you could choose.

It is important that your choice should reflect the design of the rest of the garden, and the house itself. If it is an old cottage, bricks will almost certainly look better than concrete; in a

A set of broad steps in bricks used on edge makes a steep bank seem much shallower. The patio at the top is in the same materials for uniformity. The angularity of the flight is softened by the inclusion of a mass of bushy, closely knitted plants

modern setting, however, coloured paving slabs may look better than old, weathered bricks.

If you do use bricks, choose them carefully. Not only can colour be important but also the type of brick, too. Engineering bricks, though tough and frost-resistant, may be too slippery underfoot. Flettons (the type often used for houses) and many other 'ordinary quality' bricks may be unsuitable because they will crumble with repeated wetting and freezing.

If the steps are to be near the house, it may be worth trying to match the bricks used in the house.

Steps leading to a patio will look better if they match the paving material used there. Paving slabs, for instance, are a good choice for the treads and if decorative walling blocks have been used on the patio, you may be able to use them to form the risers of the steps, too, for greater unity in design.

Where the steps are not a vital means of access to the house, garage or shed, for example, you have much more scope for imaginative design.

Timber steps give a mellow, natural look to an informal garden and, if well treated with wood preservative, can have quite a long life, despite being exposed to the weather. Wooden railway sleepers (ties) are sometimes available from specialist suppliers and you can use these to make substantial steps. They are quite laborious to cut so you would be wise to use them full length for wide, shallow flights. For a narrow, one person path, however, you can build 'stepping-stone' steps of sawn logs set end-on in the ground; you could even construct an outdoor wooden staircase with wooden treads, although this has to have just the right setting if it is not to look incongruous.

Step dimensions

Indoor steps are often steep because of the limited space available, but outdoors they should be much more shallow – it makes them easier to climb and looks much more in keeping with the scale of a garden. Of course, if the slope is very steep you will probably have to make your steps fairly steep, too; but usually it is possible to keep within the following limits.

Try to keep risers less than 180 mm (7 in) high; if they are less than 100 mm (4 in) they will be irritatingly shallow and potentially hazardous: you are likely to trip on them.

The tread should be in proportion to the riser, but at least 300 mm (1 ft) deep. For a riser as shallow as 100 mm (4 in), 450 mm (1 ft 6 in) is more appropriate for the tread.

A route that is likely to have two or more people walking abreast should have steps at least

1.5 m (4 ft 6 in) wide. Ambling paths and steps, which wind from one part of the garden to another, are the exception: they can be narrower as it does not matter if they have to be taken single-file. Nevertheless, these steps – and other small flights – still ought to be 1 m (3 ft 3 in) wide for comfort.

Basic requirements

• Paving slabs and bricks can make an attractive combination, especially for a short flight of steps linking the patio with a higher level. If you bring the steps down to a lawn, make sure there is a narrow strip of paving to make it easier to mow to the edge.

• To prevent gravel washing down a slope, logs can be used to form irregular steps. This technique is useful for a natural-looking path that does not have to be used regularly.

• Sawn-log steps can add interest to many parts of the garden, but are especially useful in woodland or a wild part of the garden, where they will not look out of place.

• Adding a curve to the bottom tread often improves what would otherwise be an ordinary flight of steps. Because paving slabs are difficult to cut to a curved shape, you will need to choose special-shaped slabs moulded with the right curve, or use paving blocks or bricks that you can lay more easily to this profile.

• Steps do not have to go straight up or down a slope – an interesting way to gain access to the next terrace is to have the steps running across the incline.

• You can make a more impressive feature of a short flight of steps by cutting them deeply into the slope and building a banking wall of bricks or walling blocks at the sides; here you must include provision for drainage from the wall.

• For a change of texture, even brick and timber can be combined. You must, however, use a rot-resistant wood and make sure it is well treated with wood preservative.

• Brick steps can look formal, but are very practical and are a sensible choice if paving slab treads are not suitable.

• Broken paving slabs are usually cheap to buy. Provided the individual pieces are securely bedded on mortar, this type of paving makes an interesting flight of steps.

• On slopes that are used infrequently, even grass treads are possible, but bear in mind the problem you will have when mowing.

• Steps that turn a corner are always more interesting than those built in a straight line. Make the turn generous so that it becomes a 'landing'. Gravel can be used to make a feature of the turn.

Above: *Railway sleepers (ties) used to form the risers of this flight of steps, also retain deep treads, which are topped with small stone blocks for contrast*
Left: *Large sawn-log rounds make up an informal flight in a steep bank*
Top right: *Split stone slabs and irregularly shaped stone block risers make a natural-looking flight of steps that blends in well in this 'wild' garden*
Right: *Large stone blocks set in a steep bank have been used to link two levels of the garden with a series of stepping-stones*
Far right: *Formal steps suit a neat, orderly plot; here, a focal point has been created with a curving centrepiece in a shallow flight. Stone slabs form the treads; layers of tile and stone make up the risers*

Building concrete steps

When planning your steps, use the following basic formula to ensure that they will be comfortable to climb. First, choose the height of rise you require (150 mm/6 in is the maximum for comfortable outdoor use) and then apply this rule to find the correct depth for the tread:
— twice the height of the rise, plus the depth of the tread, must equal 660 mm (26 in)

For example: (Riser × 2) + depth of tread = 660 *mm*
In this case it has been decided that the height of the riser will be 150 mm (6 in)
(150 × 2) + tread = 660
300 + tread = 660
660 − 300 = 360

Therefore the depth of the tread for a riser of 150 mm (6 in) should be 360 mm (14 in)

Tread

Riser

Riser (150 mm/6 in)

Although concrete is invaluable in the gardens as foundations for freestanding steps and other garden structures, it can also be used in its own right; a cast concrete flight of steps, although it can take some time to weather-in, can make one of the toughest, most durable structures where there is likely to be a lot of heavy use.

What you will need

Concrete must be cast in 'formwork', which moulds and retains the wet mix while it sets. For this you will need wide planks (such as scaffold boards) for the side 'shuttering' and lengths of 50 mm × 25 mm (2 in × 1 in) softwood for the pegs to hold it in place. You will also need lengths of softwood cut to the size of the risers.

For the concrete, use a mix of one part cement to four parts ballast (aggregate). To calculate how much you will need, multiply the dimensions of one step (length × breadth × depth), and then multiply by the number of steps.

Making the steps

1. Dig out the slope to the rough shape of the flight, allowing 50 mm (2 in) beneath the level of each tread, except for the lowest one. This is to allow the concrete to seep through to form a continuous run of concrete through the flight. Position the shuttering at each side.

2. Fix the riser board shuttering in position accurately. Use a straight-edged length of wood with a spirit level on top to ensure that the top of each riser is level with the bottom of the riser above. Nail the riser boards in position through the side shutters.

3. Shovel concrete behind each riser board and use a stout length of timber or a shovel to work the concrete into place, dispelling any air bubbles. Compact the mix further by chopping across the surface with the length of timber.

4. Leave a fairly rough surface for a non-slip finish, but if you want a smoother finish, use a steel trowel when the concrete has started to set. Remove the shuttering after four or five days and if necessary use a cement paste (cement and water) to smooth over any irregularities.

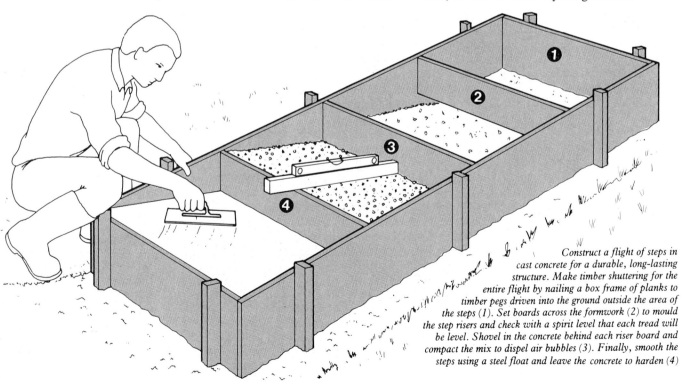

Construct a flight of steps in cast concrete for a durable, long-lasting structure. Make timber shuttering for the entire flight by nailing a box frame of planks to timber pegs driven into the ground outside the area of the steps (1). Set boards across the formwork (2) to mould the step risers and check with a spirit level that each tread will be level. Shovel in the concrete behind each riser board and compact the mix to dispel air bubbles (3). Finally, smooth the steps using a steel float and leave the concrete to harden (4)

Making steps with slabs

Paving-slab steps

If you are making steps using paving slabs as treads you will find it convenient to make the risers the depth of two bricks or blocks (plus the height of the slab and mortar joint). To save having to cut the slabs, it is best to make the steps the width of complete slabs, especially if the flight is to continue on from an existing path made from the same materials.

This type of flight is built by cutting out the shape in the bank and laying the slabs on earth or hardcore foundations.

What you will need

Order slabs of a size that will give you the right width (you may need two or three for each if they are wide steps). Bear in mind the depth of the tread, too – you should also allow a 25 mm (1 in) overhang or 'nosing' at the front to highlight the rise of the step and sufficient to go beneath the riser of the step above.

You will probably need a few bags of ready-mixed concrete for a foundation slab at the bottom step, to prevent the flight from slipping, and sufficient mortar to bed the slabs and bricks or blocks. If the ground is fairly soft, add a layer of hardcore beneath each tread.

Making cut-in steps

1. Start by excavating a shallow slope of the right angle for your steps, then use pegs and string to indicate where each step will fall. Remove the soil in steps that approximately match the size of the slabs, bearing in mind an allowance for the brick or block risers and the small overhang at the front.

2. If the ground is firm you may be able to lay the slabs on mortar directly over the earth, but if it is at all soft, add a layer of hardcore and ram it firm before laying the slabs.

3. To ensure that you start with a firm step, provide a concrete slab foundation over well-rammed hardcore beneath the first riser.

4. Lay the first tread and riser on mortar, at the foot of the flight, then level the ground carefully to take the next tread. If necessary use hardcore to firm the ground. Place the next slabs on top of the riser on a bed of mortar and use a spirit level to check levels in each direction – the tread should slope down towards the front slightly for drainage. Continue laying treads and risers as you work up the flight to the top.

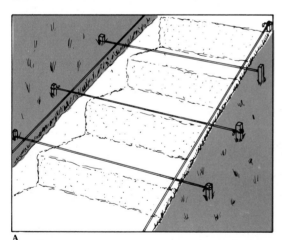

A

B

C

D

To make cut-in steps using slabs and concrete blocks, mark out the shape of the flight with strings and pegs then cut out the rough shape (A). Starting at the bottom, lay the first tread and the blocks for the first riser (B); back-fill with hardcore and tamp this down (C); lay the second slab tread on top of the riser (D)

Log and timber steps

Sawn-log steps can be an effective way to climb a fairly steep, narrow area, but they are not suitable for all-weather use. Large logs laid horizontally make a far more substantial flight of steps with, say, gravel between them as treads. But these are not easy to obtain unless you have a local supply. Old railway sleepers (ties) are sometimes available, and these can be used instead. They can be used like logs as risers and edge-retainers with gravel or earth for treads, although they can be slippery when wet.

Sawn-log steps

What you will need
Cedar is ideal because of its natural rot-resistance, but elm or other hardwood can also be used. First treat all timber with preservative.

If the ground is firm you may not need to bed the logs in concrete, but gravel and mortar will be useful to ensure that the logs are bedded firmly and level.

Laying the rounds
1. Sawn-log steps are bound to be narrow, so stagger them to make walking up them easier and to give an impression of greater width.

2. If the ground is firm, lay the first log at the foot of the slope, slightly buried for rigidity. Level the ground above, using a spirit level to check that the tread will be horizontal. If necessary, pack with compacted gravel and firm the next log on a bed of mortar. Ensure that the

edge of each log slightly overlaps the one beneath: this gives additional strength and highlights the 'ladder' effect.

Using railway sleepers (ties)
The simplest way of using railway sleepers is to make the steps full width, and to fill the 'tread' area with gravel. But they are heavy and manoeuvring them is not easy, even for two people. The timber, however, is hefty enough to keep itself in position provided you prepare firm, level earth in the first place.

1. Position the first sleeper then cut the earth away behind it to the point where you want to place the next sleeper. The size of the tread will be dictated by the steepness of the slope – the shallower the slope, the farther apart the sleepers can be. Remove the soil to a depth of about 50 mm (2 in) below the top of the first sleeper, making sure the base is level.

2. Position the second sleeper and fill the area between them with gravel.

As most sleepers are about 2.4 m (8 ft) long, there is plenty of room for plants at the sides to soften the edges.

3. Alternatively cut some of the timber, and reverse them, as shown, to form treads. This method takes up more sleepers, involves a lot of cutting and gives less flexibility for varying the tread to suit the slope.

Varying brick risers
You can alter the height of brick risers in the ways that you lay the individual modules. The standard brick (below right) can be set flat (A); on edge (B); or you can lay two bricks (C), giving risers of the heights shown

Logs can be used *to make an attractive, meandering flight of steps for a natural look in the garden. You can use them on end, cut into 'rounds', or laid across the flight, as shown above*

Making steps with bricks

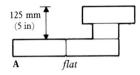

125 mm
(5 in)

A *flat*

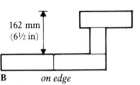

162 mm
(6½ in)

B *on edge*

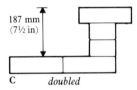

187 mm
(7½ in)

C *doubled*

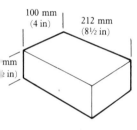

100 mm
(4 in)

212 mm
(8½ in)

mm
in)

You can use bricks to form both treads and risers in a flight of garden steps but they must be laid on a mortar base. The illustration on the left shows some of the permutations that you can use to vary the height of the treads using standard bricks.

Bricks also give you an opportunity to do something a little different, especially if there are just a few shallow steps. You could, for instance, make a feature of the steps by giving the first tread a gentle curve.

The only difficult part is cutting some bricks to shape. You may spoil a few in the process, so allow extra when you order.

Bricks and mortar

Always choose bricks that are frost-resistant. Buy a cement mortar mix suitable for laying paving (rather than the ordinary bricklaying mix). If you want to mix your own, use one part masonry cement to four parts sand.

You will need some concrete for a slab foundation below the first riser (use one part cement; two and a half parts sand; three and a half parts 20 mm/¾ in aggregate) and hardcore to pack behind subsequent steps.

Laying the steps

1. Excavate soil to an even slope, deep enough so that when the treads and risers are laid the steps will not stand proud of the surrounding ground.

2. Lay a concrete foundation for the first step, extending a little way beyond it. Once the foundation has set, lay the first complete straight row first (the one that will take the first riser) on mortar, then the cut bricks, followed by the radiating edge bricks.

3. To cut the bricks to shape, rest the brick on a bed of sand, then score the outline required with a bolster chisel and club hammer. Tap the chisel sharply on the scribed line to remove the waste part. Slight errors can be made good with the mortar. Lay the edge bricks in position loosely first; when they look right you can mortar them into place one by one.

4. Lay the bricks for the first riser, then add hardcore behind it. Level and compact the hardcore, but be careful not to displace the bricks. Spread a bed of mortar over the hardcore then lay the rows of bricks for the tread (three rows in this example), remembering the overlap for a nosing.

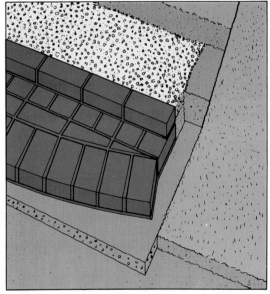

5. Repeat this operation as you work up the slope to the top of the flight. It is wise to work on just a few rows first and let those set before continuing with subsequent steps. Use a spirit level regularly as you work to check that the bricks are laid evenly, with a slight drainage fall to the front of the treads.

6. A flush mortar joint will look best on the steps. Simply clean off surplus mortar when it has started to set for a clean, neat finish.

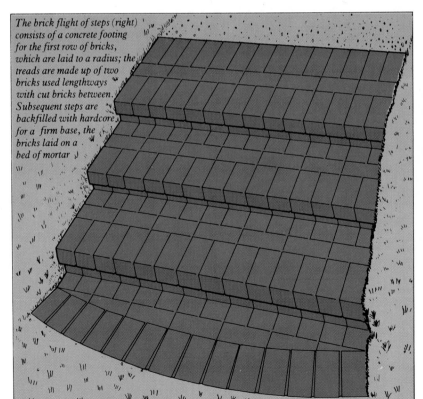

The brick flight of steps (right) consists of a concrete footing for the first row of bricks, which are laid to a radius; the treads are made up of two bricks used lengthways with cut bricks between. Subsequent steps are backfilled with hardcore for a firm base, the bricks laid on a bed of mortar

17. Garden buildings

The choice of garden buildings can be bewildering, especially if you have never owned one before. On the following pages you will find information on all the different types, along with their strengths and weaknesses, plus advice on where best to place them in the garden.

A general shed is the ideal storage for garden tools, the lawnmower and wheelbarrow, plus the usual household clutter – tins of paint, the kids' bicycles and other items too large to store indoors. If you have a fairly large site, a summer house will enable you to enjoy your garden as a place of recreation. Conservatories, too, extend living beyond the normal walls of the house and can add to the value of your property, while if you are a keen gardener, a greenhouse offers you the opportunity to get more from your garden.

The garden shed

The main types of shed are illustrated on pages 170 and 171, but you cannot always tell exactly what a particular model will be like purely from descriptions and illustrations in catalogues. Try to see as many sheds as you can at garden centres and shed manufacturers' showgrounds: the larger garden centres usually have a good range and may stock more than one maker's range.

The advantage of seeing erected buildings is that it enables you to judge quality better and may reveal irritating points that would not be obvious from an illustration in a brochure. If you are tall, for example, a roof cross-brace might be a hazard every time you enter the shed; if the walls are unlined and feebly constructed, moisture is likely to enter, and any tools you store inside will be susceptible to rusting.

When comparing prices, check whether delivery is included, if wall linings and floor and bearers are extra, whether the wood is treated with preservative or this treatment is charged as an extra (this could add more than 10 per cent to the price).

Few of us ever have enough storage space, so try to buy the biggest shed that you can afford and which will fit comfortably in your garden. A popular size is 2.4 m × 1.8 m (8 ft × 6 ft), or 2.1 m × 1.5 m (7 ft × 5 ft) in a small garden. If you want to use the shed as a workshop as well as store space, a 3 m × 2.4 m (10 ft × 8 ft) size is a better size to aim for.

Summerhouses

The same general advice about quality applies not only to sheds but also to summerhouses.

But there is another important consideration if you are buying a garden building to use as a summertime extension to the house: you have to like its appearance.

One of the most important points to bear in mind is a suitable site for a summerhouse. A shed can be tucked away in an inhospitable corner of the garden, but a summerhouse should command a good view and be in a fairly open area (not under the shade of trees, for instance).

Conservatories and greenhouses

Whether you decide on a lean-to or a freestanding greenhouse will depend on what you have space for, and what you want from your greenhouse. A conservatory combines many of the merits of a lean-to and a span greenhouse, with the bonus of elegance. The merits of the different types of greenhouse are discussed on pages 162 and 163.

Most modern greenhouses are made using an aluminium alloy framework, but you may prefer the more traditional appearance of a wooden structure. Glass is still used as the main glazing material, although acrylic sheets are sometimes used for the curved eaves in some designs. Even polythene (polyethylene) is used to clad a greenhouse and is a good choice if all you want is a cheap, productive but not particularly attractive structure in, say, the kitchen garden.

Size must reflect what you can afford, as well as the space you have available, but larger usually means better value. A greenhouse 1.8 m (6 ft) or 2.4 m (8 ft) wide and about 3 m (10 ft) long is a good size if this is your first greenhouse. But beware of the hidden costs when comparing greenhouse prices (see details on page 161).

Below: a summer house makes a cosy, relaxing place to sit on sunny days. Choose one with doors that can open fully and mount the building on suitable foundations to prevent dampness rising and rotting the floor. Lay a paved area in front of the house so you can sit out on your garden furniture

Laying a base

If you buy a greenhouse, the chances are it will not come with a base unless you buy it as an extra. But you must not skimp on this: the greenhouse must be anchored firmly. On firm ground and a sheltered site, you may be able to manage with the manufacturer's base alone, but elsewhere you should lay a concrete foundation, too.

Most garden sheds can be laid directly on firm ground on the timber bearers provided, but a concrete base may be specified for some – and it is the best way to ensure a firm, dry surface. Conservatories must have proper foundations for the side walls and a concrete base inside on which to lay paving slabs or tiles.

Making foundations
You will probably want to leave the greenhouse floor as soil, so that you can grow a crop in it. If your greenhouse has a brick base – or for any greenhouse on an exposed site – a proper foundation is necessary for the base.

Many aluminium greenhouses come with ground anchors, which you simply set in a hole dug in the ground, pour about a bucketful of concrete around and leave to set (after ensuring the framework is level).

The illustration on page 97 shows adequate foundations for a greenhouse, but be guided by the manufacturer's instructions for the exact dimensions required. If you want to get on with digging the trench before the greenhouse arrives, the manufacturer will be able to give you foundation dimensions in advance. Do not start the concreting until you know whether you have to concrete-in special anchors for the greenhouse.

A base for a shed
1. Remove 150 mm (6 in) of soil, then compact and level the base with a garden roller. Spread a 100 mm (4 in) layer of hardcore over this and compact it well using a sledge hammer or stout fence post.

2. Add a 25 mm (1 in) layer of sand then a sheet of thick, heavy-gauge polythene (polyethylene) on top as a damp-proof membrane (vapor barrier); the sand reduces the chance of it being punctured by the hardcore.

3. To provide a mould for the concrete, nail formwork of 75 mm × 25 mm (3 in × 1 in) timber to pegs driven into the ground at the perimeter of the slab; check that it is square by measuring the diagonals.

4. Use a concrete mix of one part cement; two parts sand; three parts 20 mm (¾ in) aggregate (or four parts combined aggregate). Tamp the concrete to make sure there are no air pockets and fill slightly proud of the formwork. Then use a long straight-edged board to level the concrete with a chopping followed by a sawing action across the slab.

5. Set any anchors or fixing bolts into the concrete before it sets, following the manufacturer's advice.

6. Finish the surface after about an hour by smoothing with a steel trowel. If the weather is frosty, protect it with layers of newspaper covered with polythene (polyethylene) – held down at the edges with bricks – for a few days; in hot weather cover with old sacking and spray with water to keep it damp for a few days. This prevents the concrete from cracking.

A base for a small shed
For a small shed, you may find it easier to lay a base of paving slabs instead of a concrete slab. On firm, level ground you should be able to lay the slabs direct, bedding them on a 'box-and-cross' of mortar made from one part ordinary cement; five parts concreting (sharp) sand. Leave 12 mm (½ in) joints and fill these after a few days with a stiff mortar mix.

A brick base for a greenhouse
If you choose a greenhouse that needs a brick base, it is vital that you check the dimensions carefully before you start work. If you make the base too small, or too large, the greenhouse will not fit.

Lay the bricks on strip foundations as described for bricklaying on pages 98 and 99. If you have not done any bricklaying before, this is a good starting job – as most brick bases are only two or three bricks high, you will soon see progress.

You will only need a wall one brick thick, laid in a straightforward 'stretcher' bond. You must, however, insert a damp-proof course to prevent dampness rising and affecting the structure of the greenhouse; especially important if you are mounting a timber-framed greenhouse on the brickwork. You can buy bituminous felt in rolls just the right width for the damp-proof course. Unroll it on top of the second layer of bricks, and lay the third course on top to provide an integral impervious layer.

A base for a conservatory
The same principles apply for a conservatory, but deeper footings will be necessary for a brick wall base. Consult the manufacturer for details of foundations for their buildings.

Buying a greenhouse or conservatory

Buying a greenhouse or a conservatory needs a lot more thought than buying a garden shed. The most important points to consider are your budget, the size and design of your garden and the appearance of the structure – even the type of plants that you want to grow should be taken into account.

Shape and style

Although many original and less common types are available (many are shown on pages 162 and 163), most greenhouses are the traditional 'span' design. Lean-to greenhouses are less popular, but are an ideal choice where you have limited space or want something close to the house. The difference between a lean-to and a conservatory is not great: some modern lean-to aluminium-framed greenhouses could be regarded as a conservatory if placed over French windows.

But be cautious if you are attracted to a lean-to because it seems a good idea to run an extra radiator off the central heating system to provide relatively inexpensive heating. Most of us set the heating to turn off at night, which is when the greenhouse is most likely to need heating.

Octagonal and dome-shaped greenhouses have drawbacks in practical terms (see page 163), but certainly look more striking than the traditional types if you prefer a decorative effect. A dome-shaped greenhouse, however, does have advantages on a windy, exposed site, because it offers less wind resistance.

Choosing materials

The great advantage of an aluminium alloy greenhouse is that it does not need painting. The metal may seem rather stark at first, but it does mellow eventually. The harshness of the aluminium is not a problem with some of the more expensive greenhouses that have been treated to give, say, a bronze finish.

If you simply do not like the look of aluminium greenhouses and prefer a traditional timber frame, cedar is a popular choice because it

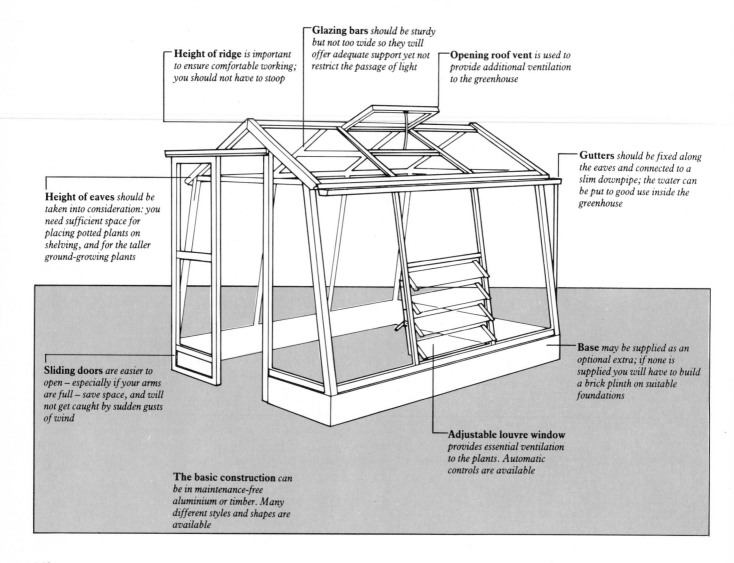

Height of ridge is important to ensure comfortable working; you should not have to stoop

Glazing bars should be sturdy but not too wide so they will offer adequate support yet not restrict the passage of light

Opening roof vent is used to provide additional ventilation to the greenhouse

Gutters should be fixed along the eaves and connected to a slim downpipe; the water can be put to good use inside the greenhouse

Height of eaves should be taken into consideration: you need sufficient space for placing potted plants on shelving, and for the taller ground-growing plants

Sliding doors are easier to open – especially if your arms are full – save space, and will not get caught by sudden gusts of wind

Base may be supplied as an optional extra; if none is supplied you will have to build a brick plinth on suitable foundations

Adjustable louvre window provides essential ventilation to the plants. Automatic controls are available

The basic construction can be in maintenance-free aluminium or timber. Many different styles and shapes are available

has a natural resistance to rot and does not warp easily. It can be left untreated, but its attractive dark colour will turn to a silvery grey; you will probably need to apply a cedar treatment every couple of years to prevent this. Cedar is also known as Western red cedar.

Deal is relatively cheap, but it will not last long unless you make sure it has been properly treated with a preservative and is well seasoned; you must also be prepared to paint it regularly. So long as you do this, the greenhouse should have a long life.

The costs

Be cautious when comparing costs. The prices of some greenhouses include a base, with others it is an extra charge. Some companies include delivery and erection by their own staff in the price, with others you may have to pay a delivery charge and erect the house yourself (or pay someone to do it for you).

Do not forget that you will need to budget for other extras such as shelving on which to stand pots and other containers (unless you are growing crops in the ground), and you will benefit from the addition of ventilators. If you can afford it, buy one or two automatic ventilator openers at the same time.

THE LEGAL ASPECTS

You are unlikely to require planning permission to erect a normal, freestanding greenhouse, but it is worth checking with your local authority before you order: some are stricter than others.

In the UK, lean-to greenhouses erected against the house, and conservatories, are likely to be subject to Building Regulations approval, which is intended to ensure that the structure is erected safely and correctly and that, when complete, it will meet certain requirements. Professionally designed structures, however, should meet the criteria of materials and construction specified by the regulations.

If the structure will bring the total area of extensions (including a garage) over a certain figure, you will need planning permission, too.

The local planning office will be able to advise you, and it is worth a telephone call or a letter if you are in any doubt.

If you are renting the land, if may be worth contacting the landlord; even if you are a freehold owner you would be wise to check the deeds in case there is a covenant that restricts what you want to do.

In the UK, a large freestanding greenhouse could become rateable, but it is most unlikely that a home greenhouse would fit into this category. A conservatory or lean-to built on to the house *could* increase your rates, but any increase is likely to be small. Again, it is worth a phone call or a letter to your local rating department.

Left: *Staging enables you to make use of the space inside your greenhouse to its fullest advantage. Typically it consists of metal 'scaffolding' or wooden trestles*
Above: *A paraffin heater makes an economical form of greenhouse heating*

Types of greenhouse

Barn or span roof greenhouses are most people's idea of a traditional greenhouse. It is the most convenient to work in, usually gives you adequate headroom and its high, vertical sides are useful for potted plants on shelving. If you want a brick base (which can help to reduce heat loss in winter), this is the most suitable freestanding type. It is a sensible choice for potted plants or as a 'mixed' greenhouse.

Dutch light greenhouses have sloping sides and a shallower roof angle. The theory is that the angle of the glass will mean that less valuable winter light is absorbed by the glass because the low winter sunshine will have the least thickness of glass to travel through. The panes of glass are usually large and you may consider this an inconvenience if they get broken.

This shape is useful for growing tomatoes and early crops, but for amateur use the benefits are likely to be marginal if you want a general-purpose greenhouse.

Lean-to greenhouses are useful if you have space on a south-facing wall and want your greenhouse convenient for the house. An easterly or westerly aspect can also be satisfactory, provided there is not too much shade. If you want to place it on a north wall, the range of

A typical Dutch light greenhouse (above) has sloping side walls and a low pitched roof – features which are intended to catch maximum useful light

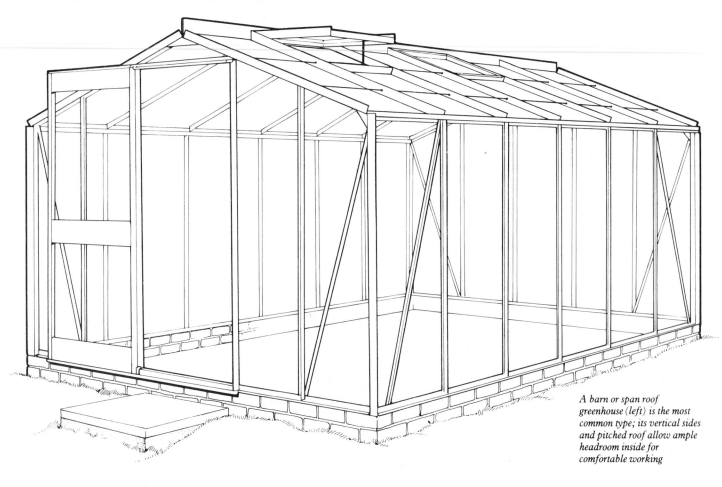

A barn or span roof greenhouse (left) is the most common type; its vertical sides and pitched roof allow ample headroom inside for comfortable working

plants that you can grow well will be reduced.

The house wall can be used for climbers, which can be more difficult to accommodate satisfactorily in a span greenhouse. A lean-to is economical to heat. Water, electricity, and even a gas supply should all be at hand.

Three-quarter-span greenhouses are uncommon, but useful if you want a little more space and scope than a lean-to. This type will give you room for a bench at the back if you want, and is a compromise between a lean-to and a span greenhouse.

Circular and dome-shaped greenhouses can be attractive if you want a garden feature, but they have practical drawbacks. You may find it difficult to make economical use of the unusual shapes, for example, and fittings such as shelving may have to be made specifically for the greenhouse: for traditional shapes you have a wide choice of equipment and accessories that you can buy from many manufacturers.

Curvilinear or mansard greenhouses are angled so that they catch more of the sun's rays (especially useful during the winter months). Not many manufacturers produce these, so you will not have as much choice as you would with a conventional barn type.

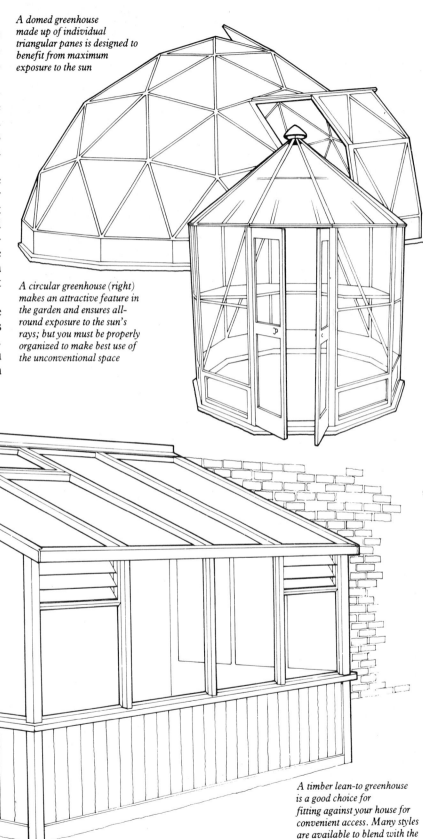

A domed greenhouse made up of individual triangular panes is designed to benefit from maximum exposure to the sun

A circular greenhouse (right) makes an attractive feature in the garden and ensures all-round exposure to the sun's rays; but you must be properly organized to make best use of the unconventional space

A timber lean-to greenhouse is a good choice for fitting against your house for convenient access. Many styles are available to blend with the rest of the building

163

Erecting a greenhouse

It is difficult to give specific advice on putting up a greenhouse: construction details vary considerably from make to make. So treat the following information only as general guidelines – not as a substitute for the manufacturer's instructions.

Timber-framed greenhouses are the easiest to put up as they usually come in sections that simply bolt together. Some have ready-glazed sections, others must be glazed afterwards.

Metal greenhouses usually come in lots of separate pieces that are more complex to fit together; the description here applies to these. If you are erecting a timber greenhouse, however, the same base preparation applies.

Preparing the site

Make sure the site is completely level, using datum pegs, a straight-edge and a spirit level. Insert the first peg so that the top is at the required finished level, then insert other pegs across the site, about 1 m (3 ft 3 in) apart, using the spirit level to ensure they are all at the same height. When the tops are all at the correct height, add or take away soil until the ground is level. Make sure it is well firmed.

Bases and foundations

If you want to make your own base, follow the advice on page 159; if you need to lay bricks over a foundation, check with the manufacturer's information for dimensions and general advice (you may have to insert bolts into the concrete or mortar, for instance).

You will, however, find it much easier to buy the manufacturer's base, which may be pre-cast concrete, steel, aluminium, or even strong plastic. A base supplied by the manufacturer can usually be anchored to the ground by pouring concrete around the ground anchors supplied.

Erecting an aluminium greenhouse

1. A metal greenhouse will probably arrive as a collection of pieces in boxes or bundles, with nuts, bolts and glazing strips.

Check that everything is included before you start assembly. Read the instructions carefully so you understand what you have to do.

2. If you are using the manufacturer's base, assemble it as the instructions advise. Make sure that it is absolutely square (measure across the diagonals, which should be the same). The pieces will bolt together quite simply. The base may have ground anchors, which are simply inserted into holes in the ground and concreted in. Alternatively you may be supplied with screws for fixing into a concrete base that has

Erecting an aluminium-framed greenhouse
Once you have identified all of the components of the greenhouse, start to assemble the wall sections. Piece together the end frame on the ground (A). Rig up the supplied base and mount the wall frames on it, securing the corners (B). The sections may be held together with special cast aluminium brackets (C); fit all the frame members to the wall sections (D). Rubber strips are fitted in the aluminium glazing bars (E) and the glass is slotted in and retained with metal clips (F). Fix the sliding door frame using the bolts provided (G) then hang the door from the top rail (H)

A

B

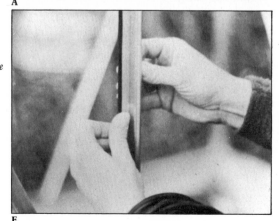

E

F

been drilled and plugged. You may be advised to do the anchoring once most of the greenhouse has been assembled.

3. Erect the sections in the sequence given in the instructions: usually sides, ends, and ventilators are assembled on the ground, then bolted into position. For many parts of the job you will need help. The actual bolting together is easy: a spanner (wrench) and screwdriver will probably be the only tools that you need; a spirit level will ensure that the sections are straight.

4. Glaze the greenhouse next. Do not leave it half glazed on a windy day, or panes may be blown out. Modern metal greenhouses usually use special glazing strips and clips instead of putty. These make fitting the precut panes straightforward, but remember to wear gloves for safety. Start by pressing the glazing strip firmly into the outer channels of the glazing sections. Cut off any surplus at the end of each bar. If the strip is not long enough, simply butt up another piece and carry on. Glaze the sides first and leave the roof until last. Insert the glass squarely between the glazing bars, leaving an equal space each side for the glazing clip.

5. Insert the spring wire glazing clip, pressing

the sides apart until it snaps into position. Use only two clips on each side of the pane, to reduce the risk of the glass cracking.

6. The upper panes of glass should overlap the lower ones by about 10 mm (⅜ in) and overlapping glazing clips are used for this. You may have to bend them to the right profile.

FINDING THE RIGHT SITE

The ideal site for a greenhouse is one where there is good light and shelter from cold winds.

Avoid overhanging or shady trees, especially evergreens. A lean-to is obviously going to be close to the house, but try to keep a freestanding type away from the shade of buildings.

On the other hand, do not tuck the greenhouse away out of sight at the end of the garden. The closer it is to the house the less expensive it will be to provide an electricity or water supply.

If you have an exposed site, you can always plant a hedge or screen as a windbreak, but make sure that it is not so close or tall that it casts too much shade.

The glazing bars of aluminium greenhouses are so thin that positioning the structure for best light is not as critical as it used to be with older wooden structures with thick bars. An east-west alignment is probably the most useful, especially if you are raising bedding plants, for instance, as it makes most use of the winter and spring sunshine.

Avoid hollow ground at the foot of slopes as these are often frost pockets.

C

D

G

H

Adding a conservatory

Conservatories are quite simply rather grand greenhouses, usually attached to the house and commonly furnished as a sun-room. Traditional brick and timber constructions are still available, although modern versions are now made in kit form for self-assembly.

Most of the old-style brick and timber conservatories are costly and are sometimes constructed – albeit from modules – to suit the particular site. They are not cheap, but you are likely to get a craftsmanlike structure, usually erected by the manufacturer or recommended craftsman. They will also provide the plans to lodge with the council for planning permission (necessary in the UK). For a fee, most companies will also take care of this legal side of construction for you.

Choose the right position

If you build your conservatory on the south side of the house, you may find that it will be too hot for comfort. You can use shading, of course, but it may be better to choose an aspect that receives a little more shade during the course of the day.

Erecting a conservatory

If you buy one of the modern aluminium-framed conservatories (really just more elegant lean-tos), erection is similar to a greenhouse. The major difference is the way it is fixed to the

Above: a modern, streamlined conservatory very much in keeping with the style of this chalet bungalow. The large glazed panels admit the maximum amount of sunlight

Right: a conservatory based on a traditional design, with a glazed sloping roof topped with decorative cresting

need careful foundations laid to a precise specification and may need a brick base. Even if the company erects the conservatory for you, they will charge a substantial extra fee if they have to lay the foundations, too. If you can do this part yourself it will reduce the cost, but it is false economy unless you work to the precise dimensions that the manufacturer will supply. Unless the manufacturer recommends otherwise, construct the base as described on page 159. If a brick base is required, follow the advice on pages 98 and 99.

Some suppliers will send a glazing specialist along after erection to do the glazing.

Fixing a conservatory to the house wall

A conservatory attached to a house must be adequately sealed against rainwater penetration at the back, where its roof connects with the wall, and down each side, where the frames meet the wall.

The exact details of how you connect the conservatory to the house walls varies according to the structure – if it has a flat, felted roof (see page 72) you will have to fit a flashing strip along the back wall, which is mortared between two courses of bricks to ensure a watertight seal; on a glass roof (see page 74) you will have to fit a wall plate and make a seal with special glass flashing strip.

The join between the conservatory walls and the house walls must also be protected against moisture penetration: frames – whether metal or wood – are fixed direct to the walls on smaller types and the gaps filled with flexible mastic (caulking compound); on larger conservatories the low brick side walls might be toothed into the house walls for an integral finish.

Above: An aluminium-framed conservatory with coloured finish is the ideal addition to any house, providing a sunroom for relaxing on hot days, a greenhouse, or a play area for the kids. They are easy to assemble on a pre-made base

house wall. Most conservatories of this type also have curved eaves, usually made of acrylic instead of glass. It will scratch, may crack, and holds condensation in a way that glass does not. It can, however, be replaced when it deteriorates, following the manufacturer's instructions for inserting new acrylic sheets.

Curved eaves means that you do not have to fit a rainwater gutter, although there may be a small channel above or below the curve of the eaves. A water butt would not look particularly attractive outside a conservatory, so it is wise to ensure that there is adequate drainage from the site, leading to a soakaway (see page 92).

If a conservatory is to look elegant and you want it to be part of the home, you must lay a proper base. Use the same principles as the base described on page 159, but finish with paving slabs or tiles; quarry tiles look particularly effective.

One of the tailor-made conservatories will

Below: Seal the gap between frame and wall with mastic (caulking compound)

Maintaining greenhouses and conservatories

If you have an old, neglected greenhouse or conservatory, perhaps in a garden that you have taken over, there may be a lot that you can do to repair the damage.

If your greenhouse is still in good condition, the maintenance tips below will help you to keep it that way.

The glass

Dirty glass looks unsightly. It also leads to poor plants, as good light, especially in winter, can be crucial for healthy growth. Keep the glass clean at all times, but take the opportunity in autumn to give it special treatment.

● When you clean off summer shading (if you have used a shading wash), wash the glass inside and out and clean between overlapping panes where dirt and algae accumulate.

If you do not let the grime go neglected for too long, you may be able to clean between panes with a forceful jet of water, perhaps aided by a thin strip of plastic that you can push between the panes.

● Very dirty glass can be cleaned with a kettle descaler based on formic acid (available from hardware stores). Add a few drops of dishwashing liquid to help it spread. Wear rubber gloves when you are using this and make sure it does not splash into your eyes. After the cleaner has been on for a few minutes, rinse with clean water (making sure you do not splash the cleaner onto plants in the greenhouse. You can also buy

products for cleaning greenhouse glass, but these are not so widely available.

● On an old greenhouse, glass that has become pitted or frosted in appearance should be removed and replaced. The glass supplier will cut a pane to size for you (if the shape of the pane is unusual it is worth making a cardboard template for him to copy), or you can cut it yourself.

● On a modern aluminium greenhouse, unhook the glazing clip to lift out the old pane (you may have to release the pane above, too, if it overlaps), and place the new glass in position. It is a quick and simple job, but the edges of the glass are very sharp, so wear strong gloves to protect your hands.

● Glass bedded on putty and held in place with glazing brads or pins is more difficult to replace. Try to remove the fixings carefully using a pair of pliers or pincers without levering on the glass. Push the glass out carefully. The old putty may lift out with the glass, but the chances are it will remain in position and you will have to chip it out with an old wood chisel. Be careful that you do not chip pieces out of the glazing bars.

● Before putting the new pane in, clean the wood, removing algae and using a wire brush or abrasive paper if necessary. You can use putty again to reglaze, but you may find a mastic or caulking compound (usually applied from a special gun) easier and less messy. The putty or mastic will stick better if you apply a coat of knotting to the glazing bars first. Glazing pins or metal brads can be bought at hardware shops, or

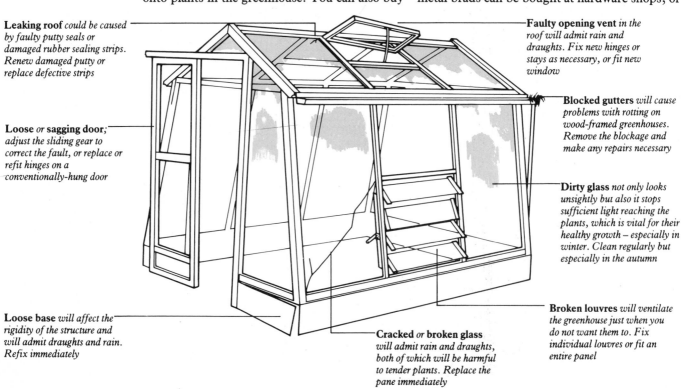

Leaking roof *could be caused by faulty putty seals or damaged rubber sealing strips. Renew damaged putty or replace defective strips*

Loose *or* **sagging door;** *adjust the sliding gear to correct the fault, or replace or refit hinges on a conventionally-hung door*

Loose base *will affect the rigidity of the structure and will admit draughts and rain. Refix immediately*

Faulty opening vent *in the roof will admit rain and draughts. Fix new hinges or stays as necessary, or fit new window*

Blocked gutters *will cause problems with rotting on wood-framed greenhouses. Remove the blockage and make any repairs necessary*

Dirty glass *not only looks unsightly but also it stops sufficient light reaching the plants, which is vital for their healthy growth – especially in winter. Clean regularly but especially in the autumn*

Broken louvres *will ventilate the greenhouse just when you do not want them to. Fix individual louvres or fit an entire panel*

Cracked *or* **broken glass** *will admit rain and draughts, both of which will be harmful to tender plants. Replace the pane immediately*

your local glass merchant should supply them.
● If you have an old steel-framed greenhouse the glass may be bedded on putty or mastic but held in place with a glazing clip, too. Make sure you do not lose any clips that you remove (they may be difficult to replace) and do not use a linseed oil putty on a steel frame: special metal casement putty is made for this job.

The timber

● You should paint your timber greenhouse before it starts to peel and look dilapidated. Regular painting (at least every second year) will improve the appearance and extend its life. Make sure you remove any old flaking paint first.
● If you have an old painted greenhouse that has become too bad to prepare by the normal washing down and sanding where necessary, you should be prepared to clean off the old paint and start again. It may sound a chore, but it is cheaper than buying a new greenhouse. To prepare woodwork for repainting, remove the old paint or varnish with a chemical stripper, blowtorch or hot-air stripper, then rub down with glasspaper. If you use a blowtorch, it might be better to remove the glass first since the heat could shatter the panes. If there are already a lot of damaged or broken panes you may feel this is

worthwhile anyway. Seal any knots with shellac knotting, prepare the wood for overpainting with primer, then apply undercoat followed by one or two coats of gloss paint.
● Western red cedar is usually left unpainted, but it will lose its attractive colour and turn silvery unless you apply a cedar wood treatment from time to time. You can treat neglected cedar by cleaning it with steel wool or abrasive paper, then restoring the colour with a preservative that contains an exterior wood stain.

Gutters

Blocked and leaking gutters can lead to other problems, such as wood rotting where it is often damp.
● Clean gutters out at least a couple of times a year, and certainly after autumn leaf fall. If you do not already have some kind of downpipe filter, make a ball of wire-netting to place in the top of the pipe.
● If a leaking gutter is only due to a poor seal at a joint, you can use one of the proprietary sealants that are available.
● If the gutter is in a very poor state it is well worth replacing it. Modern plastic gutters are not expensive and are easy to fit; 75 mm (3 in) guttering is adequate for a greenhouse.

AUTOMATION

While you are overhauling or maintaining your greenhouse or conservatory, you may want to consider ways of making the day-to-day running trouble-free.

There are many useful gadgets that you can buy for your greenhouse, but two that are particularly useful are automatic ventilator openers and some form of automatic watering. Both free you from being tied to the greenhouse every day during the summer.

Ventilator openers
These are very useful when the temperature rises dramatically in the summer. Even if you open most of the ventilators by hand, just one or two automatic ones will avoid the worst temperature rises.

Different types are available for normal roof and side ventilators, and for louvre ventilators. Most work on the principle of an expanding wax forcing the window open, but some have a metal coil that reacts to temperature changes (top left). No electricity supply is required for any of them.

Fitting instructions vary from make to make, but it should only take you about 15 minutes to fit one.

Automatic watering systems
Perhaps the most simple and effective types of watering system are capillary watering systems. You can buy simple kits, with special capillary matting and instructions, from garden centres. You can use a hand-filled reservoir (some are based on a bag that you hang up, or you could feed it from a hand-filled plastic trough). If you have a mains water supply the matting or sand can be kept moist from a water tank controlled by a float valve (*left*)

Which type of shed?

There are two basic garden shed shapes, but several materials and finishes. Here is an explanation of terms used to describe the various models plus details of their advantages and disadvantages.

Pent roof sheds have a roof that slopes in one direction. The direction of the slope will depend on the make, but usually the door and window are on the 'high' side. Think carefully where you want to put a workbench and make sure that it still gives you adequate headroom.

Apex roof sheds have the ridge in the middle. These tend to cost a bit more than pent roof sheds of a similar size. If you are tall, you may find that the headroom at the centre is an advantage if you want to use a workbench under the window.

Cladding

There are five main forms of timber cladding that you may encounter. They are described and illustrated below:

Tongued-and-grooved boards provide good weatherproofing because each board interlocks with its neighbour. They are usually used vertically.

Feather-edged weatherboards are used horizontally, the lower edge overlapping the board below: make sure they are thick enough not to buckle and warp.

Rebated weatherboard resembles the feather-edged types in appearance, but includes a lip or rebate at the overlap that gives a closer, flush fit.

Waney-edged or **rustic** cladding looks less formal than straight-edged boards, but it is not as weatherproof.

Rebated shiplap has a distinctive rebated finish between planks. It has similar qualities to tongued-and-grooved boards.

Concrete block

Concrete block sheds are generally flat-roofed and the concrete sides textured to look more attractive.

A concrete shed is most likely to be considered for a shed near the house or adjoining an existing concrete block garage, where the

Right: A typical pent-roof shed with walls clad with shiplap boards. The window and door is on the high side to make the best use of the space (and light) inside for a workbench, leaving the low side for storage of tools and equipment

material is likely to be more in keeping with its surroundings.

Other materials
You may occasionally come across a shed made from other materials that are not so readily available:

Aluminium sheds consist of sheets that lock together and usually have sliding doors, and possibly an acrylic sheet window. An aluminium shed may not be cheaper than a timber shed of the same size, but it will be virtually maintenance free. You will not have much choice of size – they are usually fairly small, intended for tool storage, and not large enough to work in.

Glass-fibre sheds are also made. Again, the design is likely to be small and box-like, but adequate for storing tools. This type of shed can be bolted together quickly and needs no maintenance.

Steel sheds normally have a shallow apex roof. Although steel may seem an unlikely material for a garden shed, it can be very durable, so long as it has been well treated to resist rust. You will

not find it so easy to hang shelves inside or to fix up hooks for tools – and there probably will not be any windows – but if you really only want somewhere to store the mower, a few garden tools and perhaps a bike, a steel shed may be perfectly adequate. They are usually cheaper than timber sheds of the same size.

Right: An apex roof shed offers excellent headroom – a boon if you are going to work inside for long periods. The door is usually in one of the end walls, reserving the long side walls for a broad window admitting good light
Top right: Concrete block sheds, although square and boxy in appearance, are durable and good where you want to match the outbuilding to a garage or the house walls

Making your own garden shed

If you are willing to improvise, you can make a garden shed yourself that will provide perfectly adequate storage space. The ideas on this page should give you some basic outlines that you can modify to suit your individual needs. Remember, though, if you have to buy all new wood it may cost you as much to make a shed as to buy one, but if you use fencing panels, or can incorporate timber and perhaps roofing felt that you have already, it should save you money.

A shed made from fencing panels is not difficult to make. In the design suggested, the carpentry has been kept to a minimum yet the structure is tough and durable.

1. Make a concrete base, or use paving slabs for the base. Set four 75 mm × 75 mm (3 in × 3 in) fencing posts in the base, making sure they are absolutely upright. You may need to provide temporary supporting struts until the concrete has set. Alternatively use metal post holders that you simply drive into the ground (if using these, insert them before laying the concrete base).

2. Depending on the type of fencing, the three wall panels may need to be fixed into position as you proceed. Closeboard panels, either vertical or horizontal, should be used, but make sure it is the type that has battens along the top (as you will want to nail into these). The type that you slide into concrete posts are usually suitable. Be sure to set the posts so that the tops will be flush with the tops of the fencing panels.

3. You can use fencing brackets (see illustration) to save the need for carpentry joints. The panels can be slid into place or temporarily held against one post, while the opposite post, with bracket fitted, is inserted.

4. The front framework can be constructed of 50 mm × 50 mm (2 in × 2 in) sawn softwood (it is cheaper than planed wood). The exact dimensions must depend on the materials that you have available. To save the trouble of trying to make a window, you can buy suitable frames from a good timber supplier and it is worth buying one plus the hinges and fasteners.

5. Make the door frame about 750 mm (30 in) wide and include a cross-brace for strength (see illustration). If you do not have any suitable spare timber for the door, use tongued-and-grooved boards about 20 mm (¾ in) thick. You will also need timber with plain edges for the horizontal and diagonal braces. Three hinges will provide a stronger fixing than two in case the door should get caught by the wind.

6. To support the roof, incorporate at least one cross-member to run from the front frame to the back fencing panel. To ensure that the roof has a slight fall, cut and plane two strips of 50 mm × 25 mm (2 in × 1 in) softwood to produce a gradual but even taper. Nail these to the tops of the side fencing panels. You will also need to use strips of the right size to fill in the gap at the front and back shed panels. Nail or screw chipboard (particle board) or plywood to the top to provide the roof, overlapping the edges slightly. Exterior-grade boards are better, but you can use the cheaper interior grades provided the timber is well protected with roofing felt.

7. Feather-edged boards (a fencing manufacturer or contractor will probably be able to supply these) can be nailed to the front frame (and you could use them for the door instead of tongued-and-grooved timber) to complete the front.

8. Whichever timber you use for the top, cover with roofing felt, overlapping the edges of the felt by at least 50 mm (2 in). Seal seams with a waterproof mastic adhesive and use clout nails every 50 mm to 75 mm (2 in to 3 in) to secure the edges.

9. Treat with a wood preservative.

10. Line the shed with an insulating paper.

Self-assembly timber sheds *come in pre-made panels that you simply screw or bolt together. It is usual to start with the base, then add one end and one side wall, followed by the remaining end and wall panels. Then complete the building by adding the roof. Door and window positions are usually optional and interior linings and flooring are offered as extras*

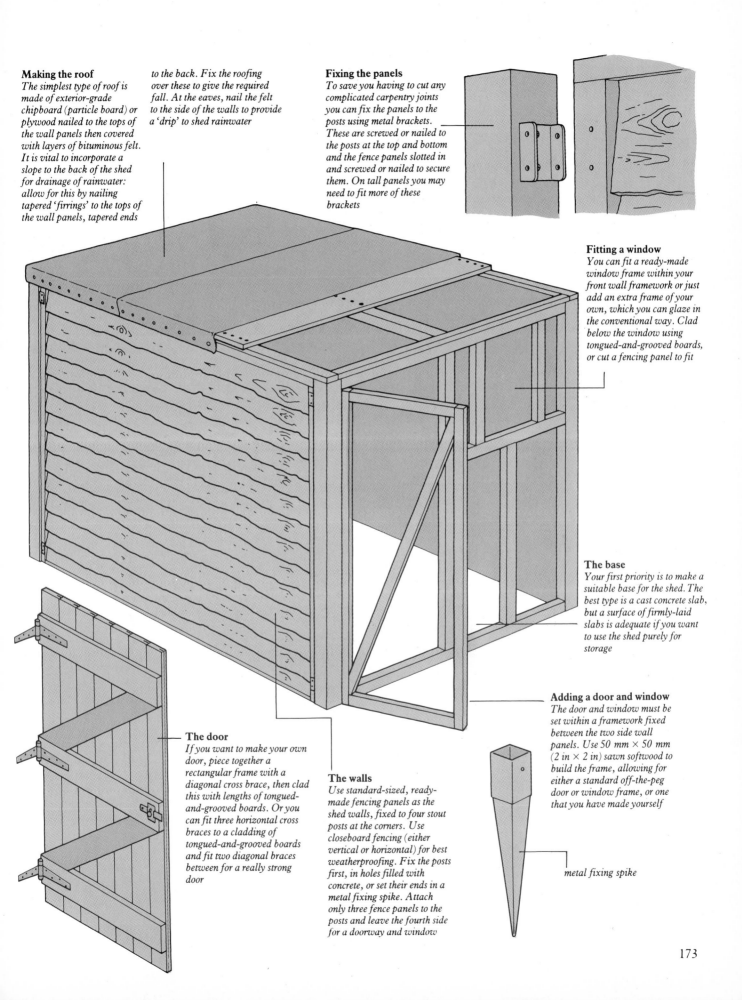

Making the roof
The simplest type of roof is made of exterior-grade chipboard (particle board) or plywood nailed to the tops of the wall panels then covered with layers of bituminous felt. It is vital to incorporate a slope to the back of the shed for drainage of rainwater: allow for this by nailing tapered 'firrings' to the tops of the wall panels, tapered ends to the back. Fix the roofing over these to give the required fall. At the eaves, nail the felt to the side of the walls to provide a 'drip' to shed rainwater

Fixing the panels
To save you having to cut any complicated carpentry joints you can fix the panels to the posts using metal brackets. These are screwed or nailed to the posts at the top and bottom and the fence panels slotted in and screwed or nailed to secure them. On tall panels you may need to fit more of these brackets

Fitting a window
You can fit a ready-made window frame within your front wall framework or just add an extra frame of your own, which you can glaze in the conventional way. Clad below the window using tongued-and-grooved boards, or cut a fencing panel to fit

The base
Your first priority is to make a suitable base for the shed. The best type is a cast concrete slab, but a surface of firmly-laid slabs is adequate if you want to use the shed purely for storage

Adding a door and window
The door and window must be set within a framework fixed between the two side wall panels. Use 50 mm × 50 mm (2 in × 2 in) sawn softwood to build the frame, allowing for either a standard off-the-peg door or window frame, or one that you have made yourself

metal fixing spike

The door
If you want to make your own door, piece together a rectangular frame with a diagonal cross brace, then clad this with lengths of tongued-and-grooved boards. Or you can fit three horizontal cross braces to a cladding of tongued-and-grooved boards and fit two diagonal braces between for a really strong door

The walls
Use standard-sized, ready-made fencing panels as the shed walls, fixed to four stout posts at the corners. Use closeboard fencing (either vertical or horizontal) for best weatherproofing. Fix the posts first, in holes filled with concrete, or set their ends in a metal fixing spike. Attach only three fence panels to the posts and leave the fourth side for a doorway and window

Deciding on a summerhouse

Unlike a garden shed or a greenhouse, which are usually bought for their functional qualities, a summerhouse must also be attractively designed and sufficiently spacious for use as an outdoor living room during summer. Some of the most popular types are shown on these pages, but you will find that there are many variations. Send for as many brochures as possible and visit showgrounds so you know what is available – there is no substitute for walking around and standing up in the real thing to know whether it is right for you and your garden.

Points to consider

Timber should be strong and durable. Western red cedar is a common choice. You may find elm and a few other woods, but be cautious of whitewood: a whitewood summerhouse is likely to be cheaper, but it must be treated regularly with a preservative and this will add considerably to the cost during its lifetime.

Floor and base A summer house will normally stand on treated bearers, but if the building appears raised above ground level it will seldom look right. You could make a firm base for the house a little below the surrounding ground level to lessen this effect, but you must ensure that the surrounding ground does not come into contact with the timber. It is also worth fixing

An octagonal summerhouse such as this is ideal for a moderate-sized plot – it is glassed all round for maximum admission of sunlight, and its steeply pitched roof ensures good weatherproofing

close-mesh wire-netting between the ground and the floor to reduce the chance of rodents and other animals setting up home there.

The floor may be of a different and less expensive timber than the rest of the structure, but this will not matter provided it is treated with a preservative.

Windows that open are vital. You need a much larger area of ventilation than you would in a shed if it is to be comfortable to sit in during the summer. Large windows that do not open may increase the problem; you may not want to sit with the doors open. Some models have shutters, and you may feel this is a useful extra if you want to use the summerhouse as a storage shed during the winter.

A verandah adds an extra dimension to a summerhouse and when it is too hot to sit inside you will be able to sit more comfortably outside. Some verandahs have a slatted timber floor to reduce the risk of water lying and increasing the chance of rot.

Doors can make a difference to both appearance and convenient day-to-day use. If you plan to use your summerhouse for family meals you will find double doors more useful, also giving more of an open, airy feeling. Some summerhouses have sliding doors, which save on space.

Roofs As with sheds, summerhouses come with apex roofs (sloping both ways from a central ridge) and pent roofs (sloping one way). Apex roofs are the most popular as they tend to give more scope for design. Although many are covered with ordinary roofing felt, some have asphalt roofing tiles, which resemble conventional roof tiles.

Metal construction Some steel summerhouses are available. They usually consist of steel framework with a wood cladding. Visually there is little to choose between these and a timber summerhouse.

Erecting a summerhouse

As with sheds and greenhouses, most manufacturers will erect their models for you, but this may involve extra cost.

Even if you have it erected, the supplier will expect you to have prepared a level base. Unless you are setting the summerhouse on a paved area such as a patio, you should prepare a suitable footing for the bearers.

If the ground is firm, and you do not want to lay a cast concrete base, you could simply lay bricks or paving slabs bedded on mortar over the

bare earth, where the bearers are to lie: you will need to check the positions of these with the manufacturer. If you lay a concrete base, make this the same size as the overall area of the building, but no wider: the wall cladding should oversail the base so that rainwater is shed beyond it.

If you do erect the summerhouse yourself you will need an extra pair of hands to help hold the panels while you bolt them together, but you should have no difficulty. Bolt holes are usually pre-drilled and each section will be easy to identify by its shape, or may be numbered. All you have to do is hold one section up to the other, slide the bolts through the holes, then secure with a washer and nut.

A light and airy summerhouse (top) with plenty of space inside for sitting in the shade
A spacious summerhouse like this (above) is only really suitable for a large garden – but if you have the space you will find it excellent as a summer retreat and a winter store for garden furniture, the barbecue and any other garden equipment that needs to hibernate. Special features on this model include a covered verandah and window boxes to make the summerhouse a home-from-home

Maintaining garden buildings

There is a lot of timber in a garden building and unless you maintain it well it will start to rot. Even timber that is treated initially will succumb sooner or later to the effects of the weather. There is, however, a lot you can do to ensure that your building gives a long and trouble-free life.

Stopping the rot

The fungi that cause wood to rot need air and moisture, so any parts in contact with damp ground are particularly vulnerable. That is why fence posts tend to rot at ground level first, and likewise the bearers of sheds are likely to rot.

If you buy fence posts, or bearers for a shed or summerhouse, try to buy pressure- or vacuum-treated timber: the preservative penetrates the wood more effectively in these processes.

You can do much to reduce the risk of rotting by making sure that soil and garden refuse is not piled against the building to act as a bridge for moisture to rise. Leaking gutters and downpipes should also be repaired as a matter of urgency.

Preservative applied as a routine treatment by brushing or spraying will stop surface moulds and provide ample protection if carried out every two or three years. Follow these tips, and it should prolong the life of your shed or summerhouse.

● Remove algae spores from the surface of the building by scrubbing with a fungical solution. Allow to dry thoroughly before applying preservative.

● Apply preservative when the timber is dry (and therefore more likely to absorb the liquid); in practical terms this usually means during the summer.
● Be generous, whether brushing or spraying on preservative. Let the first application soak in, then give it another coat. You can give it a third coat, but two is the minimum.
● Be particularly thorough at joints, at exposed

Paint on preservative from the bottom of the building up, so that you do not have to paint over drips, which would show through on the finished surface

ends, and where the wood has been cut, to ensure saturation.
● If you have plants growing against your shed or summerhouse, choose a water-soluble preservative, which is not harmful to plants (check with your supplier or the container label). Creosote or one of the organic solvent preservatives are usually used for sheds and summerhouses where plants do not have to be considered. These will all be harmful if splashed on to plants, and have vapours that are noxious.

Rotting timber

Once timber has started to rot (it will be soft and spongy) there is no point in using a wood preservative on that part.

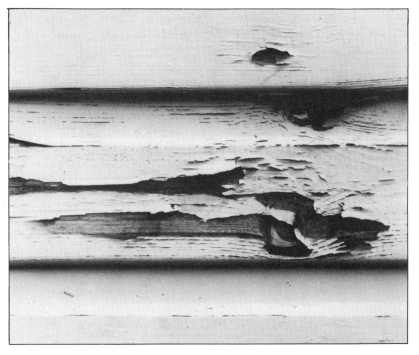

Flaking paint, spongy timber and mould growth are signs of an attack by rot

Remove the affected section, cutting well back into sound wood. You may have to remove sections of good timber too so that you can replace the affected section. The problem may be finding suitable replacement timber to match the cladding.

Remember to use galvanized nails when you replace the section and treat the new wood with preservative.

Timber shrinkage

Sometimes the timber of a poorly made shed may begin to part where the boards shrink and buckle. You will be able to see light between the boards (this sometimes happens with new sheds), and there is easy access for moisture.

Your tools and equipment will soon start to rust if you do not improve the insulation of the shed. You can buy a special type of insulating lining paper from a builder's merchant, which you can use to line the shed. If you use the shed as a workshop, too, the lining should make it more comfortable in bad weather.

Draughts

Draughts can be a particular nuisance in a summerhouse. Even in warm weather you may find a piercing draught through a crack annoying. These are most likely round the framework, doors and windows. Obviously you do not want to seal up doors and windows, but if the draught is coming from a non-opening part you might find a waterproof sealing tape useful. You can buy these from hardware stores and they can also be used to temporarily seal leaking gutters. Poorly fitting doors and windows may

benefit from a strip of plastic-backed self-adhesive foam draught-proofing tape, sold in reels.

The roof

Roofing felt will last for many years, but it can crack and tear so check it once a year (or as soon as you notice any sign of dampness seeping through).

If the tear or damage is only in a small area, the simplest solution is a small patch. Seal the edges and use galvanized clout nails to hold it in position. If it is beginning to deteriorate in several places, it is wise to refelt the whole roof.

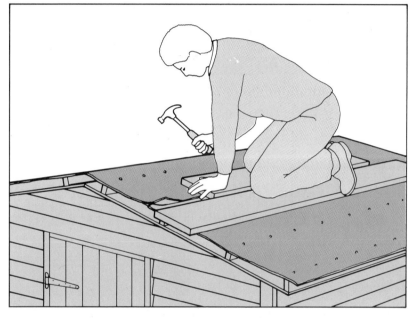

Refelt a shed roof if the old covering has deteriorated badly. Work from boards spanning the roof to spread your load and protect the surface from damage

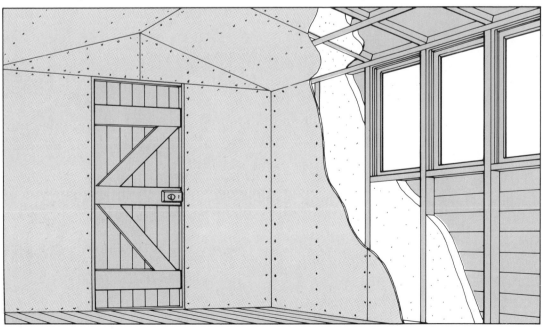

Lining the inside of your shed or summerhouse with building paper will keep out draughts and help to protect your tools from rusting, but if you plan to spend a lot of time inside, working or simply relaxing, it is worthwhile cladding the walls and roof with slabs of polystyrene covered with sheets of hardboard. This treatment also gives you a good surface for fixing shelves, racks or other fittings

Garages and carports

A garage is a definite asset for two main reasons. First, it provides protection for your car – both from weather and from vandals (although there is some evidence to show that your car will actually suffer less from rust if it is left out in the open). Second, it allows you to work on the car under cover – a distinct benefit in winter especially. If the garage is big enough, it can also provide welcome extra room for a workshop, for large appliances such as chest freezers and for bikes, garden tools and equipment and d-i-y materials. If it is linked to the house, it can save you getting wet when you arrive home. And it certainly adds to the value of your house, as anyone who has tried to sell a house without one will tell you.

A carport is often regarded as a poor substitute for a garage, and up to a point it is. However, it can still keep the worst of the weather off your car, especially if a side or end is enclosed, too. It can also be useful in other ways – for example, in providing covered parking in front of an existing garage, or a covered area where you can work on the car far more easily than in a cramped garage. It will also be far cheaper than a garage to build.

So if you have nowhere to keep your car, or the existing garage, built at a time when family cars were rather smaller than they are today, is now too small, then it is time to consider building a garage or carport. Which you choose depends on the site available and on how much you are prepared to spend.

Planning restrictions

You may need planning permission to put up a garage or carport. In general terms (in the UK) a garage built next to your house (or within 5 m/16 ft of it) is treated as a home extension for planning purposes, which means that it must not add over 15 per cent to the volume of the original house, must not protrude in front of the building line facing the roadway and must not result in more than half the original garden being covered with buildings. A garage or carport more than 5 m (16 ft) from the house is treated as an outbuilding for planning permission purposes; here the restrictions apply to the building's height (not more than 4 m/13 ft high if it has a ridged roof, 3 m/10 ft high otherwise), position (not in front of the building line) and size (again, not more than half the original garden to be covered by buildings).

The question of access may also have to be considered unless the new garage or carport will use the existing access to the property. A new access will usually need planning permission unless it is onto an unclassified road and is required for a garage or carport that does not itself need permission.

A detached, modern-style, *low-maintenance garage can fit into any corner of the garden as long as access to it is easy. Trees and bushes can be used to help screen it from view*

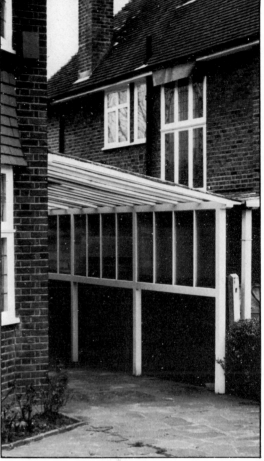

2. The second layer of wall panels is lifted and bolted into place next, to complete the walls. Personal doors and windows can be incorporated into the structure in place of some of the wall panels, if required.

3. Check the structure for squareness, fit the main door frame and add the roof trusses, ready for the roofing to be fixed. The job is quite straightforward, but needs two fairly strong people to lift the upper wall panels into place.

By contrast, building a kit carport is a much lighter job. Such buildings can be freestanding, but are usually built alongside the house or garage, so one side or end of the roof is supported by a wallplate attached to the building. The other end is supported on metal or timber posts either sunk into the ground or fitting into metal 'shoes' that are bolted to the concrete surface on which the carport is being built. Horizontal beams are then added to form the perimeter of the roof, and purlins are fixed between them to support the roof covering – usually translucent pvc sheet. Finally, fascia boards and gutters are added.

Above left: an integral garage built onto the side of your house often looks attractive and provides sheltered access to and from your car

Above right: a cheap but effective alternative to a garage is a carport attached to the side of the house. This one, constructed from a timber structure, looks more in keeping with its house than a flat-roofed aluminium model would

The building work

You can either build a garage or carport from scratch – yourself, or with the help of a builder – or you can buy a prefabricated building and erect it on a prepared base. The former allows you to have exactly the building you want, but is likely to cost rather more than using a prefabricated building.

Prefabricated garages consist of a number of wall panels that are slotted together to form the garage walls, plus pre-assembled roof trusses that carry a corrugated roof of asbestos cement or pvc sheeting. The following is a general indication of what is involved and is not a substitute for specific manufacturer's instructions.

1. Start erecting the garage at one rear corner, bolting two lower wall panels together at right angles. Then add adjacent panels until the garage door is reached.

18. Garden furniture

Your choice of garden furniture will be dictated to some extent by how you like to use your garden: sun lovers will want something comfy to stretch out on; barbecue fans will sacrifice comfort for an upright chair and a decent table. Yet ease of maintenance must be an important factor, too.

Your furniture's resistance to weathering depends on what it is made of and it tends to fall into two categories: the sort you can leave outside permanently and virtually forget and the kind you have to bring indoors when you are not using it.

The rugged outdoor type is usually least comfortable; commonly hardwood garden seats, ornate cast metal chairs and tables and basic picnic tables with integrated bench seats. All need occasional maintenance (see our guide) but are highly resistant to weathering and can be made more comfortable if you use soft cushions from indoors.

Hardwood seats, like those in parks, are ideal tucked away in leafy corners of the garden from where you can sit and admire the view. Decoratively patterned cast metal chairs, invariably with a matching table, look elegant on a paved patio, whereas wooden picnic tables with built-in benches are great for family use – they are often inexpensive and usually extremely hard-wearing in use.

Also at the budget end of the market are tubular steel and plastic tables and chairs. These can be left out all summer but must be brought indoors when the season ends. Most have facility for a sunshade in the centre of the table and are good for drinks and meals on the patio or lawn. Chairs can usually be stacked for storing and sometimes the table can be folded away, too. They do not look as attractive as the hardwood and cast metal ranges but they are slightly more comfortable to sit on for a considerable length of time.

If you are looking for something you can snooze in on long, sunny summer afternoons there is quite a selection of more comfortable furniture. It must be brought indoors at the end of the day, so make sure you have somewhere to store it. Some of the luxury padded chairs and loungers at the top of the range can be bulky. Remember, you will need somewhere dry to store them in winter, too.

At the bottom of the luxury scale is the good old deckchair. Do not dismiss it as outdated: it is adjustable, fairly comfortable for lounging in the sun (you can even get a matching clip-on footstool if you want to put your feet up) and it

Left: *Distinctive metal-patio table and chairs like these were typically made in cast-iron, a material that required regular maintenance to prevent rusting. Modern manufacturing processes allow the moulds to be used to cast these ornate patio sets in aluminium, which, when plastic-coated, is virtually maintenance-free*

folds away flat for storage. If you already have a couple that have seen better days, clean and re-varnish the frames and replace torn seats (see overleaf). If you need to buy them from new you are not restricted to the traditional stripes these days; there is quite a variety of attractive modern designs available.

For lightness and easy storage you cannot beat a lightweight aluminium-framed chair with canvas or plastic fabric seat. They are not as comfortable as a deckchair but they are cheap, easy to maintain and perfectly adequate for reading in the garden or outdoor meals. Not quite as easy to care for but generally better looking and serving the same purpose is the side folding or 'director's' chair. Normally with a wooden frame construction and strong canvas seat, the side folding chair is surprisingly comfy and folds easily for storage. They come in quite a range of colours and could double as extra seating in the dining room if you really want to get your money's worth.

If you spend a lot of time in the garden it is worth paying extra for the flexibility of a reclining chair. Usually well padded and very comfortable, recliners are like outdoor adjustable armchairs and can be used sitting upright, or with feet up and head back – whichever is required. They do tend to be bulky to handle and store and the cushions at least should be kept indoors when not being used to prevent them becoming damp.

Sun-worshippers will find plenty of loungers varying quite considerably in comfort and in cost. Very basic pool-side beds are available, which you could leave out all summer and their hardness can be softened a little with covered foam pads. You can often buy foam offcuts from specialist suppliers, which are ideal.

More common is the lightweight aluminium-framed sunbed with fabric stretched across it and adjustable head rest. They are cheap and easy to fold away and repair but not particularly comfortable. Some can be very smart with thick, comfy padding, attractive designs and various adjustable positions. If you buy one of these remember you will have to look after it and find plenty of space to store it. At the top of the range is a luxury model, complete with wheels and fitted drinks holder.

Top row, left to right: A selection of garden furniture consisting of a folding canvas chair; a metal-framed collapsible patio set with checked upholstery; a wheelbed and adjustable chair with padded cushions. **Bottom row, left to right:** *a traditional park bench style seat; a hardwood bench and table; a swing hammock and awning*

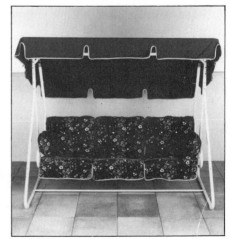

Maintaining garden chairs

Your garden furniture should last you for years if you look after it. Maintenance and repairs are best done at the end of the season when the furniture can be properly stored away in good condition.

As a general rule fabric-covered furniture should be allowed to dry naturally, if possible, before storing. Keep it in a well-ventilated shed or garage when not in use during the summer, but in winter it is probably better to keep it in the house, away from any damp. Lubricate all pivots and hinges with a little thin cycle oil and check and tighten screws regularly. To tighten a rivet, support one side on a hard surface and hammer its head firmly. Any wooden parts should be treated with a colourless preservative once a year, preferably when the wood is absorbent after a spell of dry weather.

Teak and iroko Paint or preservative should not be used on these woods. They are extremely waterproof but will benefit from an application of teak oil once or twice a year. Remove dirt by scrubbing first with soapy water, rinse and allow to dry. Remove stubborn surface grime with white spirit.

Beech and elm Clean with detergent once a year then rub down with fine glasspaper and treat with linseed oil.

Softwood Treat initially with a colourless preservative, and repeat every few years.

Cast metal Scrub clean occasionally and forget about it until it needs repainting.

Plastics Most are treated to prevent cracking and colour fading and can be left out during the summer. Scrub clean and bring indoors for the winter.

Aluminium Smear lightly with a little oil before storing away for the winter but remember to wipe off before use.

Fabric Clean cushions using an upholstery shampoo (providing the foam filling does not get soaked). Wipe over plastic and synthetic fabrics. Patch tears or replace the fabric using new lengths (available from hardware stores and garden centres).

Deckchair

If the fabric of a deckchair rips, it can be easily replaced with a new length, which is readily available in both traditional canvas and rot-proof synthetic fibre. It can be bought either by the metre or in pre-cut lengths.

1. Remove existing fabric by prising out the tacks with a screwdriver, using a hammer or mallet if they are driven in too hard.

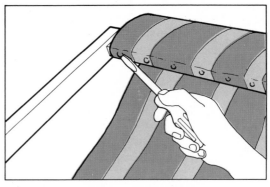

2. Measure the length of the cover and buy a new one to match. Fold one end under 25 mm (1 in) and tuck it round the top rail of the chair. Hammer a tack in to hold the centre of the cover to the underside of the top rail.

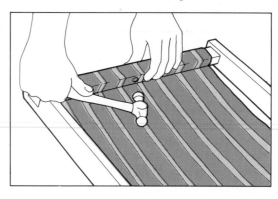

3. Hammer in tacks at each end, then two more midway between. Take the other end to cover the bottom rail, which is narrower than the top. Taper each side until it fits and fold the edge under 25 mm (1 in). Align the edge of the fold with the inside edge of the rail underneath and tack first at the centre, then the edges, then midway, as before.

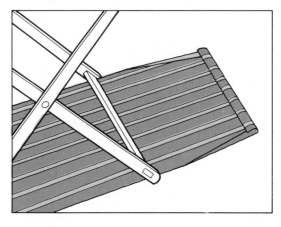

Sun lounger

If a sun lounger tears the fabric can be replaced in the same way as any other fabric chair, or repaired by overstitching the tear with doubled 60 gauge thread.

If you are replacing the fabric, buy a new cover to fit and slide the ready-made pockets over the tubular ends of the lounger. Lay it on its side and refit the cords underneath through the lacing holes in the flaps.

Tears typically occur where the cord flaps are doubled over and stitched to the single thickness of the fabric. To repair a tear, undo the retaining cords, remove the cover and cut the loose threads from the tear. Fold under the torn fabric about 6 mm (¼ in) and butt the fold against the cord flap. Overstitch along the tear, extending 12 mm (½ in) beyond the ends.

Often the support cord under the metal frame snaps or over-stretches and is difficult to repair with any other kind of cord. It is best to buy a special repair kit (available from hardware shops and garden furniture departments). Remove the broken or worn cord from the eyes in the cover flaps; check that the cover is sound. Fix a hook at each end of each rubber band in the sun lounger repair kit, leaving the hooks open. Locate one hook in each eye of one flap, checking that the cover is straight. Working from the centre hook, stretch the bands and secure with the free hooks in the other flap.

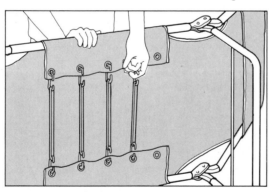

Aluminium-framed chair

Torn fabric on an aluminium-framed chair can be quickly replaced, following this simple procedure. Cut through the existing stitching and remove the damaged chair cover. Buy a new length to fit, allowing 25 mm (1 in) on the length for turns.

1. With the chair open, fold the new cover strip over the top bar. Knot your thread and, from the back, push the needle through the fold and front of the cover (A). Backstitch neatly the length of the cover finishing off with a double

stitch at the back to give a firm and strong seam. (B).

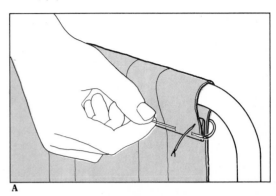

A

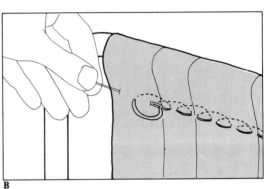

B

2. Take the cover down behind the bar at the back of the seat and over the top of the front bar. Fold under 12 mm (½ in) of the front edge. Pin temporarily along the folded edge about every 40 mm (1½ in).

3. Fold and unfold the chair to check that the cover is correctly fitted, then backstitch across the front hem in the same way as before, finishing with a double stitch. Remove the tacking pins.

Patching damaged covers

Garden furniture covers can be patched if they rip some distance from a seam or side flap and cannot be overstitched. Try to obtain a similar piece of canvas or synthetic fabric for the patch.

1. Remove the cover and start stitching 12 mm (½ in) from the tear, pushing the needle up from below. Fold under 6 mm (¼ in) of the edges and overstitch, taking care not to overlap the edges. Finish stitching 12 mm (½ in) beyond each end of the tear.

2. Cut a patch to overlap 50 mm (2 in) all round. Fold under 12 mm (½ in) round the edges of the patch and tack stitch the edges. Lay the patch on the underside of the tear and overstitch tightly to the cover.

Making your own garden furniture

Making or adapting old items of furniture for garden use is simpler than you might think, and original and highly successful results can be achieved. Scour junk shops or friends' attics for unusual patio furniture such as the ubiquitous washstand, usually on a wooden stand with marble or wooden top (or an old wrought-iron sewing machine trestle). Old beer barrels make excellent tables, as do the huge wooden reels used for storing heavy-duty cable. You can quite often pick up large, scarred kitchen tables quite cheaply, which look perfectly in character in the garden or on a patio. Treat all wooden items for woodworm and give an annual application of colourless preservative. Cheap folding wooden chairs are light and easy to store and can be made more comfortable with soft cushions or covered foam pads.

If you prefer to construct your own furniture, it is relatively easy to build seats and tables in convenient corners of your garden or patio that will look totally in keeping with their surroundings. Garden seats are particularly quick to build using specially made walling blocks that give the impression of being made up of separate 'stones', like a dry stone wall (see page 104). They can be integrated with other features such as planters, barbecues and matching table areas, too.

Pine and hardwood such as iroko make sturdy, weatherproof furniture; if you have an attractive tree in your garden, you could build a wooden seat around it. You could even construct your own picnic tables and chairs.

For a very personal corner you can build and grow your own moss or herb seat – comfier than any cushion, it is completely weatherproof and will reward you with a wonderful scent when you sit on it.

Garden furniture, *and even simple garden buildings, can often be made from spare timber and materials you may have around the house and garden*

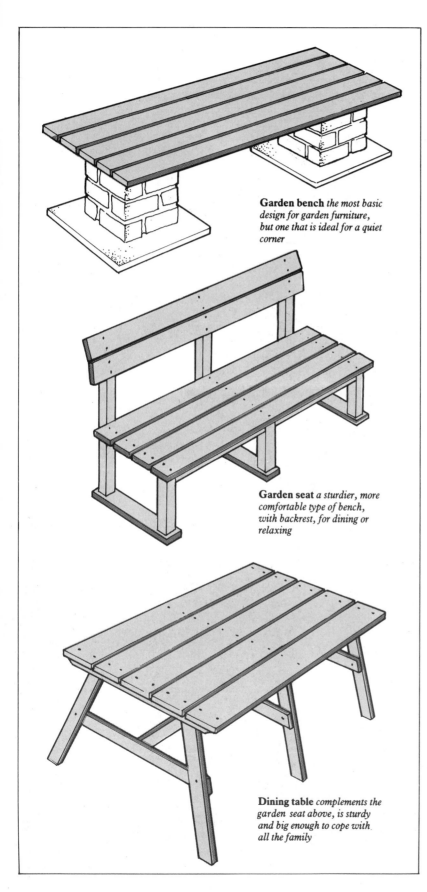

Garden bench *the most basic design for garden furniture, but one that is ideal for a quiet corner*

Garden seat *a sturdier, more comfortable type of bench, with backrest, for dining or relaxing*

Dining table *complements the garden seat above, is sturdy and big enough to cope with all the family*

The beauty of custom-built garden furniture from walling blocks, bricks or wood is that you can make and match all your other garden and patio accessories: barbecues, tubs, troughs, patio walls and planters – all at a fraction of the cost you would find them at in the shops.

Garden bench

For informal seating in a quiet corner of the garden, this basic garden bench is the simplest design and easy to make.

Build two piers of concrete, bricks or garden walling blocks to give a finished seat height of about 450 mm (18 in). They should be set on shallow footings (small cast slabs or pre-cast slabs) approximately 150 mm (6 in) into the subsoil and extending by 150 mm (6 in) beyond the edge of your piers.

Cut lengths of hardwood to just over the span of the piers and bolt these planks to a pair of parallel supports at each end, spaced to slot over your piers. Finish the seat with several coats of exterior grade polyurethane varnish.

Garden seat

Make a more ambitious garden seat with a back rest, using a stout timber framework joined with simple woodwork joints.

The back rest is 1.5 m (4 ft 6 in) long: you will need lengths of nominal 62 mm × 35 mm (2½ in × 1½ in) timber clad with rails of 100 mm × 32 mm (4 in × 1¼ in) timber. Before screwing to the framework, round off the top edges of the cladding rails. Finish with exterior grade varnish.

Three frames are required to support the seat, each pair of legs being joined with a halving joint. Bolts and timber connectors are used for jointing leg frames to the top horizontal member.

Legs should be stiffened with either cross or longitudinal members (or both).

Garden table

If you plan to dine outside during summer you will need a sturdy, durable table: this one is designed to complement the style of the garden bench (above).

A table for outdoor meals must be a comfortable height in relation to the chairs being used: usually anything between 650 mm and 730 mm (26 in and 29 in) will be adequate.

Make a top of 150 mm × 35 mm (6 in × 1½ in) planks set with a 20 mm (¾ in) gap between each, supported on two or three leg frames of 62 mm × 37 mm (2½ in × 1½ in) timber. The lowest part of each leg frame should be braced to the next by means of a central longitudinal member.

Picnic table

You can make a larger picnic table in the same style, and add integral benches too, for a permanent feature on the patio.

Construct a picnic table with built-in benches along the same lines as the garden table, then add bench seats at each side made from 150 mm × 35 mm (6 in × 1½ in) planks supported by 62 mm × 35 mm (2½ in × 1½ in) battens. It does have the advantage that the benches provide additional longitudinal bracing to the structure as a whole.

Tree seat

If you have a fine tree growing in your lawn or patio area you can make a special feature of it by building a seat round the trunk. The simplest design to tackle is a triangular rather than circular plan.

Construct the tree seat by making up three chair-section frames and linking them with rails for the seat base and back. The size of timber used will, of course, depend on the girth of the trunk (which will determine the span from frame to frame). Usually 62 mm × 35 mm (2½ in × 1½ in) timber will be sufficient for the framework and 75 mm × 32 mm (3 in × 1¼ in) timber for the seat base and back rails. On a lawn it will be necessary to distribute the weight of the legs by setting them on bricks below the lawn surface.

Herb seat

A scented seat is a lovely idea for a secluded corner of the garden – on the patio or terrace, tucked into a hedge or arbour, or even cut into an earth bank.

Build a low bank of earth and lay slabs of stone paving, slates or wooden planks along the top, leaving spaces in between for the herbs. Plant it in the spring for a complete covering in a carpet of scented plants by the end of the first year. You will have to keep it well weeded at least once a fortnight until the plants are established. Don't worry about crushing them by sitting on them – they will flourish under such treatment, releasing a lovely scent.

Choose your plants to suit your seat's position: a sunny aspect will favour creeping varieties of thyme such as the *Thymus serpyllum* varieties, or *Thymus azoricus*, which smells of pine needles and forms a compact cushion with pale purple flowers. Roman chamomile *Chamaemelum nobile* will also make a fine scented seat in a sunny position and is available in single- and double-flowered varieties. If the spot is shady, choose one of the creeping mints such as pennyroyal, *Mentha pulegium*, or the tiny *Mentha requienii*.

Picnic table *with integral bench seating makes a permanent feature on the patio for dining outside*

Herb seat, *grown in a secluded corner of the garden, gives a delicately scented place to relax*

Tree seat *for a shady place to sit under the branches of an attractive, imposing tree*

Sundeck

A simple but effective construction for sun-bathing fans is a hardwood platform built to whatever size suits your garden. A raised area can be added to make an excellent low table for drinks and sun tan lotions, and the addition of cushions and mats makes it a comfy suntrap. A great advantage is that it can easily be moved round the garden as the sun changes position.

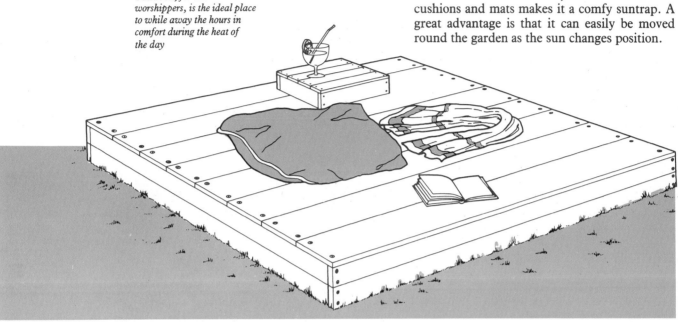

Sundeck, *for sun worshippers, is the ideal place to while away the hours in comfort during the heat of the day*

Planter seat

An integrated planter and paved seat make a lovely addition to a patio, especially if you can match the walling blocks to your patio walls. For a structure like this you will need: 16 × 530 mm (21 in) blocks; 8 × 260 mm (10½ in) coping; 2 × 450 mm (18 in) square paving slabs.

Planter seat, *ideal for the patio, is one way of providing informal seating plus a growing area for shrubs and flowers*

1. Chalk out the shape of your seat and planter, making allowance for simple concrete footings to a minimum of 100 mm (4 in) deep × 500 mm (20 in) square.

2. Build the first course using a mortar mix of 1;1;6 of masonry cement/lime/sand or 1;4 masonry cement/sand. The most natural effect is achieved by keeping mortar joint thickness to a minimum, but ensure that all the blocks are firmly embedded in the mortar by tapping with the handle of your hammer or trowel.

3. Continue to build up courses and check throughout that the structure is level using a spirit level. Finish the pointing carefully, brushing away any loose mortar before it has time to dry.

4. Cut coping stones to fit on top of the planter by scoring with a bolster then hitting firmly with a club hammer until it breaks along the line. Add the seat slabs and allow the mortar two days to dry before using.

5. Plant small evergreen shrubs such as juniper or dwarf conifers for year-round greenery, or plant with annuals for a blaze of summer colour and bulbs for spring. You will get best results if you fill it with a proprietary compost mix.

Barbecue Seat

A complete, permanent preparation/barbecue and seating area can be constructed using bricks or decorative walling blocks with paving slabs laid on top. Design and build it specifically to suit your patio.

1. Chalk out the shape of your design, making allowance for suitable concrete footings (as described for the planter seat). Do not forget to take into consideration prevailing winds when siting your barbecue.

2. Build up your basic seating and food preparation areas course by course, using bricks or walling blocks. Take special care that it is level by using a string guide-line and spirit level.

3. Top with paving slabs. If slabs are not the correct size cut them by scoring with a bolster at the required position on sides and edges. Lay the slab on the ground, place the bolster on the score mark and hit it firmly until the slab breaks along the line.

4. Build up your barbecue stand in the same way to one side of your preparation area, again topping with a slab. Remember it will have to be the correct size to take your barbecue equipment. It is a good idea to raise the structure slightly higher on the windward side to provide a windbreak. For a really smart finish you could finish off the food area by bedding frost-proof ceramic tiles in mortar.

Brick barbecue
You can make a barbecue from bricks without using mortar: simply stack the bricks one on top of the other in a circular or square shape to the height you want the cooking area. Cut a panel of sheet metal to fit between two courses of bricks as the ash tray (or use an old oven tray with the sides beaten flat to fit between the bricks). Build up another course of bricks then set the slatted grill tray in place. Continue to build up courses of bricks to form a windshield around the cooking area. If you eventually want to move the barbecue it is a simple matter to dismantle it and rebuild it elsewhere – and you can experiment with different designs as you wish

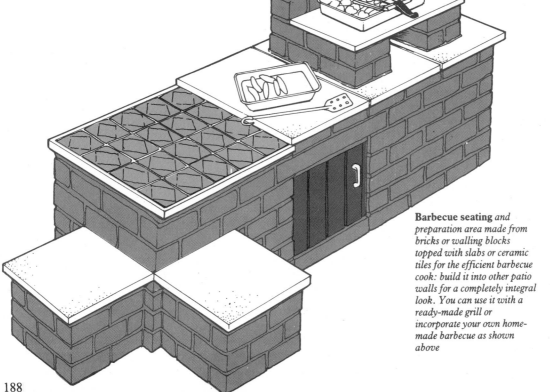

Barbecue seating *and preparation area made from bricks or walling blocks topped with slabs or ceramic tiles for the efficient barbecue cook: build it into other patio walls for a completely integral look. You can use it with a ready-made grill or incorporate your own home-made barbecue as shown above*

19. Gardens for children

If you have children they should ideally be allotted a corner of the garden to call their own. There is no point in planning a beautiful lawn surrounded by well-tended flower beds and expecting your offspring not to tear up the grass and flowers with their balls and bikes.

A paved area is harder wearing and provides a firm, dry surface for playing; if properly drained, puddles will dry quickly after rain and extend precious playing time. Try not to site in a draughty corner or you will be plagued by snuffles and sneezes for nine months of the year, but fencing on the northern and eastern sides should screen off any chill winds.

Most children will clamour to play outdoors even when it is wet, and it is easy enough to rig up rick tarpaulin over the play area if you provide stout vertical supports on either side. If you can get hold of a translucent plastic sheeting rather than black tarpaulin, it will keep the area lighter too.

Once you have decided where your play area is going to be you can have fun devising and building your own play equipment. Remember that the simpler it is, the more imaginative possibilities it offers: a climbing frame can be a castle, mountain or pirate ship; a simple table and bench becomes an eating area, play table or shop counter.

The vital aspect is that everything is strongly built and safe to use. Toys should be smooth and well-sanded to avoid splinters, and should be painted in bright weatherproof paint or wood-stain followed with at least three coats of tough exterior varnish. For complete peace of mind while your children are playing, check the twelve-point safety plan below.

When choosing what toys and games to make, remember that a very active child will get more hours of fun from a climbing frame than a sandpit or play table, while an intricate arrangement of slides, bridges and tunnels will be a waste of your time and effort if your child prefers to play quiet games.

To offer your child a good opportunity to develop both agility and imaginative skills, you should really have some form of exercise equipment – climbing frame, parallel bars or the perennially popular swing; an area where favourite toys can be brought out of the house and played with without them getting too dirty; and a 'get messy' activity corner – sandpit, paddling pool in summer, or a plot of soil for mud pies and sunflower growing.

Twelve-point safety guide

1. Make sure that any timber-constructed equipment is strongly made and well anchored to the ground. Check regularly to satisfy yourself it has not deteriorated or become damaged through use.

2. All timber should be sanded down really smooth to avoid splinters and wood catching skin and clothes. Give at least three coats of exterior or yacht varnish for a smooth, safe and durable finish.

3. Use rustless screws and hinges in all construction and check there are no screws or nails protruding by sinking them below the surface.

4. Home-made climbing frames and wooden-constructed swings are safer for older children; but younger children should be given a steel-framed swing with a special seat to prevent them falling off.

5. Do not site your play area too near glass frames and greenhouses. A boisterous game or an unlucky ball could lead to a nasty accident.

6. If you have young children, garden ponds should be fenced off or covered with netting for safety. Always supervise play in paddling pools; a child can drown in only a few inches of water.

7. Do not have poisonous shrubs and plants in the garden. Teach your children which leaves and berries are dangerous. Common culprits are: rhubarb leaves, seeds and pods of lupins, and laburnum, yew, cotoneaster, foxgloves and all the nightshade family.

8. Do not leave old kitchen equipment such as fridges or cookers (ovens) abandoned in the garden, and make sure any toy boxes and chests do not have catches on the lids.

9. Slides and seesaws need extra care: slides must be enclosed at the top and sides with something to hold on to; seesaws need buffers fitted under the seat to prevent jarring.

10. Check that fences and gates are secure before allowing your children to play in the garden unsupervised. Take particular care if your gate opens onto a busy road: fit child-proof locks and latches.

11. Garden tools and chemicals are not toys and can be very dangerous. Do not leave rakes, forks and spades lying around – lock them away in a shed or cupboard with all fertilizers and weed-killers on a high shelf.

12. Never use slug bait or sprays unless specified safe for use with pets and children.

Making toys for the garden

Sandpit

Construct a raised box using second-hand skirting boards (base boards), well sanded and painted in bright weatherproof colours. A locker built at one end by adding rustless-hinged lids of marine plywood provides a handy place to sit as well as storage for buckets and spades. Fill with river-washed sharp sand rather than builder's sand, which will stain clothes. You will need a piece of board, a fine net or a fitted lid to cover the sandpit when not in use to keep out animals and garden debris.

Paddling pool

This can be built in the same way as the sand pit above but lined with a plastic pool liner to make it waterproof. Take care to empty during winter to prevent freezing, and again provide a board or net cover for when not in use.

Combined sandpit and pool

You can make a combined sandpit and paddling pool in much the same way as the individual units: construct a basic rectangle from old floorboards nailed together at the corners, and divide it up into three areas using boards nailed between the sides.

Make up a slatted seat for the central area, and hinge this to one side of the dividers as a storage area for garden toys.

Set the unit on a base of paving slabs that extends about 600 mm (2 ft) all round the unit; set the slabs about 75 mm (3 in) below the surrounding area by building a low brick step: this will help to contain the sand within the play area.

Lastly, make two slatted covers to fit over the paddling pool and sandpit to keep out animals and debris.

A private beach for your children: *the combined sandpit and paddling pool is easy to make from reclaimed floorboards or skirting boards (base boards) – or new timber if you have nothing suitable. Cut the pieces to length and fix together the basic rectangle with nails driven in at the corners. Cut two lengths to fit between the sides and nail these in place to form the three sections. Staple a plastic pool liner in one of the end sections, making sure they are above the water line. Make a slatted lid-cum-bench seat for the central section by screwing several thin battens to two frame pieces and hingeing the assembly to one of the dividers. Use the compartment for storing beach balls and other toys that can be left outside*

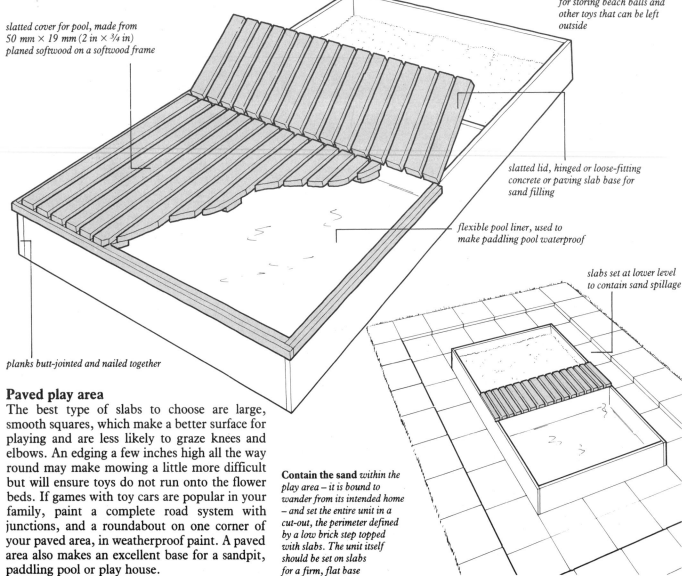

slatted cover for pool, made from 50 mm × 19 mm (2 in × ¾ in) planed softwood on a softwood frame

slatted lid, hinged or loose-fitting concrete or paving slab base for sand filling

flexible pool liner, used to make paddling pool waterproof

slabs set at lower level to contain sand spillage

planks butt-jointed and nailed together

Contain the sand *within the play area – it is bound to wander from its intended home – and set the entire unit in a cut-out, the perimeter defined by a low brick step topped with slabs. The unit itself should be set on slabs for a firm, flat base*

Paved play area

The best type of slabs to choose are large, smooth squares, which make a better surface for playing and are less likely to graze knees and elbows. An edging a few inches high all the way round may make mowing a little more difficult but will ensure toys do not run onto the flower beds. If games with toy cars are popular in your family, paint a complete road system with junctions, and a roundabout on one corner of your paved area, in weatherproof paint. A paved area also makes an excellent base for a sandpit, paddling pool or play house.

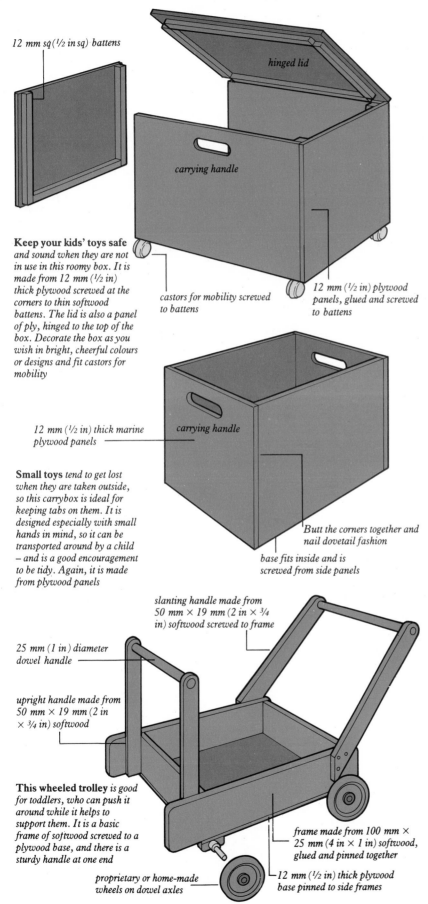

12 mm sq (½ in sq) battens

hinged lid

carrying handle

Keep your kids' toys safe *and sound when they are not in use in this roomy box. It is made from 12 mm (½ in) thick plywood screwed at the corners to thin softwood battens. The lid is also a panel of ply, hinged to the top of the box. Decorate the box as you wish in bright, cheerful colours or designs and fit castors for mobility*

castors for mobility screwed to battens

12 mm (½ in) plywood panels, glued and screwed to battens

12 mm (½ in) thick marine plywood panels

carrying handle

Small toys *tend to get lost when they are taken outside, so this carrybox is ideal for keeping tabs on them. It is designed especially with small hands in mind, so it can be transported around by a child – and is a good encouragement to be tidy. Again, it is made from plywood panels*

Butt the corners together and nail dovetail fashion

base fits inside and is screwed from side panels

slanting handle made from 50 mm × 19 mm (2 in × ¾ in) softwood screwed to frame

25 mm (1 in) diameter dowel handle

upright handle made from 50 mm × 19 mm (2 in × ¾ in) softwood

This wheeled trolley *is good for toddlers, who can push it around while it helps to support them. It is a basic frame of softwood screwed to a plywood base, and there is a sturdy handle at one end*

frame made from 100 mm × 25 mm (4 in × 1 in) softwood, glued and pinned together

proprietary or home-made wheels on dowel axles

12 mm (½ in) thick plywood base pinned to side frames

Toy box

A sturdy marine plywood toy box with rustless screws and hinges encourages children to put their toys away and saves cluttering up the shed or garage. Adjacent parts can be joined with 12 mm (½ in) square wooden strips screwed and glued into the corners. First glue and screw wooden strips to the bottom and the ends, then glue and screw through the strips into the back and front. Do not forget to saw out a handle grip hole at the front (or attach a sturdy thick rope handle). The lid should be constructed in the same way, using wood strips and being fitted to the box by screwing at least three rustless hinges into slots chiselled into the underside of the lid and top edge of the back. Castors screwed under each bottom corner will allow the box to be pulled easily from one part of the garden to another. Paint in bright colours and give several coats of exterior varnish.

Carrybox

A small sturdy wooden carrybox makes it easier for children to transport small toys to their play area and doubles as a shopping basket for pretend games. Make a simple box construction from marine plywood, taking care that each pair of opposite sides are of equal length and their ends sawn or planed accurately square. Corner butt joints should be nailed dovetail-fashion for strength. Gluing between the parts, particularly between the bottom and sides, will make the box even stronger.

You could fit rectangular handle supports, and glue and pin them to the sides with 19 mm (¾ in) oval nails or panel pins. Glue a length of dowel to the supports to complete the handle.

Blocks trolley

A simple wheeled cart for bricks, blocks or other heavy toys should be strongly made as it will invariably be used for ferrying other children and pets as well as a support for toddler's first steps. Larger wheels will allow extra clearance over rough ground. Shape end pieces and handle supports to avoid any sharp corners, and assemble a simple box shape using pva wood glue and panel pins. Glue and pin the bottom from below for strength. Fit handle and wheel bearing supports using glue and screws.

A short, straight support at one end and a longer, angled support at the other enables the cart to be used by children of varying heights. Fit and glue lengths of dowel rod between the supports to serve as handles. Cut four wheels using a jig-saw (sabre saw); glue a wheel onto a length of dowel at one end only, then insert the dowel through the wheel/handle supports and glue on the other wheels.

Swings

For older children construct a stout three-bar wooden frame (protected from rot with wood preservative) with 100 mm × 100 mm (4 in × 4 in) support posts firmly anchored to the ground using cement or mild steel bars, two to each post. Available from builders' merchants, these should be 900 mm (3 ft) long, 30 mm (1¼ in) wide and 6 mm (¼ in) thick, with holes bored in each to take 55 mm (2¼ in) carriage screws, galvanized against rust. Bore holes in the post to line up and tighten screws using a spanner. A third of the post's length should be below ground level for extra stability. A variety of swings and ropes can be attached, allowing several children to play at one go: old car tyres, a length of dowel rod for a trapeze and large metal rings all make good additions. The conventional swing is notoriously bad at wearing out the grass beneath – a piece of plastic netting below will resist wear but still allow the grass to grow through the mesh.

Seesaws

Seesaws are simple to make from a single plank, well sanded and varnished to prevent splinters. Pivot the plank at its exact centre on a frame securely fixed to the ground, and make sure both ends are fitted with a handle for safety. A simple semi-circular back rest and buffers beneath the seat help prevent jarring.

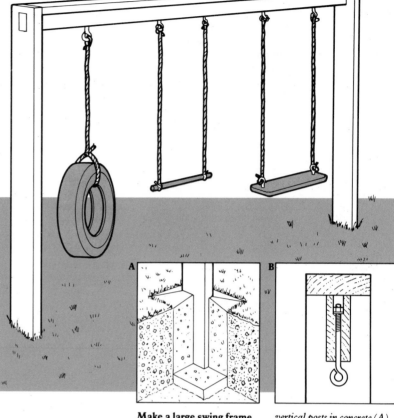

Make a large swing frame *from stout timber and suspend tyres, trapeze bars and seats from strong ropes. Set the* vertical posts in concrete (A) and use eye bolts (B) set in pre-drilled holes in the cross bar to attach the ropes

Make a seesaw *from a plank pivoted on a base and secured to the ground by setting in concrete. Cut out two uprights from 150 mm × 50 mm (6 in × 2 in) softwood and cut notches in the top to take a length of steel rod or iron tube as the pivot. Retain the rod at the top with metal brackets screwed on top, and at the* ends with wood blocks screwed on to the uprights. Fasten the plank to the pivot with U-shaped metal brackets

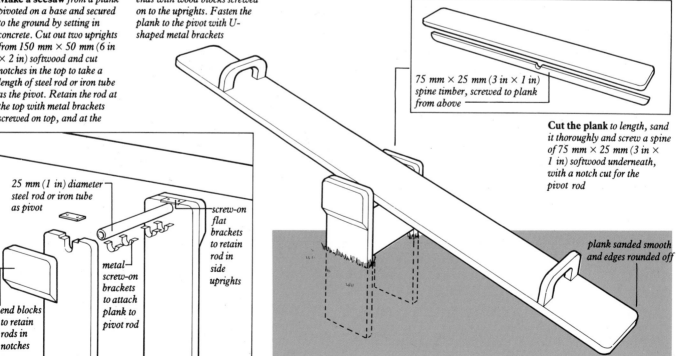

25 mm (1 in) diameter steel rod or iron tube as pivot

metal-screw-on brackets to attach plank to pivot rod

screw-on flat brackets to retain rod in side uprights

end blocks to retain rods in notches

75 mm × 25 mm (3 in × 1 in) spine timber, screwed to plank from above

Cut the plank *to length, sand it thoroughly and screw a spine of 75 mm × 25 mm (3 in × 1 in) softwood underneath, with a notch cut for the pivot rod*

plank sanded smooth and edges rounded off

Table and chairs

If you are confident enough to tackle something a bit more ambitious than a simple picnic bench and table, a proper child-sized table and chairs are not as difficult to construct as they seem – and they are ideal for playing 'house', tea parties and picnics. Mark out a circular table top from a piece of pre-laminated (that is, veneered chipboard) wood, accurately marking leg frame positions to form a cross on the underside. Use a jig-saw (sabre saw) to cut the circle and round off the top and bottom of the cut edge with a plane. Sand the top until smooth. To prevent warping and to anchor the legs, make one long and two short rounded leg frames, and glue and pin them to the underside of the table top to form a cross. Remember to pre-drill the holes for the legs. Cut legs to equal length and glue in position measuring the first one at both ends to check that it is level.

Mark two legs at equal distance from the bottom and glue a round-ended leg brace in position, checking it is square. The other leg brace should automatically find its own level and can be glued onto the first where they cross. Cut seats and legs for the chairs, remembering to pre-drill all holes for the legs and making sure they line up. Glue supports to back and front of the underside of each seat and round off seat edges with a jig-saw (sabre saw). Drop legs into position and glue, spreading slightly to allow braces to be fitted and glued. Cut a back rest to shape using a jig-saw (sabre saw) and sand smooth, then glue into position using three dowel rods as supports. Finish the table and chairs with a good sanding and a couple of coats of paint or varnish. As a finishing touch you could stencil a child's name on the back of each chair before varnishing.

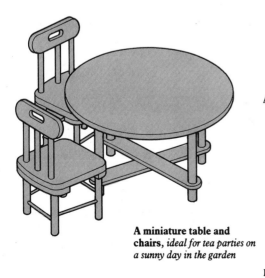

A miniature table and chairs, *ideal for tea parties on a sunny day in the garden*

Play table

A generously sized tabletop attached to frame legs for stability has a number of uses: a picnic table, play table, workbench, shop counter and so on. Attach a row of box seats along one side with hinged lids for storage, and screw or nail a couple of wooden boxes to the table edge to serve as non-spill bottle holders, toy receptacles and shop storage bins.

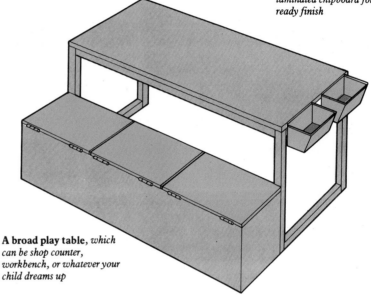

A broad play table, *which can be shop counter, workbench, or whatever your child dreams up*

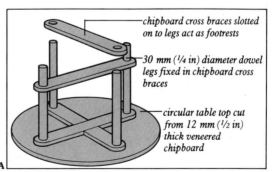

chipboard cross braces slotted on to legs act as footrests

30 mm (1/4 in) diameter dowel legs fixed in chipboard cross braces

circular table top cut from 12 mm (1/2 in) thick veneered chipboard

A

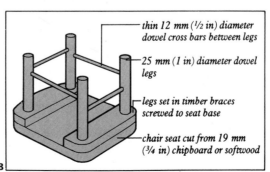

thin 12 mm (1/2 in) diameter dowel cross bars between legs

25 mm (1 in) diameter dowel legs

legs set in timber braces screwed to seat base

chair seat cut from 19 mm (3/4 in) chipboard or softwood

B

Make a play table *from sheets of chipboard fixed to a softwood framework. Construct a basic skeleton by butting together lengths of timber and fixing with glue and screws or nails. Screw a chipboard table top to the frame and make a smaller frame for the box seats. Clad these with chipboard, hinging the lids for storage. Sand all sharp edges smooth and paint as you wish. Alternatively, use laminated chipboard for a ready finish*

A child-sized table *and chairs can be made with chipboard and dowels. Cut out a circular table top and fix one long and two short braces underneath in a cross-shape. Fix the dowel legs into pre-drilled holes. Brace the legs near to the base with two more cross braces (A). Cut out a rectangular chair seat and fit with two leg fixing braces to the underside. Drill holes for the legs and insert them, using glue to secure. Fit thinner dowel cross bars between the legs (B). The chair back is made from three lengths of thin dowel set into the back of the seat. A back panel is fitted on top*

Play house

A fine house can be built on a corner of your paved area, or you can make a floor from old floorboards nailed onto 75 mm × 25 mm (3 in × 1 in) joists spaced at an interval of about 330 mm (13 in). Use second-hand timber, which is less likely to warp than new, to construct a simple wooden framework with sloping roof. Cover in exterior plywood to make walls and roof, with holes cut for door and windows. Windows should be covered in demountable polythene (polyethylene) or acrylic so that they can be removed for ventilation. Go to town with the weatherproof paint for pseudo black beams and trailing roses copied from any Hansel and Gretel picture book for a real fairytale gingerbread house. You will find a play house useful for storing bikes, dolls' prams (carriages) and other items when not in use; use a padlock and key on the door but no catches or bolts.

Climbing frames

Erect a sturdy rectangular framework well anchored to the ground as for the swings. Narrow crossbars set at an easy child's arm span across the top make good overhead swinging bars, while ladders and climbing frameworks can be built along the sides. Somersault bars and ladders can be hung from the centre rails. Take special care that all wooden surfaces are smooth and free from splinters. Rick tarpaulin spread over the framework also makes a fine impromptu marquee for showery summer parties.

A good, sturdy climbing frame *will provide your children with hours of active entertainment. Construct a rectangular frame from 75 mm × 50 mm (3 in × 2 in) softwood, the verticals driven into the ground, the corners notched for strength, secured with glue and screws. Fix intermediate cross bars and suspend ladders and swings*

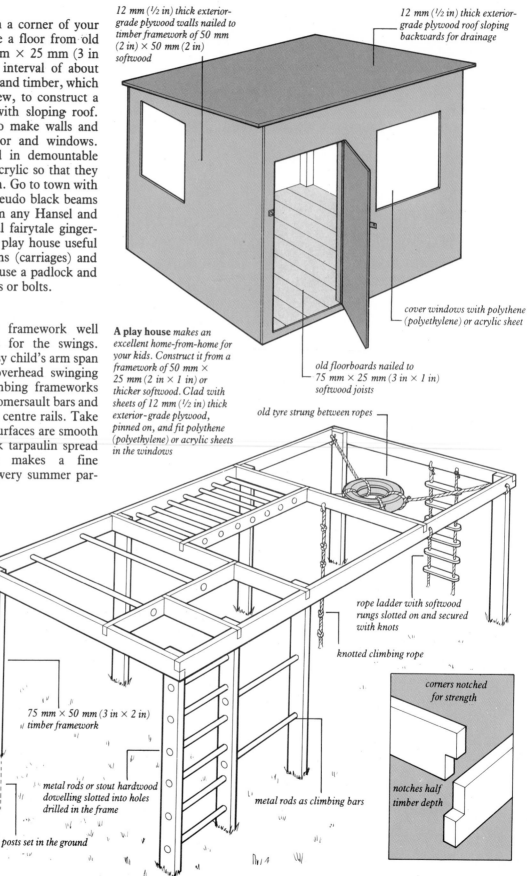

12 mm (½ in) thick exterior-grade plywood walls nailed to timber framework of 50 mm (2 in) × 50 mm (2 in) softwood

12 mm (½ in) thick exterior-grade plywood roof sloping backwards for drainage

cover windows with polythene (polyethylene) or acrylic sheet

A play house *makes an excellent home-from-home for your kids. Construct it from a framework of 50 mm × 25 mm (2 in × 1 in) or thicker softwood. Clad with sheets of 12 mm (½ in) thick exterior-grade plywood, pinned on, and fit polythene (polyethylene) or acrylic sheets in the windows*

old floorboards nailed to 75 mm × 25 mm (3 in × 1 in) softwood joists

old tyre strung between ropes

rope ladder with softwood rungs slotted on and secured with knots

knotted climbing rope

corners notched for strength

notches half timber depth

75 mm × 50 mm (3 in × 2 in) timber framework

metal rods or stout hardwood dowelling slotted into holes drilled in the frame

posts set in the ground

metal rods as climbing bars

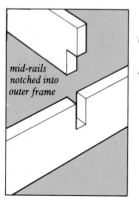

mid-rails notched into outer frame

Ballboard

A ballboard makes an excellent windbreak and screen, and saves all the irritation of rescuing stray balls from irate neighbours. Clad three fence panels with sheets of exterior-grade hardboard and make a goal area with softwood edging. Paint the inner and outer areas a bright colour for contrast. Fix a stout framework on top of the fence and cover with fine netting.

joints glued and pinned

frame of 50 mm × 25 mm (2 in × 1 in) softwood butt-jointed at corners

exterior-grade hardboard nailed to fence posts

white-painted softwood edging defines goal area

paint goal green

paint outer section same as goal

Shop

A simple box structure made from a timber frame, filled in with marine plywood to waist level, and roofed with a panel of plywood or draped with a waterproof cover, offers endless possibilities as shop, chuck wagon and so on. A hinged counter suspended on chains at each side folds up as a shutter and adds to the fun. It can double as dry storage for toys when not in use, or you could install a floor of plastic-covered foam so that it can be used as a sheltered playpen for toddlers.

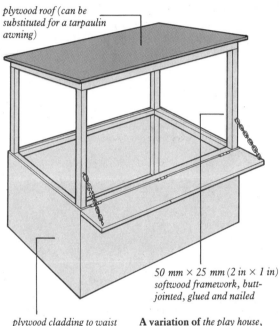

plywood roof (can be substituted for a tarpaulin awning)

50 mm × 25 mm (2 in × 1 in) softwood framework, butt-jointed, glued and nailed

plywood cladding to waist level

A variation of *the play house, this kids' shop is made from a softwood frame clad with plywood to waist level and fitted with a ply roof, or simply draped with a sheet of tarpaulin*

Make a slide *from reclaimed timber, anchored securely to the ground in concrete. The chute itself must be free from any rough edges, nails or other protrusions, which could snag a child's skin or clothing. The size of the unit depends on the age – and height – of your children, but in any event you should aim for a gently sloping chute rather than a steep one, which could cause accidents*

stout handrail screwed to verticals at top of slide

ladder made from softwood stiles with dowel rungs

softwood sides screwed to chute from below

box in the slide with plywood on a wood frame for toy storage

main timbers set below ground in concrete

Slides

Build the basic frame from seasoned, second-hand timber filled in with a weather-proof material such as marine plywood. Crossbars across the 'tower' provide a suitable ladder, but check they are near enough together for a child's stride. A marine plywood slide chute should be free from protruding nails or splinters and have enclosed sides. The top should also be enclosed, with proper hand holds. The slide can double as a handy store for large toys if boxed in beneath with plywood doors on weatherproof hinges and easy-open catches.

20. Designing a garden

No matter how hard you work in a garden and no matter how much you spend out buying good quality garden plants, nothing will ever turn it into a place of beauty and an area of relaxation unless it is properly planned.

Planning a garden may seem a daunting task that is best left to experts but, so long as you follow a few basic rules of design, there is no reason why you should not be able to create a garden to be proud of.

Whether you are starting from scratch with an area of plain earth or turf as left by the house builder, or whether your garden was started many years previously, the first necessity is for an overall plan.

Start by listing exactly what you want from the garden, bearing in mind your interests, activities and family needs. Head the list with those features that are important to you and try to gauge the space that each requires. You should also work out how long each feature is likely to be used. It pays to plan for the future as

well as for the present. For example, a patio or paved terrace will probably be used by the whole family for the foreseeable future, while a sandpit for the children may be fine for a year or two but it may then be redundant when they have moved on to bikes and go-karts. It may well be that a temporary structure is ideal for a sandpit, or if a permanent sandpit is made then at least it should be built so that it is relatively easy to clean out and convert to a garden pond as soon as the children are older.

Other features that you may wish to include on your list are such things as a pergola, play area, pool and rock garden. Also add to this list the garden buildings and utility features that will be required. This list might include a greenhouse, shed, summerhouse, compost heap, dustbin area (trash can storage), and clothes-drying area or washing line.

You also need to list the types of plants you want to grow – roses, fruit trees, herbaceous plants, shrubs, vegetables, lawns, and so on.

Below: *Bold planning can produce some striking effects. This walled garden utilizes every bit of available space to the full, with a formal, steep flight of steps in brick flanking a lush pond as a centrepiece; on the raised level there is a spacious terrace and pergola for sitting out*

Right: *You can plan a 'wild' garden by grouping together leafy shrubs and bushy trees around a meandering path of irregularly shaped crazy paving. Here the illusion of a much larger area has been created by taking the path through the undergrowth to a small paved area, which contains the table and chairs. A high boundary wall prevents the garden from being overlooked*

Drawing up plans

Once you have listed your requirements and assessed your existing garden you are in a position to draw up a detailed plan of the new garden. But first you need to look once more at the list of requirements to ensure that everything you wish to include is feasible.

A small garden will limit possibilities and in this case it is best to reduce the number of features to be included in order to avoid the garden from looking a hotch-potch of too many small elements. Even so it may be possible to plan a paved area so it can serve many purposes, such as for sitting, entertaining, play, washing line, and so on. It will probably be best to make the final list of features according to your priorities and then, when drawing up the detailed plan, you can work down this list including as many features as possible.

Another limiting factor will probably be cost. It is very easy to plan a lavish summerhouse, paved area, pool, shrub border, and so on, but paying for it may be another matter. So forward planning is essential, allowing the garden to develop over the years as plants are bought or given and major items such as greenhouses, sheds and paving are purchased. All these various items should be planned for initially and even if the garden starts as a large lawn area it will be possible to plant trees, shrubs and flowers, and lay paving and put up garden buildings as you can afford them, until the garden develops following the initial plan.

Remember that for a good deal of the time the garden will be viewed from indoors, so design the garden so that it looks good from your favourite armchair, or from the kitchen window.

It is best not to have just one dominating feature such as a large lawn, but to plan various features such as sitting area, lawn, pool, vegetable garden, and so on, so they are fairly well balanced with each other and therefore do not give the garden a lopsided appearance. It is also a good idea to plan the garden so that all parts are not visible from just one place as this will give the design an element of interest.

Adding the details

You can draw up your final detailed plan of the garden on plain paper, but you will probably find it easier to work to a scale using graph paper. The scale to use depends on the size of your garden; you should, however, work to as large a scale as possible, if necessary joining small sheets of paper together to allow all the boundaries to be marked. For a small garden work to a scale of 100 mm to represent one metre (about 4 in to 3 ft).

Draw in the boundaries of the plot, and indicate window and door positions on the house walls. Mark the North point clearly and add the existing features, such as garage, shed, walls and existing trees. Remember that existing trees are not always worth preserving. Some may be too close to the house, damaging foundations and blocking light to the windows. Others may be obliterating a desirable view or simply be declining due to old age. You may wish to remove such trees, but first check with the local authority in case they are subject to a preservation order, in which case permission will be required before they can be felled.

Once the bare bones of the garden have been noted on the plan, you can draw in the various features. But first you need to decide what style the garden should be. An informal garden should be based on gentle, but not fussy, curves. Most gardens are based on this style because curves have a softening effect, which goes well with the loose, informal habit of most plants, and allows plants of all types to be mixed together in beds and borders.

Choosing a style

A formal garden should contain strictly geometrical shapes – squares, circles, rectangles, hexagons and so on. Such gardens look best with shrubs such as roses, and clipped hedges.

A third, compromise style is semi-formal because it features areas that are informal in design and those that are formal. For instance, you may want to have a formal terrace and rose garden area leading on to an informal shaped lawn and mixed border.

Another important consideration is to include an 'axis': this is an invisible line to which the main features are aligned and which ideally leads the eye to a focal point. This may be a distant view, a summerhouse, a fountain or a statue. Try to set the focal point off-centre to create an angled axis, which, in a narrow plot in particular, helps to disguise the dominant rectangular shape.

If there is a view that is worth preserving, the layout of the garden can enhance this. Borders can be shaped and plants grouped to frame the view and ensure it becomes a natural focal point.

Remember also that the view of the garden can be completely different when standing than when sitting, so plan the garden so that when it is viewed from your favourite armchair, or when standing at the kitchen sink, the important features are not hidden behind the glazing bars.

In some cases the view of the skyline can be undesirable – such as when there are high-rise buildings nearby, for example – and in this case it can be a good idea to screen the view by building a pergola close to the house and planting trees to blot out the unwanted view. If

Making a plan of your garden

Before you can decide on a finalized plan of your garden you must make some rough sketches of the existing plot, drawing in all permanent features – such as the house, outbuildings and mature trees – in their correct proportions.

Measure up the garden from a fixed point such as a boundary wall, which makes a ready baseline for plotting all the information. If there is no suitable baseline, set one up yourself with stringlines stretched between pegs driven into the ground. Indicate the north-facing direction so you can plan the patio and planting areas with the most suitable aspect.

Transfer the measurements to a scale plan drawn on graph paper for accuracy – use a scale of 1:50 – and include all features. Any parts that are difficult to position on the plan from the baseline can be plotted by taking two measurements from already fixed points, such as the corners of the house. Use a compass to transfer the dimensions to your plan, by marking intersecting arcs to indicate the centre of the object – a technique called 'triangulation'.

Use this method to draw in other remote features such as trees, hedges, paths or a garden pond. Draw in items you cannot move, such as manholes.

Where there are curved paths, walls or other features, triangulate from your baseline, marking off all major changes in direction, then join up the dots to form the curve.

Once you have included all the relevant dimensions and have drawn movable and immovable features on your plan, you can start to adapt the shape of the garden to your new design. Here it is best if you stick tracing paper overlays to the scale plan and draw your new schemes on these, to avoid cluttering the plan with pencil marks.

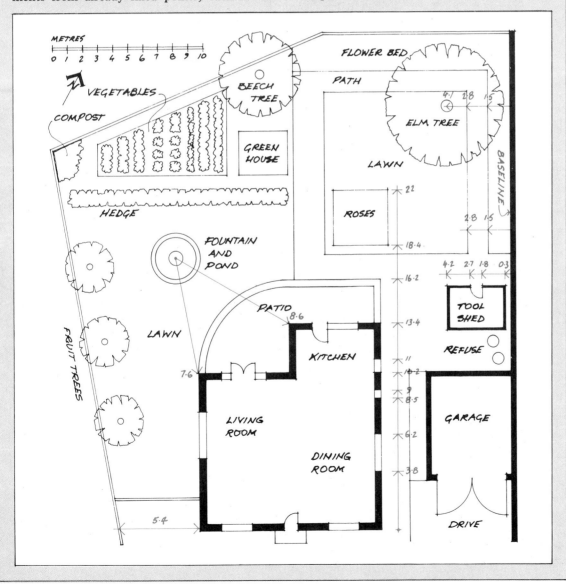

Drawing up plans

paved and linked to the rest of the garden by one or two shallow, broad steps.

Probably most of the garden will be devoted to lawn or paving, in the latter case particularly if the garden is small or surrounded by trees, where a lawn will probably not grow satisfactorily. The shapes of those areas should be kept as simple as possible – gentle curves, or squares or rectangles, which can be broken up by using the soft forms of plants around or within the shape to give contrast. In the paved areas contrast can be achieved by planting in raised beds and using tubs and vases.

You can also use different building materials together to soften the design. For example, reconstituted stone paving can be relieved with areas of bricks, stone chippings or pebbles.

When choosing a site for a patio or other seating area, or considering where to site a greenhouse, it is most important to consider the aspect of the garden. It is best to study the

Left: *brick pavers laid in a simple running bond make a narrow border path*

Below: *A patio made up of bricks in intricate patterns leads to an ornate pond*

these screens are close to the normal viewpoint they will obliterate the distant view far more effectively than by planting a tall hedge on the boundary.

In a small garden in particular, paths tend to be dominant, so site them with care as they can easily seriously affect the appearance of the garden, in many cases detrimentally. Try to keep paths as straight and as direct as possible when they are purely functional, such as leading from the gate to the front door, but otherwise you can use gentle curves, especially if the path is just for strolling around the garden. In fact, a meandering path is a good design feature: it helps to create an element of surprise in the garden design; it can wander round a screen formed partway across the garden to give a garden extra interest by providing a new view as you walk round. The screen can be created by taking a shrub border partway across the garden, or by planting a hedge, for example.

Very steep slopes can be dangerous, but shallower ones can be an asset rather than a liability in garden design. Gentle slopes look attractive whether planted with shrubs, rock garden plants or grassed over, while steeper slopes can be terraced with low retaining walls to make planting and maintenance an easier task.

If a site is flat it will look much better if a change in level can be created, even if this means only digging out part of the garden by about 150 mm to 225 mm (6 in to 9 in) to create a partially sunken area, which can be turfed or

garden over a period, noting where the sun rises and reaches the garden, and where it sinks and disappears. You need to bear in mind the seasonal variations also; the summer sun is much higher in the sky than the sun in winter, which may entirely fail to reach the garden. Whether an area of the garden is sunny or shaded for most of the day will also affect your choice of plants.

If possible the patio should adjoin the house so it is convenient for taking meals outside. Ideally it will receive sun for the greater part of the day. Part of the patio can be screened with a pergola to give shade on hot days and it will also give some privacy from neighbouring houses. Generally in the UK and most of Europe it is best to choose the sunniest, hottest spot possible for sitting out, and on those comparatively few scorching days, shade can easily be arranged, by using sun umbrellas or a temporary awning; but in many parts of the USA a permanent shelter will be needed.

When designing a front garden practial considerations should be the first priority. You need easy and convenient access to the front door and to a garage if there is one, and if the garden is large enough a car turning area will avoid danger of having to back on to the road. Unless it is essential to maintain an open-plan front garden it will probably be desirable to have a boundary wall, fence or hedge. This should blend in with the style used on neighbouring properties. On main roads there is the problem of traffic noise to contend with and while double-glazing the windows at the front of the house will reduce the problem it will still be beneficial to plant shrubs and small trees in the front garden to act as a sound baffle.

With all these various design considerations in mind you should be able to produce a detailed

Left: *A small, secluded plot, fenced off for privacy, has a freeform lawn with tree centrepiece*

Above: *A patio designed for relaxation, with a sheltered and shaded paved area*

plan, if necessary using paper shapes to represent the various features you require and arranging them jigsaw fashion on the outline plan until you achieve a satisfactory design. You can then transfer the design to tracing paper, which will allow you to finalize the master plan.

At this stage it is sensible to physically try out the design on the site using long canes and string to represent screens, walls, fences and tall plants and short canes to represent the boundaries of paved areas and grass. View the plot from the downstairs windows, take a chair and try sitting in various parts of the garden, and finally take a look from an upstairs window, which will give a semi-plan view. At this stage it is easy to move canes and make adjustments as necessary.

A rectangular plot

Typical of many houses is to have a plain rectangular plot some 12 m (40 ft) wide and 36 m (120 ft) long. Often such plots have a concrete path running the length of the garden and in this case it is probably best to retain the path; not only is it hard work to break up, but also it would be expensive to replace. Such a path also has the advantage of allowing access down the garden at all times of the year, without getting your feet wet. The path forms a natural division in the garden, so it is sensible to grow vegetables to the east of the path and keep the decorative areas to the west side. A low lavender hedge running along the side of the path makes the vegetable plot less obtrusive.

This decorative side of the garden is divided into four distinct areas by plantings of evergreen shrubs and a mixed planting, which give visual breaks and a hint of what lies beyond to tease the onlooker into thinking that it meanders on for a long way.

The first section is a sitting area near the house, using paving to form an extension to the path with an irregular edge to soften the hard outline. The hardness of the paving is also softened with pockets of low-growing herbs, while the group of conifers and taller flowers screens the shed and almost all of the vegetable area from the sitting area.

The second section, bordering the paved area, is a good quality lawn bordered by flower beds planted with annuals and perennials and divided from the next section, a grassed play area, with evergreen trees to form an irregular-shaped all-year screen to be least like a formal clipped hedge.

Another evergreen screen separates the final area which is partially paved for wet weather play and partially enclosed with a fruit cage, which allows soft fruit to be grown.

Privacy is provided by fences at each side of the garden planted with espalier fruit trees. If privacy on the seating area is required, then a pergola could be erected here, or a gazebo could be constructed that is partially glazed to allow sitting out in wet weather. Alternatively, the pergola can be covered with a canvas awning to give shelter and shade.

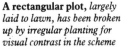

A rectangular plot, *largely laid to lawn, has been broken up by irregular planting for visual contrast in the scheme*

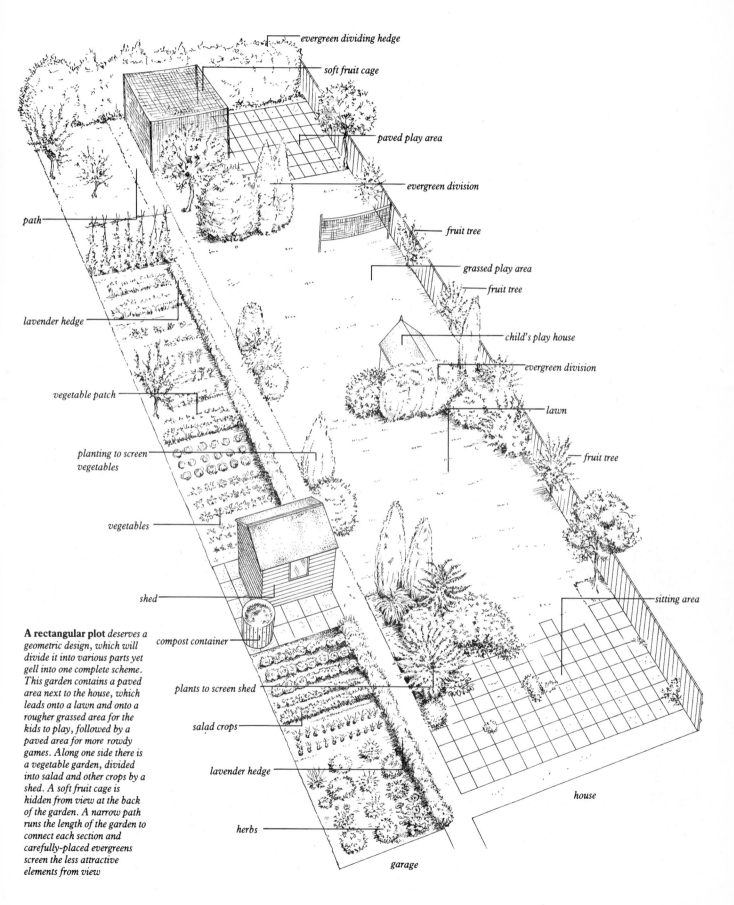

evergreen dividing hedge

soft fruit cage

paved play area

evergreen division

path

fruit tree

grassed play area

fruit tree

lavender hedge

child's play house

evergreen division

vegetable patch

lawn

planting to screen
vegetables

fruit tree

vegetables

shed

compost container

plants to screen shed

sitting area

salad crops

lavender hedge

house

herbs

garage

A rectangular plot *deserves a geometric design, which will divide it into various parts yet gell into one complete scheme. This garden contains a paved area next to the house, which leads onto a lawn and onto a rougher grassed area for the kids to play, followed by a paved area for more rowdy games. Along one side there is a vegetable garden, divided into salad and other crops by a shed. A soft fruit cage is hidden from view at the back of the garden. A narrow path runs the length of the garden to connect each section and carefully-placed evergreens screen the less attractive elements from view*

A small plot

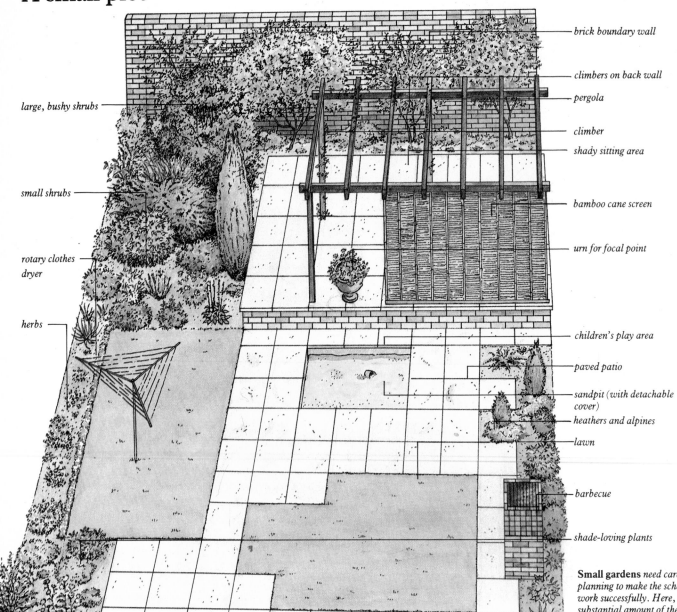

brick boundary wall

climbers on back wall

pergola

climber

shady sitting area

bamboo cane screen

urn for focal point

children's play area

paved patio

sandpit (with detachable cover)

heathers and alpines

lawn

barbecue

shade-loving plants

large, bushy shrubs

small shrubs

rotary clothes dryer

herbs

Small gardens *need careful planning to make the scheme work successfully. Here, a substantial amount of the plot has been given over to paving, making regular maintenance easier. For the kids, there is a sandpit enclosed within the paving to prevent the contents from wandering. A slightly raised terrace at the back of the garden contains a paved sitting area partially screened from view from neighbouring houses or roads by a bamboo trellis arrangement. Shrubs provide a colourful, bushy show at one side of the terrace and flowering climbers lessen the harshness of the brick boundary wall. A rotary clothes dryer is an excellent choice where space is limited. Sensibly, the barbecue is located near the house for convenience*

Most town gardens are restricted in size and this design makes the best use of the available space. The extensive use of paving makes the garden simple to run and to maintain and despite the lack of room it has been possible to divide the garden into four distinct sections – for sitting, playing, clothes-drying and entertaining.

The paved area near the house is used for entertaining, since this part of the garden receives sun in the evenings. The main sitting area is at the far end of the garden on a slightly raised area of paving. This area was chosen because it is the sunniest part of the garden during the day.

The two areas are linked by square paving across a grass area with a play area and sand pit on a slightly lower level, which allows sand to be easily swept back in. (Incidentally, the pit should have a slatted cover to keep pets out of the sand when the pit is not being used.)

A focal point is provided by a flower-filled urn positioned under the pergola, which is partially screened with a bamboo trelliswork arrangement on one side for privacy – an important factor in a garden of this type.

Herbs are allotted to the sunny area next to the sitting space, while the shady bed by the house is planted with shade-loving plants such as hostas, mahonias, camellias and flowering quince (*chaenomeles*).

An awkward-shaped plot

Although most gardens tend to be either rectangular or square, you may be faced with the problem of an odd-shaped plot. An area with a curving boundary calls out for an informal design, as shown here.

In this case the garden sloped towards the house: by terracing the garden it was possible to form a raised bed with a serpentine front wall to complement the curve of the boundary wall. For privacy this boundary is planted with a conifer and evergreen hedge and the raised bed, which is retained by a 750 mm (30 in) high wall, is planted with bedding plants and bulbs, which can be changed twice a year. At the foot of the retaining wall is a 75 mm (3 in) wide strip of concrete set slightly below the lawn level, which

enables the grass to be trimmed up to the wall without damaging the mower blades.

The circular seating area is constructed with hard bricks laid on mortar on a firm base with a gentle fall to allow rainwater to run off freely. A permanent seat is built into the retaining wall and the fabric-covered foam block seat cushions are stored indoors when the seating is not in use.

A greenhouse is placed to one side of the seating area, where it will catch the maximum amount of sun.

The rest of the garden is given over to lawn apart from a narrow bed on the south-east side, which has some espalier fruit trees planted against the boundary fence. A morello cherry is the best choice for the shady section.

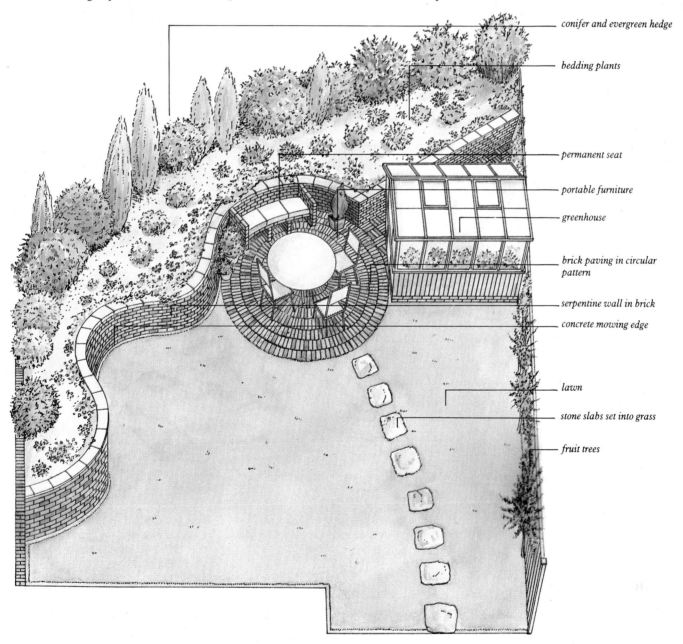

conifer and evergreen hedge

bedding plants

permanent seat

portable furniture

greenhouse

brick paving in circular pattern

serpentine wall in brick

concrete mowing edge

lawn

stone slabs set into grass

fruit trees

21. Garden machinery

Maintaining your mower

The lawnmower is one of the most neglected pieces of garden equipment, often put away at the end of the mowing season and brought out the following spring, with no thought of overhaul or maintenance. We just expect it to work.

A well adjusted and maintained mower will make the work easier and will do it more efficiently and reliably, too. Follow these simple tips to keep your type of mower running smoothly.

WARNING: Before you attempt any repairs or cleaning operations on an electric lawnmower, you must disconnect it from the power supply.

Cylinder mowers

● Clean the blades after each mowing. Always clean them, including the curved deflector plate, before you put the mower away for the season. Brush these parts with paraffin or light oil to discourage rust.

● Periodically, throughout the season, check that the height of cut is set properly. There may be two controls for this – one at each side of the blades. Make sure both are set evenly: it is easier to check on a firm surface than on grass. The exact height of cut will depend on the type of lawn that you want and the time of year.

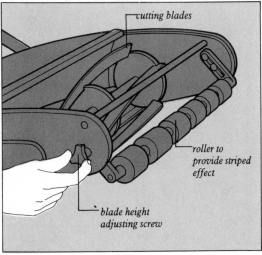

cutting blades

roller to provide striped effect

blade height adjusting screw

● Lubricate the mower's working parts occasionally, and certainly at the beginning and end of the season. The exact points to oil vary slightly with different makes of machine, but even if you have lost your instruction manual it will be obvious from the position of dust caps where the main lubrication points are. Do not forget the roller bearings, cutting height adjusters, front rollers and cylinder bearings.

A hand-powered *lawnmower is still a popular choice for smaller lawns or remote areas where a flex will not reach and where a petrol type is uneconomic*

A typical lightweight *electric lawnmower with detachable grass box. This type usually has a roller to produce the familiar striped effect*

For the larger lawn *a petrol mower gives you the freedom to wander from power points without the need for trailing extension leads. This type usually has a large-capacity grass box*

A hover mower – *either petrol- or electrically-driven – is a boon for awkward shaped gardens with steep grassed banks and hollows, where a conventional mower could not go*

● At the same time, see that the blades are correctly adjusted to cut cleanly and evenly along their length. Use a piece of writing paper, moving it along the fixed blade and turning the cylinder by hand (be careful not to trap your fingers). The paper should be cut cleanly along the whole length. Follow the instruction manual for any necessary adjustment.

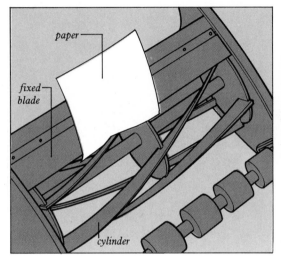

● If you notice a small nick in the blade – possibly caused by a stone – remove the blade, clamp it in a vice and try to file it out, using a coarse metalworking file. If the blade is in poor condition, it may need regrinding. This should be done by a specialist.

Electric mowers

● Before you use an electric mower at the beginning of the season, inspect the whole length of the cable carefully. If it is damaged in any way, renew the cable. If you want to join the cable, always use special waterproof fittings: never just tape them together.
● If you have a battery mower make sure that the battery is kept charged. Even if you are not using the mower, top up the charge every six weeks. Check the level of the distilled water periodically and keep it filled.

Rotary mowers

● Clean the underside of a rotary or suction mower with a brush before you put it away each time. Before putting the mower away at the end of the season, wash the underside of the hood.
● Check that the cutting height is correct and adjust if necessary. Lubricate the adjusting lever or handwheel.
● If the blade becomes nicked, remove it, place it in a vice and use a fine file to smooth the edge. Check that the blade is balanced by rotating it on a pencil. If it needs slight adjustment you may

be able to balance it with a little more filing on the heavy side.

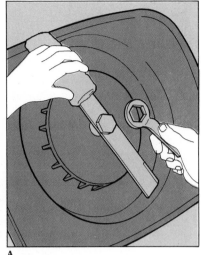

A   B

Petrol mowers

● If the engine is reluctant to start, or is not performing normally, remove the spark plug, clean the points and check the gap. Use a feeler gauge (25 thousandths of an inch is normal, unless otherwise stated in the handbook). If the plug is very worn and dirty, buy a new one. Always check the plug before starting a new season.

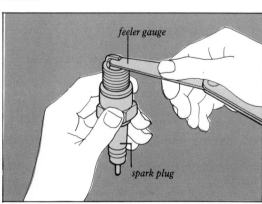

● For winter storage, remove the spark plug and store it in a dry place indoors. Pour 5 ml (1 teaspoonful) of engine oil into the plug hole, turn the engine by hand, then block the hole with a clean, fluff-free rag.
● Keep the oil sump topped up (check the dipstick). After winter storage, drain the sump and renew the oil (unless it is a two-stroke engine). SAE 30 oil is more suitable than multigrade car oil.
● Before winter or at the beginning of the season, remove and clean or renew the air filter. It can usually be cleaned in a detergent, dried, then moistened with cycle oil.

To remove the blade of a rotary mower for sharpening, turn the mower on its side and grasp the blade with a wad of thick cloth – take care not to cut your hands. Loosen the central retaining nut with a hexagonal spanner (A) then pull out the nut and lift the blade from its spindle (B). Reverse the procedure when fitting the sharpened blade

Dealing with other garden tools

All garden tools will benefit from a little routine care and maintenance. It does not take long to clean your tools before you put them away and a little extra effort before storing them for the winter is always worthwhile.

Follow these quick checklists to make sure you keep your tools in good order and ready for action. If your tools should become damaged, there are some quick and easy ways to make lasting repairs to prolong the life of the implements.

Remember, if you are carrying out any repairs to electrical equipment, to unplug it from the mains first.

Digging tools *(left) usually have no moving parts, so deterioration occurs in the metal parts, which rust, and the wooden shafts, which may break. If you are buying new tools it is sensible to choose non-rusting types with metal or tough plastic shafts. Cutting tools such as shears (below) and clippers may need adjustment or replacement parts*

Rotary Cultivator
After use
● Clean off dirt and mud from around the rotors and shield, then wipe the blades with an oily rag.
● Dry with an old cloth.

Periodically
● Check belt drive for tension (if applicable); make sure cable controls do not need adjustment.

Before storing
● Remove rotors, together with other accessories, and wash them. Dry and spray with a proprietary protective coating.
● Remove rotor pins and clean socket. Grease shaft before replacing rotors.

Hedgecutter
After use
● Wipe over the teeth with an oily rag.

Before storing
● Lubricate the blades.
● Check cables (if electric).
● Spray blades with a proprietary protective spray coating.

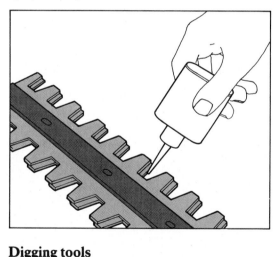

Lubricate all the blade sections of a hedgecutter to prevent rust and corrosion

Digging tools
Spades and forks will last for years with little attention, but make a point of cleaning the soil and mud off them before putting them away. Wipe the metal parts with an oily rag to discourage rust: the action of digging, however, will usually keep the blades or prongs polished.

Repairing a broken shaft
One of the most likely problems with a spade or a garden fork is a broken shaft. Metal shafts are unlikely to break, but if they do you will not be able to do anything about it. Wooden shafts are the most likely to break but are fairly easy to replace.

● Remove the stump of the old shaft. It is possible that you may have to drill out the old rivet.
● Taper the end of the new shaft with a plane and glasspaper until it fits snugly into the socket.
● Knock the shaft firmly into the socket then secure it in place with rustproof screws through the rivet holes.

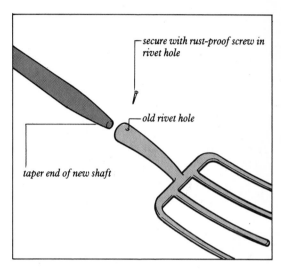

secure with rust-proof screw in rivet hole

old rivet hole

taper end of new shaft

Shears and trimmers
Do not try to sharpen your own shears or trimmers – setting the angles of the cutting edge is difficult. You should be able to get this done professionally if it is necessary. You should, however, keep the blades well lubricated and the pivot of secateurs tightened to prevent any sideways movement (this will depend on the type and make of secateurs). Those that can be tightened usually have a nut or screw.

keep pivot point well lubricated for easy action

keep blades sharp and at correct angle of cut

22.Water in the garden

Adding a pond

Ornamental ponds provide such pleasure in the garden and are so easy to install and maintain. They have a lot to offer even the smallest suburban garden, which can enjoy a few beautiful miniature water lilies, the odd fish swimming lazily between the weeds in addition to tiny frogs, water beetles and even dragonflies.

A small, formal pond can be incorporated into a patio or paved area with great success. It will remain looking good with little maintenance, making it ideal for anyone who does not have a lot of spare time. And if you install a waterfall or fountain you will have the added feature of running water.

A word of warning though: if you have very young children a pond can be dangerous and it may be better to wait until they are older before you add one to your garden.

A curved garden pond, *such as this distinctive figure-of-eight style, can be made using a flexible liner. This attractive pond complements the broad, flat lawn and its circular planting bed, and makes an interesting focal point when viewed from the patio area beyond. Turn to the following pages to see how the pond was created*

Siting a pond

Your pond can be as simple or complicated in shape as you wish; it is a good idea to visit your local water-garden centre before you start planning to get inspiration on designs, plants and fish available. Whatever type of pond you decide, it must be sited carefully: most important is that it should be positioned well away from any trees, which can be a problem in autumn when the leaves fall. Overhead trees will also inhibit water plants from flourishing and encourage mosquitoes.

Your pond should also be in a fairly sunny location if you want your flowering pond plants to grow vigorously – sunlight for at least half the day is the minimum. If you intend to have a fountain, waterfall, or underwater lights, bear in mind that the nearer the house it is sited, the closer it will be to an electricity supply.

A level site is not essential – you can install a pond on a gently sloping site quite easily if you use rocks above and below it to retain the soil. But make sure the pond itself is perfectly level.

Calculating size

Size will be limited not only by how much you can afford to spend and how much time you have, but also by available space in the garden. Try to keep it in proportion to the surrounding area. A minimum surface area of 3.5 sq m (38 sq ft) is recommended to maintain harmony between water, plants and fish and to keep the water well aerated. Any smaller than this and you may find the water remains cloudy. The recommended depth is between 380 mm and 600 mm (1 ft 3 in and 2 ft) with a planting shelf about 230 mm (9 in) below the surface and 230 mm (9 in) wide around the edge of the pool. Plants will be planted in plastic baskets stood on the shelf. Water less than 380 mm (1 ft 3 in) deep is prone to overheating in hot weather, leaving the fish short of oxygen, and may freeze solid in winter. Aim at excavating a hole big enough to give a minimum of five gallons of water per square foot of surface area, although the optimum is eight gallons of water per square foot. Even in large ponds there is no need to exceed a depth of 760 mm (2 ft 6 in). The sides of the pond should not be vertical but slope outwards at about 20 degrees to the vertical. This ensures that if the pond freezes, the ice will tend to move upwards as it forms, thus reducing pressure on the sides.

Pond shapes

Shape will be purely a matter of personal preference. Formal ponds are usually square, circular or rectangular, usually the centrepiece of a formally designed garden or paved area such as a patio. More popular, however, are informal ponds, irregularly shaped and intended to follow the natural contours of the garden. If you choose the informal type keep it fairly simple and stick to bold sweeps and curves, with nothing elaborate. A variation of the broad kidney shape is the most economical in pond lining material. To get some idea of whether the size and shape are suitable, mark out the ground with pegs or lay a garden hose in varying shapes and sizes.

Pond types

Ponds can be constructed from concrete but they are difficult and laborious to build and unless great care is taken, they are also prone to cracking and leaking.

The quickest pond to install is the rigid plastic, pre-formed type. It is less likely to leak than other types, but you are limited by size and shape. The thicker, more expensive of these ponds are made from rigid glass fibre and are self-supporting so need not be buried.

The most flexible system is using waterproof liners, which are available in a variety of materials of differing qualities; so choose with care. The cheapest and least suitable is heavy-gauge polythene (polyethylene) with a minimum thickness of 150 microns (600 gauge), but this is not really durable or flexible enough. PVC is stronger and has more elasticity, particularly if you select the nylon-reinforced variety, which should last more than ten years; these are usually stone coloured on one side, blue on the other. It is best to use the stone-coloured surface uppermost in the pond for the most natural effect.

The best, and most expensive, lining material is butyl rubber, which is extremely durable and stretches easily to fit the contours of your pond. It is available in black, grey or stone-colour.

Calculate the size of liner required by measuring the overall length of the pond and adding twice the maximum depth to give the liner depth, and the overall width of the pool plus twice the depth to give the liner width.

Plants and fish

Planting can be done a few days after the pond is filled if you use a rigid or flexible liner, but it is a good idea to wait a month before introducing any fish. This allows the plants to become established and the water to settle; you will find any murkiness will begin to disappear after this period. Plant out any time between late April and early September. As a rough guide you will need one marginal (pool-side) plant per 1.5 sq m (5 sq ft) of surface area; one floating plant per 3 sq m (10 sq ft); one deep marginal (positioned in crates on the pool bottom) per 4.5 sq m (15 sq ft); and one water lily per 7.5 sq m (25 sq ft).

Pond shapes
Informal ponds are usually the most popular, because they look more natural in most garden settings. You can fit a liner pond in virtually any shape you like, or a rigid plastic pre-formed type (above): these come in a range of designs

Constructing a pond

Installing a pre-formed pond

1. Rigid pre-formed plastic ponds are easy to install. Dig a hole about 100 mm (4 in) larger than required all round then place a compacted layer of sand in the bottom. Place the pond temporarily in position to check that the hole is the right depth and to make sure that its edges are level using a spirit level and straight-edge; adjust the sand bed if necessary.

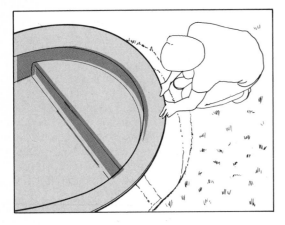

2. Once you are satisfied the pond is level, pack soil tightly round the base section. Be very careful there are no sharp objects in the soil likely to puncture the lining (especially important if installing one of the cheaper, semi-rigid types). When the lower section of the pond is fixed, half-fill with water to help keep it steady while you fill in the rest of the soil, making sure you compact it well.

3. Finish off by edging with coping stones. These should overlap the pond edge by 30 mm to 45 mm (1¼ in to 1¾ in) and be firmly bedded into mortar. For a more substantial edge, lay the stones on a concrete foundation. Dig out a strip all round the pond 100 mm × 300 mm (4 in × 1 ft) before installing the liner. Pour a 1:2:4 mix of concrete into the excavated strip, fit the liner and fix slabs on top.

Installing a liner pond

1. Before you start to excavate for the pond, decide on an approximate shape, using a length of rope or garden hose. If the pond is to be set into a lawn, remove the turf 50 mm to 60 mm (2 in to 2½ in) thick to the shape of the pond plus the width of the paving stones that will be set round the pond edge. Drive in pegs at the extreme corners of the site and level them off accurately using a straight-edge and spirit level.

2. Dig out to a level of about 230 mm (9 in), sloping the sides inwards by about 75 mm (3 in) for every 230 mm (9 in) of depth to save damage during freezing and to reduce the likelihood of soil subsidence. Now excavate the rest of the hole to about 230 mm to 300 mm (9 in to 1 ft) deep, again with sloping sides, leaving a 230 mm (9 in) wide planting shelf all the way round. Remove any sharp objects which may puncture your lining.

3. Lay a 25 mm (1 in) thick layer of compacted sand in the bottom of the pit and carefully unfold and place the liner squarely across the hole. Try to lay the liner during warm weather, so that it will stretch more easily. Weight the edges with bricks, blocks or slabs at regular intervals all the way round, leaving a slight sag in the middle. Begin filling the pond slowly with a hose.

4. The liner will gradually sink into the hole, partly due to stretching: you should ease the weights at intervals until the liner fits snugly in the hole. Try to smooth out any wrinkles as they occur, although most should have disappeared by the time the pond is full of water. When it is full, trim off any excess liner material, leaving about 200 mm (8 in) around the edge for fixing down. In corners and tight bends fold bunched sheeting neatly to hide the surplus; never cut it or it will invariably tear later. Finish off the edges as described above.

Building a raised pond

1. A formal square or rectangular raised pond can be constructed using decorative walling blocks. Mark out the site as before then lay footings for the walls according to your soil conditions and height of wall. Walls of approximately 300 mm to 760 mm (1 ft to 1 ft 6 in) high need a concrete foundation around 200 mm (8 in) wider than the wall – 100 mm (4 in) each side. The concrete should be 70 mm to 100 mm (3 in to 4 in) thick; a mix of one part cement ; six parts mixed aggregate will provide a suitably stong surface.

2. Build up the walls a course at a time, checking that each is level. They should be double-skinned, allowing a 25 mm (1 in) gap between each skin. For maximum stability, 'key' the walls into each other at the junctions. Lay the flexible pond liner and build it into the structure by completely overlapping the inner wall skin one course above the surface of the water. Walls should be capped with 270 mm (10¾ in) coping stones mortared firmly into place.

3. Set deep marginal plants and water lilies in plastic planting crates with open pattern sides. Line with hessian sacking (burlap) and fill with ordinary soil to which as much clay as possible should be added. Top with washed gravel and lower the crates into the pond. Suitable marginal plants should be placed in pots or crates on the shelf at the sides of the pond to help give it a finished look. Floating plants simply need placing on the surface of the water to provide shade below and to help prevent a build-up of algae, which would suffocate the other plants and make for a generally unhealthy pond.

Repairing a concrete pond

The hard work involved in installing a concrete pond really does not merit using this method of construction. However, if you have inherited a pond that leaks, it can be repaired. Rescue any surviving fish with a fine net and keep them in a plastic bag or bowl with some of the pond water. Empty all the water out of the pond'– it will be easier to work at if you can stand in it, and this gives you the chance of cleaning it also.

Fill any cracks wider than 9 mm (⅜ in) with mortar, than apply a proprietary sealing compound. To prevent any future problems you may prefer to fill the cracks with mortar and install a flexible liner over the concrete. Refill with water and reintroduce your fish by floating the plastic bag in the pond for a couple of hours. This will help acclimatize them to the pond temperature.

Plants for a garden pond

There is a wide selection of plants available for garden ponds, but not all are suited to every situation. It is best to check with your local water-garden centre for suitability.

Marginal plants

Acorus calamus (sweet flag): fragrant, narrow leaves. 760 mm (30 in) high.

Acorus calamus variegatus (variegated sweet flag): leaves striped with cream and gold.

Galtha palustris (marsh marigold): buttercup-like flowers in May and June. 300 mm (1 ft) high.

Iris laevigata (water iris): white, blue-mauve and pink flowers in June. 460 mm to 760 mm (1 ft 6 in to 2 ft 6 in) high.

Myosotis palustris (water forget-me-not): clusters of blue flowers in summer. 150 mm (6 in) high.

Ranunculus lingua (greater spearwort): buttercup yellow flowers July to September. 600 mm (2 ft) high.

Scripus zebrinus (zebra rush): green and white banded stems. 760 mm (2 ft 6 in) high.

Typha latifolia (great reed mace): large chocolate-brown flower bosses often mistakenly called bullrushes. Plants can grow up to 1.3m (4 ft 6 in) high.

Typha minima (miniature reed mace): small rusty brown flower bosses. 460 mm (1 ft 6 in) high.

Deep marginals

Aponogeton distachyus (water hawthorn): long, oval floating leaves. White scented flowers 50 mm (2 in) high in spring and autumn.

Hottonia palustris (water violet): lilac flowers in May. 150 mm (6 in) high. Feathery submerged foliage active October to May but breaks up in summer.

Nymphaea (water lilies): many varieties with flowers in red, pink, white or yellow floating on the water among large leaves.

Ranunculus aquatilis (water crowfoot): white buttercup-like flowers above the water in May. Floating and submerged divided leaves.

Sagittaria sagittifolia (common arrowhead): arrow-shaped leaves and three-petalled white flowers. 460 mm (1 ft 6 in) high.

Floating plants

Hydrocharis morsus rannae (frogbit): round, floating leaves with small, white flowers in July and August.

Lemna triscula (ivy-leaved duckweed): useful for clearing water. Masses of pale green leaves.

Oxygenating plants

Callitrich verna (water starwort): masses of green starry foliage. Active in winter.

Ceratophyllum demersum (hornwort): delicate bristly foliage.

Myriophyllum spicatum (water milfoil): brownish stems with feathery green leaves.

Potamogeton crispus (great pondweed): rampant but a good oxygenator. Wavy-edged leaves.

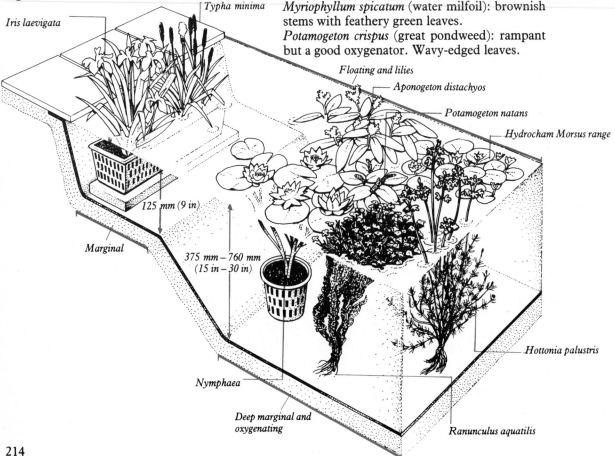

Iris laevigata

Typha minima

Floating and lilies

Aponogeton distachyos

Potamogeton natans

Hydrocham Morsus range

125 mm (9 in)

Marginal

375 mm – 760 mm (15 in – 30 in)

Hottonia palustris

Nymphaea

Deep marginal and oxygenating

Ranunculus aquatilis

Waterfalls and fountains

A fountain will add an extra dimension to the charm of your pond. It will also help oxygenate the water, especially useful in hot, dry weather when the rate of evaporation is high. Your most important consideration will be size: a large powerful fountain in a small pond will not only look ridiculous but also is likely to spray water over the rest of the garden, particularly if caught by gusts of wind. You will have to circulate the water used in a fountain because constant fresh water would upset the natural balance of the pond and probably kill your fish, too.

There are two types of pump you can use. The simplest and cheapest is an electric submersible model; a simple motor-driven centrifugal pump with a plastic impeller. A strainer fitted to the inlet prevents debris being drawn into the pump and the outlet delivers either to a jet fixed onto it or to a remote jet via an extension hose.

The other type, for larger fountains or to run several features, is housed at the side of the pond and draws water from it by suction hose before delivering it by hose to the sprayhead. The size and pattern of spray is determined by the capacity of the pump and some friction loss is inevitable in long, small-bore hoses. Most pumps now feature a nozzle adjustment allowing you to find the optimum flow and pressure for your needs. There is a wide range of nozzles available giving different spray patterns as well as ornamental spouts and illuminated models for night-time.

Waterfalls can be used to create a lovely natural effect of running water and are most effective when they form part of a rock garden set on a natural incline with the water finally pouring into a larger, informal pond at the bottom. However, more formal, raised ponds of different levels can be used very successfully to create small falls using decorative walling blocks, or contours created on a flat site using soil usually excavated from the main pond.

The basic principle is to build a series of small, sealed ponds at least 75 mm (3 in) deep. Three or four are usually sufficient for a small garden. These are made to overflow as sheets of water from one to the next by means of a circulation pump. However, the waterfall should be designed to look attractive even when the pump is turned off by retaining a minimum of 70 mm to 100 mm (2¾ to 4 in) of water. The front edge of each pond should have a flat ledge or row of boulders enabling the water to spill clear of the vertical fall beneath it. A more natural effect can be achieved if the ponds are staggered rather than falling in a straight line.

A formal-style pond *and ornate fountain makes a striking centrepiece in a courtyard garden or paved area, reminiscent of a Roman atrium. Seating centred around the pond and fountain focuses the attention on the feature, while lights in the pond played on the fountain give a spectacular effect at night*

215

Waterfall and fountain construction

Fountains can be grand or simple in the effect they create. The bubble fountain, for instance, quietly gurgles and looks most natural in an informal pond. Other fountains can be made to give jets of water of differing heights and spray patterns; they can be combined with waterfalls and underwater lights for a spectacular effect, especially at night.

A bubble fountain: Bed down paving slabs sloping slightly to form a shallow saucer. An angle grinder, available from a hire shop, will help cut the slabs to a taper. Dig a flat-based hole about 375 mm sq (15 in sq) and 300 mm (12 in) deep. Remove any sharp stones and lay a 25 mm (1 in) layer of compacted sand on the base and sides. Buy a suitable pool liner the length and width of the hole plus twice the depth of the hole added to both dimensions.

Buy a simple submersible pump and strainer and stand it in the hole, placing a planting crate upside down over them to protect them. Feed the pump cable through 12 mm (½ in) tubing and fix a piece of 12 mm (½ in) tubing along with the flow adjuster to the pump outlet and cut off just below water level. Lay a piece of welded wire mesh across the top of the hole and edge with paving slabs to hide the edges. Top with large, smooth pebbles allowing the fountain to come up between them and using an interesting piece of wood or rock as a focal point.

A pond fountain: To install a submersible fountain pump in your pond, simply place the pump in the water and run the electric cable to a convenient position outside the pool, where it can be connected to an extension cable with an outdoor weatherproof connector. The extension cable is then connected to the most convenient earthed power supply. The weatherproof con-nector should be covered with a small paving slab. Nozzles should be positioned just above the water surface; you will probably need to provide it with a support to keep it at the correct height.

A surface pump has to be housed in a dry, well-ventilated chamber outside the pond. If this is above pond water level you will also need a foot valve and strainer on the suction tube to retain the prime. If housed below water level only a strainer is needed as the prime will be maintained by gravity. Delivery can be divided for both fountain and waterfall by adding a tee fitting into the pump delivery. You will need to fit a control valve for each outlet to control the flow.

Waterfalls make an attractive addition to a pond and they are not difficult to construct. Water can be made to fall from one or more ponds into the main pond and their size and shape is up to you.

The ponds can be made from flexible liners or semi-rigid units with specially made cascade lips. Using flexible liners is more difficult but it gives far more scope for design and allows a more natural effect to be achieved. Informal waterfalls are constructed so as to give a natural appearance, whereas the formal waterfall is used as a design feature.

Whatever the design water is pumped from the main pond up to the top pond and allowed to fall naturally under gravity, so creating a closed circuit into which fresh water is not introduced.

The formal waterfall was often a feature of the gardens built for the great houses of the past. The small stepside waterfall was originally used in the Middle East where it was used to please the eye and the ear and to cool the air, but the feature makes an attractive centrepiece to any garden.

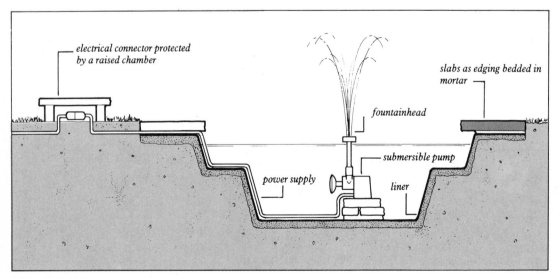

electrical connector protected by a raised chamber

slabs as edging bedded in mortar

fountainhead

power supply

submersible pump

liner

A fountain *is powered by a submersible pump to which the fountainhead is fixed. It receives its power from an electrical supply connected via a weatherproof connector. This connection must be completely weatherproof and protected from damage by a sturdy chamber made from bricks and slabs*

An informal waterfall Unless you have a natural incline you will have to build a mound of soil using earth excavated when constructing the main pool.

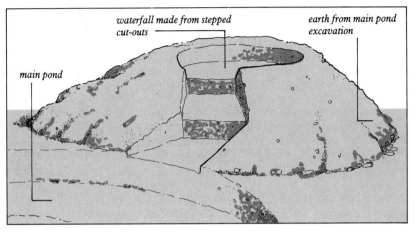

main pond

waterfall made from stepped cut-outs

earth from main pond excavation

1. Construct three or four small, sealed ponds in series, staggering them for the most natural effect. When measuring for liners, allow 150 mm to 225 mm (6 in to 9 in) extra and remember that the side walls must be higher than the anticipated water level. Overlapping liners and a flat stone at the front of each pond should rest on a firm foundation, preferably of concrete.

2. The most difficult part of the construction is sealing the gaps between the pools. This can best be achieved by overlapping the front edge of the flexible liner sheet of the top pond over the back edge of the next, lower pond and bedding them under the lip stones. The pump should be sited in the lower pond with the hose and cable concealed by rocks.

3. Stones and rocks are useful for concealing edges of the waterfall and building a surrounding rock garden, but check they have no sharp edges when used near the liner. You can lay stones bedded on mortar to form the watercourse, the type of stone determining the fall; a flat stone will give a weir effect while cobbles produce a rippling cascade.

A formal waterfall A series of formal raised ponds can be constructed using the decorative walling blocks and liner method described previously.

1. Build up additional courses of walling onto the liner to produce ponds at different levels. Position the water pump in the lower pond, screening its position and the path of the waterproof electric cable with plants. Lay the water feed pipe to the upper ponds over the liner and through the mortar joints above water level, again using plants to hide its position.

2. Paving laid flat over the liner and on the joining walls of each pond will form a curtain of water as it falls over. Height of falls can be adjusted as required. The level of water in each pond can be reduced by adding smooth pebbles to the required level and laying the liner over them. Boulders and pebbles placed carefully in the pond will also cover the liner and give a firm base for growing plants.

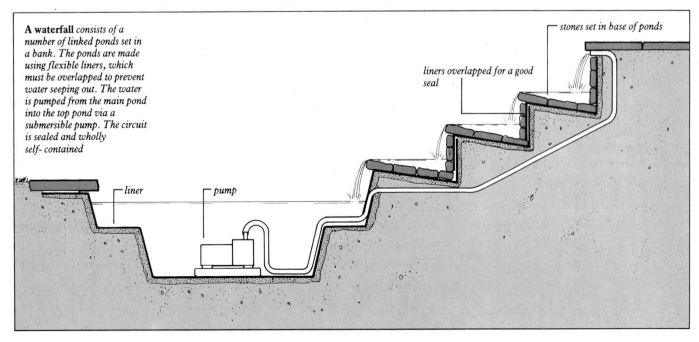

A waterfall consists of a number of linked ponds set in a bank. The ponds are made using flexible liners, which must be overlapped to prevent water seeping out. The water is pumped from the main pond into the top pond via a submersible pump. The circuit is sealed and wholly self-contained

liner

pump

liners overlapped for a good seal

stones set in base of ponds

23. Electricity in the garden

Electricity is needed in the garden as a temporary supply for powering tools such as lawnmowers and hedge trimmers, and as a permanent supply to outbuildings (greenhouses and sheds) and fixtures such as outdoor lights and pumps and fountains in garden ponds.

The temporary supply will almost always be taken from one of the house's power circuits via a plug-in extension lead, since few people will go to the trouble and expense of putting in special outdoor sockets for power tools that are used only infrequently.

A permanent supply, on the other hand, has to be a permanent job – the wiring regulations do not allow temporary cables to trail unprotected all over the garden because of the huge dangers of shock. Putting one in will be well worth the effort, however. It means that you can heat your greenhouse efficiently all the year round, work in your garden shed on long winter evenings, light up your garden subtly or spectacularly and enjoy the pleasure of hearing the sound of running water in the humblest pond.

Never use an extension lead or power tool out of doors when it is raining, or after rain when foliage is wet and moisture could get into the tool or the trailing plug, socket and cord.

Permanent supplies

As already mentioned, a permanent electricity supply to an outbuilding or an outdoor light or appliance has to be connected us as a proper sub-circuit – unless it is run as a low-voltage supply from a transformer.

Temporary supplies

1. All you need to provide a temporary supply of electricity is an extension cord. Make one up long enough to reach right to the end of your garden, using orange three-wire-core cable and toughened plugs and sockets (even though most garden tools are double-insulated and have only a two-wire core, you never know when someone might use the extension cord to power a piece of equipment that does need grounding).

2. For added protection, install a ground fault circuit interrupter (GFCI or GFT) in the place of the conventional plug, or install a GFCI-protected outlet in the house, into which the extension cord can be plugged to power tools out of doors. It's recommended that such an outlet be provided in new houses or when complete rewirings are carried out, and it is an excellent idea to provide one anyway for your own (and your family's) protection. You can fit one in place of any existing double outlet, or run a cable near the back door and insert the new outlet there where it will be most convenient.

Installing porch lights

There are three good reasons for lighting up the approach to your front door. It will look more welcoming to night-time callers, they will be able to see any obstacles such as steps on their way to the front door, and burglars are more likely to look elsewhere – they dislike houses with lights outside. You can choose from a wide range of fixtures to install by your front door, from simple wall lights to ornate carriage lamps and globes. One thing to remember, whatever you choose, is that a little light goes a long way in the dark – a 40W bulb looks at least as bright out of doors as a 100W one does indoors, so your outside lights are not going to add dramatically to your electricity bill.

Wall lights are neat and functional. The cover may be toughened glass covered with a metal cage, or plastic.

Globe and cube lights have a wall-mounted bracket holding the fixture upright, and have a soft glow rather than a bright beam. The most popular type of fixture is the decorative lantern, often seen on 'period-look' houses and either mounted on a wall bracket or hung from the porch roof.

When buying lighting fixtures for your porch,

it is vital that you choose a type designed and recommended by the National Electrical Code (NEC) for outdoor use – unless your porch is completely enclosed, and even then the damp conditions in any porch make an exterior-quality fixture the best bet.

Wiring in a porch light is quite straightforward. All you have to do is locate a nearby lighting circuit – probably the one feeding the hall light – and pick up a feed from that circuit to power the new light. Open up the hall light ceiling box to identify the type of wiring system you have (see box).

House lighting circuits are wired in one or two ways:

● *loop-in system:* the cables from the service panel are connected to the first in a series of special loop-in ceiling boxes; another cable then loops out to the next ceiling box in the series, and so on. A second cable runs from each box to its light switch.

● *junction box system:* an older arrangement, in which the cable runs from the service panel to a series of junction boxes above the ceiling. Additional cables run from the boxes to the fixtures and switches.

Identify which type of system you have by unscrewing the ceiling box cover. If there is only one cable entering the box you have a junction box system; if there are two or three cables connected to the box you have a loop-in system.

How to add a porch light

1. Connect the wires of a length of 14-2 armored cable (BX) or 14-2 non-metallic sheathed cable (Romex) with ground to the live (black), neutral (white) and ground (green/bare) wires in the ceiling box. Run the cable in the ceiling void, stapled neatly to the side of the joists, to the porch light position. In this arrangement the porch light will be controlled by the hall light switch.

2. For independent switching of your porch light, run a length of BX or Romex to a 4 × 4-in junction box located near the light and switch position. Connect up the black, white and green/bare wires to the live, neutral and ground wires. Run another length of cable from the box to the porch light position; in the box, connect the white wire of this cable to neutral, the green/bare to the ground and the black wire to the switch terminal. Connect another length of cable between the box and a new single-pole switch, positioned near the front door – set the cable in a channel cut in the wall or fish the cable through the wall. At the box, connect the green/bare core to ground; the black to live and the white wire to the switch.

3. On the junction box system cut the main circuit cable at a convenient point and connect up the wires to a junction box. Run in a new length of BX or Romex from the junction box to the porch light position.

4. At the point where you want the porch light, drill a hole through the house wall and feed the new cable through. Connect the cable to the light's junction box.

5. If you want a pair of porch lights, simply run two cables from the junction box to the live lights in a parallel circuit.

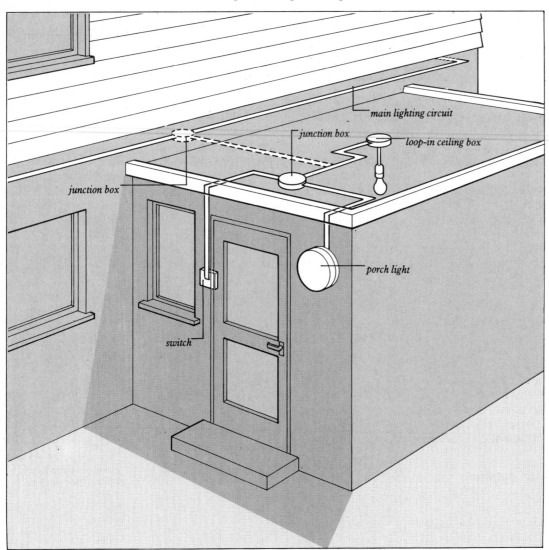

main lighting circuit

junction box

loop-in ceiling box

junction box

porch light

switch

Power for a porch light
Take your power for a porch light from an existing loop-in ceiling light supply, or from the main lighting circuit (shown as a dotted line in the diagram). Provide independent switching with the former method by installing a junction box in the supply from the ceiling fitting, and run a switch supply from this

Outdoor circuits

Except for extensions of lighting circuits to power lights installed to the exterior of the house, you are not allowed to extend existing circuits in the house to supply outbuildings or exterior fixtures; a separate circuit must be run in. You can use a spare open circuit or fuse in your service panel if you have one; otherwise you will have to install a new panel alongside the existing fuseboard, run your new circuit(s) from this and call in a licensed electrician to link the unit to the supply.

If the new circuit is simply to power remote lights, then it can be run from a 15-amp fuse in No. 14 wire. Run appliances on a 20-amp circuit in No. 12 wire.

You can run the section of the circuit that is inside the house in BX or Romex. When it leaves the house, you have to decide whether you want an overhead or an underground supply. In both instances, use UF or USE underground cable. Codes may vary on this, but most overhead cable (UF or USE) must be in conduit. UF or USE cable can be run underground without any further protection, such as conduit, except where the NEC dictates otherwise.

If your new circuit is running to outside lights on posts or pillars, you may be able to run the cable directly to the fixture. However, use conduit to protect the cable where it leaves the house and enters the ground. The cable (UF or USE type) can then run unprotected to the lamp post.

If the circuit is running to, for example, a pond fitted with a pump or submerged lighting, you can run the circuit in the same way as for outside lights; an underground cable is obviously less obtrusive than an overhead one, but you may be able to run it along boundary walls to the pond if it is close to the house. *Never* attach cables to fences, which can blow down and sever the cable. A better alternative is to use low-voltage supplies and pond equipment designed to run at only 12 volts.

In this case you need a suitable transformer, sited under cover (ideally indoors). From there the low-voltage cable can be run underground or on the surface (there is no shock risk as 12V if the cable is cut) to the pump itself. The transformer can be simply plugged into an outlet in the house, or can be permanently connected to the service panel.

Adding a new circuit – the options

1. If you have a spare fuse in your service panel turn off the main switch, open up the unit and connect the black wire of the circuit cable to the terminal of the spare fuse, the white wire to the main neutral terminal and the ground wire to the

ground terminal. Run the cable to where it is needed as an overhead run, fixed to the house walls (but NOT to fences or hedges) or as an underground run. Be certain to use UF or USE underground cable for outdoor runs. Finally, fit the new circuit fuse.

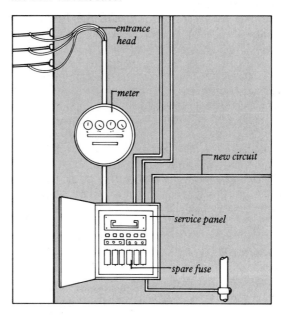

A new circuit can be run directly from the main service panel, if there is a spare fuse. The circuit cable wires are simply screwed into the relevant terminals and the circuit run onto the new fitting

2. If you don't have a spare fuse, you have to add a new fuse panel alongside the main service panel. Choose one with two or four circuit fuses or circuit breakers so you have spare capacity for future extensions. Mount it near the panel board, connect in the new circuit cable as in 1 and complete the new circuit. Connect two meter tails to the new fuse panel and link them to a service connector box. Then call a licensed electrician to disconnect the existing meter tails from the service panel, link them to the service connector box as well and fix new tails from the service connector box to the meter. You are not allowed to do this job yourself.

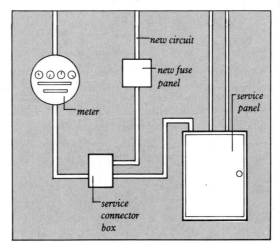

If there is no spare fuse you can add a new circuit by installing a new fuse panel alongside the main service panel. The unit is connected to the meter via a service connector box. A licensed electrician must make the final connections to the meter

Index

Acknowledgements

Swallow Books gratefully acknowledge the assistance given to them in the production of
The Outside Handyman by the following people and organizations. We apologize to anyone we
may have omitted to mention.

Photography

Amdega *166B, 174;* Black & Decker *41T;* Blue Circle Industries PLC *84;* Michael Boys/Susan Griggs Agency Ltd *2;* Bradstone *100;* Bracknell Buildings *50B;* Sue Brinkhurst *50T;* Butterley Pavers, *59, 62, 63, 127;* Camera Press London *6, 48; 136, 148, 151* (Jan Tennek) *152T, 184R;* Cement and Concrete Association *17, 18, 19, 103 T, BL & BR, 105, 132;* Bruce Coleman Ltd *37T;* The Country Garden *181 TR, BL & BM;* Critall Warmlife Ltd *162;* Crosby Doors Ltd *28R;* Crown Paints *42 L & R;* Ellard Sliding Door Gears Ltd *24TR;* Feb GB Ltd *75T;* Flymo *206BR;* Susan Griggs *36;* Grosvenor Products *166T;* Halls *164, 165, 172;* ICI Paints Division *7, 24TL, B, 40, 176;* Magnet & Southerns *28L;* Marley *53, 171T, 179L;* Marshalls *94, 102, 124;* Peter McHoy *93, 95B, 104, 109, 125B, 137, 152T, 153 BL & BR, 158, 160, 161, 169, 180, 186, 188, 202T, 215, 219;* Tania Midgley *23, 149, 153T, 197, 201B;* Qualcast *206TL, TR & BL;* Sears & Nelson *178;* Spear & Jackson *208;* Spectrum Colour Library *81, 125T;* Stapley Water Gardens *210, 211T & B, 212, 213;* Sterling Roncraft *37B, 41B;* Syndication International Ltd *36T;* Texas Homecare *181TM, TR & BR;* Velux Windows *76, 77;* Elizabeth Whiting & Associates, *56, 95T, 121R* (Ron Sutherland) *141, 146, 196, 201T, 202B, 218.*

Illustration

Rick Blakely, *22, 58, 62, 63*
Robert and Rhoda Burns, *38, 39, 46, 47, 48, 49, 68, 69, 78, 79, 80, 84, 85, 86, 87, 88, 89, 90, 91, 92, 99, 126, 128, 130, 131, 132, 133, 134, 135, 140, 160, 168, 173, 187 T.*
Steve Cross, *16, 17, 18, 19, 20, 21, 25, 26, 29, 30, 31, 33BR, 40, 41, 54, 55, 60, 61, 65R, 70, 71, 73 TL & R, 74, 75, 104, 105, 110, 111, 114, 115, 116, 117, 129, 138, 139, 154, 155, 157, 167, 176, 177, 182, 183, 190, 191, 192, 193, 194, 195, 206, 207, 209, 212, 216, 217, 220, 221.*

Kevin Dean, *203, 204, 205.*
Andrew Farmer, *10-11, 14-5, 32, 33 L & BL, 42, 43, 45, 57, 64-5, 66, 67, 72, 73, BL & R, 82, 83, 96, 97, 98, 102, 106, 108, 109, 112, 113, 118, 119, 120, 122, 123, 142-3, 144, 145, 162, 163, 185, 186, 187B, 188, 212, 214.*
David Parr, *34, 35, 147, 150.*
David Tetley, *199.*

T: Top *B:* Bottom *M:* Middle *R:* Right *L:* Left